Intelligence-Led Policing

Intelligence-Led Policing

Jerry H. Ratcliffe

WILLAN
PUBLISHING

Published by

Willan Publishing
Culmcott House
Mill Street, Uffculme
Cullompton, Devon
EX15 3AT, UK
Tel: +44(0)1884 840337
Fax: +44(0)1884 840251
e-mail: info@willanpublishing.co.uk
website: www.willanpublishing.co.uk

Published simultaneously in the USA and Canada by

Willan Publishing
c/o ISBS, 920 NE 58th Ave, Suite 300
Portland, Oregon 97213-3786, USA
Tel: +001(0)503 287 3093
Fax: +001(0)503 280 8832
e-mail: info@isbs.com
website: www.isbs.com

First published 2008
Reprinted 2008, 2009

ISBN   978-1-84392-339-8 paperback
ISBN   978-1-84392-340-4 hardback

British Library Cataloguing-in-Publication Data

A catalogue record for this book is available from the British Library

Project managed by Deer Park Productions, Tavistock, Devon
Typeset by GCS, Leighton Buzzard, Bedfordshire
Printed and bound by T.J. International Ltd, Padstow, Cornwall

To Philippa

Contents

List of acronyms   *xi*
Preface and acknowledgements   *xiii*

1 Introduction   1

Reimagining policing   3
What is intelligence-led policing?   6
    What makes intelligence-led policing unique?   7
    A holistic approach to crime control   9
    Case study: Operation Nine Connect   11
The structure of this book   12

2 Origins of intelligence-led policing   15

Drivers for change   16
    Complexity in policing and the performance culture   16
    Managing risk   18
    The demand gap   18
    Limitations of the standard model of policing 20
    Organised and transnational crime   22
    Changes in technology   23
The US policing landscape   24
    Fragmented and uncoordinated   24
    Viewpoint: Fragmented policing and the role of fusion centers   26
    Demonising intelligence   27
    The community policing era   29
    Slow emergence of problem-oriented policing   30
    Rapid emergence of Compstat   31
    9/11 and homeland security   32
The British policing landscape   33
    New public managerialism and oversight   33
    Sporadic emergence of problem-oriented policing in the UK   34
    Helping with enquiries and policing with intelligence   36
    The National Intelligence Model   38
Summary   39
Notes   40

3   The magnitude of the crime challenge   42

The crime funnel   43
     How much crime gets reported?   43
     Case study: Calls for service in America's most dangerous city   47
     Crime-prone places   49
     Completing the crime funnel   50
The offender problem   52
     Individual offending and recidivism   53
     Predicting prolific offenders   56
     Can the police identify prolific offenders?   58
     Organised crime   59
     Viewpoint: Threat measurement techniques for organised crime   61
Summary   62

4   Defining intelligence-led policing   64

Related policing frameworks   65
     Community policing   66
     Problem-oriented policing   70
     Compstat   76
Conceptual confusion   79
     Viewpoint: Policing conceptual frameworks from the analyst's
       perspective   82
Intelligence-led policing defined   83
     Original tenets   83
     Revising the original model   84
     Intelligence-led policing components   85
Summary   88

5   Analytical frameworks   91

Awash with terminology   91
     What is criminal intelligence?   92
     What is crime analysis?   93
     Data, information and knowledge?   94
     DIKI continuum   96
     From knowledge to intelligence   98
Levels of crime intelligence   99
     NIM levels   101
     Viewpoint: A practitioner's perspective on the National
       Intelligence Model   103
Conceptualising analysis   104
     NIM business model   107
     The 3-i model   109
Can models reflect reality?   113
Summary   114

6 Interpreting the criminal environment 115

Target selection 116
  Recording crime details 116
  Threat assessments 118
Objective targeting and offender self-selection 120
  Playing well with others 122
  Viewpoint: Information sharing at the national level 126
Information collation 127
  Improving information sharing 130
  A role for liaison officers? 132
  Confidential informants 133
Analytical tehcniques 135
  Strategic thinking 137
Summary 139
Note 140

7 Influencing decision-makers 141

Who are decision-makers? 142
  Front-line officers 143
  Police leadership 144
  Non-law enforcement 146
  The general public 148
  Security networks 149
  Viewpoint: The responsibilities of intelligence-led police
    leadership 152
Understanding the client's environment 153
  Working with the audience 157
Maximising influence 158
  Embracing networks 159
  Recommending action 160
Summary 162

8 Having an impact on crime 165

Revisiting the crime funnel 166
  Estimating prevention benefits 169
Reduction, disruption and prevention 171
The changing leadership role 173
  Viewpoint: The leadership role in intelligence-led policing 175
  Steering the rowers in the right direction 177
The police impact on crime 178
  Does police targeting prevent crime? 178
  Does increasing arrests reduce crime? 180
  Intelligence-led crime reduction 182
Summary 183

9   Evaluating intelligence-led policing — 186

Evaluation concepts and practice — 187
    What are we evaluating? — 188
    Types of evaluations — 189
    Operation Vendas and Operation Safe Streets — 190
    Evaluation skills — 192
    Pure evaluations and realistic evaluations — 193
    Case study: Operation Anchorage — 195
    Viewpoint: Refining strategy after Operation Anchorage — 199
Measuring success in different ways — 201
    The cost-benefit of surveillance and confidential informants — 202
    Measuring disruption — 204
    Measuring success in changing business practice — 206
    Measuring success in performance indicators — 207
Summary — 210
Notes — 212

10   Challenges for the future — 213

The challenges of covert activity — 214
    The risks of greater informant use in covert activities — 215
    Principle of proportionality — 217
    Storing private information — 219
    Human rights and surveillance — 220
    Viewpoint: Intelligence-led policing and public trust — 222
The widening security agenda — 224
    Greater strategic application — 225
    Merging criminal intelligence and national security — 227
An agenda for the future — 230
    Conceptual training for analysts and executives — 230
    Disseminating success — 232
    Looking beyond the tactical imperatives — 233
    Engage the next cohort of police leaders — 234
    Ten yardsticks for intelligence-led policing — 235
Summary — 237
Note — 237

References — 238
Index — 257

List of acronyms

ABCI	Australian Bureau of Criminal Intelligence
ACC	Australian Crime Commission
ACPO	Association of Chief Police Officers (UK)
BCS	British Crime Survey
CISC	Criminal Intelligence Service Canada
DEA	Drug Enforcement Administration (US)
FBI	Federal Bureau of Investigation (US)
HIDTA	High-Intensity Drug Trafficking Areas (US)
IACA	International Association of Crime Analysts
IACP	International Association of Chiefs of Police
IALEIA	International Association of Law Enforcement Intelligence Analysts
ILP	intelligence-led policing
JTTF	joint terrorism task force
NCIS	National Criminal Intelligence Service (UK)
NCPE	National Centre for Policing Excellence (UK)
NCVS	National Crime Victimization Survey (US)
NIM	National Intelligence Model (UK)
NJSP	New Jersey State Police (US)
NPIA	National Policing Improvement Agency (UK)
NYPD	New York City Police Department (US)
POP	problem-oriented policing
RCMP	Royal Canadian Mounted Police
SOCA	Serious Organised Crime Agency (UK)
ViCAP	Violent Criminal Apprehension Program

Preface and acknowledgements

The central aim of this book is to bring the concepts and processes of intelligence-led policing into better focus, so that students, practitioners and scholars of policing, criminal intelligence and crime analysis can better understand the evolving dynamics of this new paradigm in policing. The main audience is professionals within the law enforcement environment; senior officers, middle management, analysts and operational staff. With this in mind, each chapter contains a 'Viewpoint' from a professional in the field. These expert views are drawn from specialists from around the globe, and I am indebted to the authors for agreeing to share their insight.

The book also aims to be a resource for the growing number of academics and students interested in intelligence-led policing. To enable readers to make more effective use of this book as a learning resource, a series of PowerPoint slides is available on the publisher's website at www.willanpublishing.co.uk and mirrored at the author's website (www.jratcliffe.net). These slides reproduce many of the tables and graphics found in the book. The websites also contain suggestions for further reading and some related links.

I'm immensely grateful to John Eck, R. Mark Evans, Tim John, Eric McCord, Deborah Osborne, Philippa Ratcliffe, Nick Tilley, Jennifer Wood and John Cohen, for providing valuable and insightful comments on early drafts or sections of this book; Peter Gill and Toni Makkai for permission to reproduce some of the figures found within; John Goldkamp and Ralph Taylor for picking up much of the slack and helping me find the time for this project; my graduate students for tolerating a slower-than-normal turnaround in their work; Kip and George at Philadelphia's Southwark bar and restaurant for providing the ideal haunt to de-stress; Jerry and Alia and the staff at Philadelphia Java Company, where half the book was written; and Brian Willan for encouraging this whole thing from the start. Furthermore I would particularly like to thank the authors of the viewpoints: R. Mark Evans, Robert Fahlman, Rick Fuentes, Ray Guidetti, Corey Heldon, Deborah Osborne, Lisa Palmieri, Russ Porter and Peter Stelfox. Further thanks are necessary to Roger Gaspar, Frank Rodgers, and

Tim Connors from the Manhattan Institute, for being such strong supporters of intelligence-led policing.

All these fine people are far too busy to have helped as much as they did; however, the book is much better for it. It should go without saying that the opinions expressed in the rest of the book are solely those of the author, and my opinions are not necessarily shared by the many government bodies or police departments that I have worked with over the years (though they should be!).

1

Introduction

What is intelligence-led policing? Who came up with the idea? Where did it come from? How does it relate to other policing paradigms? What distinguishes an intelligence-led approach to crime reduction? How is it designed to have an impact on crime? Does it prevent crime? What is crime disruption? Is intelligence-led policing just for the police? These are questions asked by many police professionals, including senior officers, analysts and operational staff. Similar questions are also posed by students of policing who have witnessed the rapid emergence of intelligence-led policing from its British origins to worldwide movement. These questions are also relevant to crime prevention practitioners and policymakers seeking long-term crime benefits. The answers to these questions are the subject of this book.

Questions of how the police should respond to crime have plagued scholars and practitioners of policing for decades. It is still a constant source of discussion and is perhaps debated more so now than at any time in the history of law enforcement. When the first officers of a modern police service walked out on to London's streets in September 1829, one of their first commissioners stressed that the primary role of the police was the prevention of crime (Mayne 1829), and the job of the police officer remained – at least until the 1960s – a relatively simple one. In these halcyon days, the constable or patrol officer (often on foot) had to avoid getting into trouble with the sergeant, and then take care of two constituent groups; local offenders and potential victims. His (all early police officers were male) job was to inhibit the former and reassure the latter (Flood 2004). This required the officer to develop community contacts, act to prevent crime, reassure local people, and catch offenders when crime occurred.

The police officer was the epitome of the Hobbesian ideal, the thin blue line that represented societal order and governmental legitimacy in the face of crime and anarchy (Wood and Shearing 2007). However, since the 1960s, many aspects of the policing world have changed. Society transformed rapidly, criminals developed new ways to commit crime, public expectations changed, and the police adjusted in response. Radio-directed rapid response, criminal investigations and crime fighting became the dominant model of law enforcement. Public attitudes to the police changed, as did their attitude to the role of the police. With rising crime rates and greater information availability regarding police performance, the job of a police chief became one of managing risk, trying to keep the public happy, and responding instantly to crime threats once they emerged. Crime fighting and making arrests came to define the role of the police, while crime prevention was relegated to an occasional hobby. To put this gulf in perspective, one survey of UK police forces found that, while 40 per cent of personnel were assigned to investigation, only 1 per cent addressed crime prevention (Audit Commission 1993: 14).

Reactive, investigative policing became the order of the day and, at least in the US, this is still the dominant model of policing (Weisburd and Eck 2004). This strategy is founded on the assumption that more detections will reduce the number of offenders and act as a deterrent to the criminal still at large; thus having a preventative role. To the public and many within policing it seems a simple argument: increased crime detection will lead to increased crime prevention, and therefore increasing the number of arrests will prevent crime. Unfortunately, the police do not arrest at a rate even close to making this a reality. If they did, the jails would overflow and the criminal justice system would grind to a standstill.

Clearance rates have stayed steady over the last few years in both the US and the UK, with rates hovering between 20 and 26 per cent, leaving the vast majority of crime unsolved. If police were to increase arrests, the criminal justice system would certainly need more resources and funding. We would need more courts and jails, more probation staff and more parole boards. Police stations would need to be larger and the police would need more staff.

Irrespective of the almost perpetual law and order debate that sees politicians and the media exploiting public fears on a regular basis (Weatherburn 2004), recent trends suggest that taxpayers are unwilling to fund the substantially greater numbers of police that are necessary to reduce crime simply through a universal increase in incarceration. For while police strength in England and Wales increased 50 per cent from 1970 to 2004, recorded indictable offences increased by over 250 per cent in the same period.

This explosion in criminality did not affect the UK alone. From the 1970s, in both the US and the UK, crime rates soared and public confidence in the police was eroded as a result. With the crime problem outstripping the available resources, many in policing began to recognise that the traditional role of reactive, investigative policing was not a satisfactory response. There is a common saying within law enforcement that 'you can't arrest your way out of a problem'. If not, then what options are left to the police?

Reimagining policing

The first attempt to 'reimagine policing' (Wood and Shearing 2007) took law enforcement back to a mythical age of cheerful beat cops chatting with store owners and clipping misbehaving kids around the ear. Community policing initially appeared to hold the promise of reconnecting the police with the public, and through this increased contact would flow greater information about crime problems, a re-engagement of neighbourhood issues by police, and an improvement in police legitimacy. In the UK, progressive officers such as then Chief Constable for Devon and Cornwall, John Alderson, not only moved their forces toward a more community-oriented organisational structure, but were also highly vocal advocates for community policing, engaging in considerable public debate about styles of policing. By the 1980s, most police agencies in the UK claimed to be committed to community policing (Morgan and Newburn 1997). In the US, the breakdown in the relationship between many communities and the police in the 1960s and 1970s drove American police – with considerable support from the federal government - to embrace the community policing ethos to a far greater extent.

With the primary aim of restoring police legitimacy, community policing is a partnership philosophy that increases collaboration (or at least consultation) between the community and the police, decentralises police organisational hierarchy, gives greater discretion to lower ranks, places greater influence in the hands of the community in determining police priorities, and promotes a social service ethos (see, for example, Bennett 1994; CPC 1994; Trojanowicz 1994; Cordner 1995; Skogan and Hartnett 1997; Edwards 1999; Skogan 2006b). While many police departments have more or less subscribed to this philosophy, research evidence suggests that police departments that have moved to a general community policing ethos have not been successful in converting that strategy into measurable crime reduction (Sherman *et al.* 1998).

Police chiefs, while retaining the rhetoric of community policing, are now exploring different managerial styles and strategies. New strategies have been made possible through a broad movement in policing that has discovered the benefit of using data to influence decisions and drive crime control strategy. This movement has produced problem-oriented policing, Compstat, and now intelligence-led policing.

The problem-oriented policing approach recommends that police identify clusters of repeat crime incidents and use these as indications of underlying problems within the community (see the Center for Problem-Oriented Policing at www.popcenter.org). Police – armed with the results of a thorough analysis of the crime problem – target the specific cause of the problem, often (though not always) with the help of the community both to identify problems and figure out solutions (Goldstein 1990; Leigh *et al.* 1996). Problem-oriented policing has been instrumental in educating a

3

generation of police leaders in the importance of analysis as a foundation for decision-making (see Chapter 4).

Originating in the New York City Police Department in early 1994, Compstat is an accountability process that seeks to empower mid-level commanders to seek a rapid response to emerging crime problems and hotspots. The central medium is crime mapping, where recent crime data are mapped, viewed and discussed by police commanders. After a much-publicised drop in crime in New York City, interest in Compstat spread around the world (again, see Chapter 4).

Most recently, intelligence-led policing has become the latest wave in modern policing: 'intelligence-led policing does not re-imagine the police role so much as it re-imagines how the police can be "smarter" in the exercise of their unique authority and capacities' (Wood and Shearing 2007: 55). Intelligence-led policing has a lineage that can be traced back to many of the same key drivers that influenced the development of problem-oriented policing and Compstat. Originally formulated as a law enforcement operational strategy that emphasised the use of criminal intelligence when planning police tactics, in the last few years it has come to take on a broader definition and scope. While still stressing that police should avoid getting fixated on reactive case investigations, intelligence-led policing has evolved into a management philosophy and movement.

Intelligence-led policing holds out the promise of a more objective basis for deciding priorities and resource allocation, and many in policing are beginning to see the benefits of using an analysis-driven approach to decision-making. As one of the latest analysis-driven models, intelligence-led policing has commonalities with problem-oriented policing and targeted, proactive policing. These strategies attempt to be 'strategic, future oriented and targeted' in their approach to crime control and are more than just catchy phrases; they are representative of a significant and widespread change in the business of policing (Maguire 2000: 315–317).

Intelligence-led policing has become a significant movement in policing in the twenty-first century. In the UK, the concept is enshrined in legislation that demanded all forces adopt the National Intelligence Model by April 2004; by 2003, every police service in Australia, including the Australian Crime Commission, had reference to intelligence-led policing on their websites (Ratcliffe 2003); the New Zealand Police were committed to intelligence-based policing by 2002 (NZP 2002); and in the US, a 2002 summit of over 120 criminal intelligence experts brought together by the International Association of Chiefs of Police called for a national policing plan to promote intelligence-led policing (IACP 2002).

Intelligence-led policing has emerged at a time when crime threats have become less parochial. The growth of international organised crime continues to defy any attempts by national and locally organised police bodies to contain its pervasive tentacles. Organised crime groups now dominate the illegal arms, drug and people smuggling industries and provide significant challenges to containment, let alone suppression: 'Locally based policing, although it has a role in tackling organised crime … is not structured to combat transnational and global-scale criminality' (Harfield 2000: 109–110). And international organised crime is not the only significant new challenge to policing.

Since 11 September 2001, the task of terrorism prevention has challenged all aspects of the criminal justice system, creating a post-9/11 homeland security era where the focus continually threatens to shift from everyday crime to terrorism, and where information needs are deemed to be real-time. Information and intelligence sharing has emerged as a key element in law enforcement strategies to prevent terrorist incidents and control organised crime. The growth of regional information-sharing partnerships and the recent development of 'fusion centers' in the US suggest the promise of real-time data sharing and access in the near future, with real-time intelligence linkages expected to play a key role in preventing future terrorist incidents. These intelligence linkages rely on agencies sharing information among themselves, yet a key shortcoming recognised by the 9/11 Commission was the failure of agencies to share vital information. They identified not only the technological barriers to information sharing, but, perhaps more importantly, also the organisational and cultural barriers. Their recommendations spoke of 'unifying strategic intelligence' (p. 399), yet the barriers to be overcome are sizable.

> Current security requirements nurture overclassification and excessive compartmentalization of information among agencies. Each agency's incentive structure opposes sharing … [and] few reward for sharing information. No one has to pay the long-term costs of over-classifying information, though these costs – even in literal financial terms – are substantial. There are no punishments for not sharing information. Agencies uphold a 'need-to-know' culture of information protection rather than promoting a 'need-to-share' culture of integration. (9/11 Commission 2004: 417)

The 9/11 Commission could easily have been discussing the wider field of criminal intelligence and the way that many police services currently handle information. The 9/11 Commission's concerns led them to propose that 'information be shared horizontally, across new networks that transcend individual agencies' (p. 418). The structure of law enforcement in most places militates against horizontal information sharing, both between agencies and within. The challenges for information sharing, arguably a component of a strategic, intelligence-led crime control strategy, are therefore substantial; but (contrary to the views of some in US federal law enforcement) intelligence-led policing is not just about better information sharing or information collection. It is also about better resource allocation, priorities and crime reduction decisions.

Law enforcement is being asked to tackle a range of threats and risks that were never an issue when the current crop of police leaders entered the police service. These managers are having to adapt rapidly to the new policing environment. It is certainly a challenging time to be in policing.

What is intelligence-led policing?

When first proposed, intelligence-led policing was an operational tactic that would reduce crime through proactive policing targeted by criminal intelligence. Kent Police (UK), under the leadership of Sir David Phillips, moved resources from reactive, crime investigation departments to proactive units, began tactical operations that were directed by criminal intelligence analysis, and promoted greater intelligence gathering. As a whole department, they were among the first to practise 'genuine' intelligence-led policing (John and Maguire 2003). This information-based strategy focused heavily on active and prolific offenders.

Some began to see that the business model required to manage crime analysis and criminal intelligence would also work as a broader management model for policing in general. From these early UK developments in intelligence-led policing grew the National Intelligence Model, which has evolved into a business and management model for resource decisions affecting a wide range of police activities. As a result, the interpretation of intelligence-led policing appears to be broadening in scope, and has evolved into a management philosophy that places greater emphasis on information sharing and collaborative, strategic solutions to policing problems at the local and regional level.

While it now appears clear that intelligence-led policing is evolving into a framework to encompass most operational police activity, police departments are at varying stages of development. Furthermore, the paradigm of intelligence-led policing is being interpreted differently in some places. While there is certainly a lineage that can be traced, a single unifying definition may prove elusive under these circumstances. In case the reader is seeking a quick answer, I will endeavour in this book to argue that intelligence-led policing is a business model and managerial philosophy where data analysis and crime intelligence are pivotal to an objective, decision-making framework that facilitates crime and problem reduction, disruption and prevention through both strategic management and effective enforcement strategies that target prolific and serious offenders. This definition (explained and expanded on in Chapter 4) recognises the evolution from whack-a-mole policing that arrests offenders with no overarching strategy, to one that places significant emphasis on data and intelligence analysis as the central component of police strategic thinking. This requires a wider interpretation of the information resources that police can draw upon. In this book, 'crime intelligence' is used as a collective term to describe the result of the analysis of not only covert information from surveillance, offender interviews and confidential human sources (informants), but also crime patterns and police data sources as well as socio-demographic data and other non-police data. It also centralises the role of the crime intelligence analyst (or police analyst) at the core of police decision-making.

What makes intelligence-led policing unique?

The next chapters go into greater depth in attempting to clarify what intelligence-led policing is, and how it compares with other crime-control strategies. However, at this point, it is necessary to state what it is not. This book is about intelligence-led policing. It is not about intelligence-led police. The police are a specific institution common across the world, whereas 'policing' is a term that suggests a set of processes within society that fulfil specific social functions related to regulation and control (Reiner 1997). As such, it is theoretically possible to conduct intelligence-led policing without involving the traditional public police force. Policing is now being widely offered by institutions other than the state, including private companies and community volunteers (Bayley and Shearing 1996). To understand the role of analysis in this expanding security field, it may be necessary to pay as much attention to 'knowledge and power, information and action' (Ransom 1980: 148) as to the formal structures of the policing environment.

Some of the perceived problems with intelligence-led policing lie with the name. Some people have a tendency to see the word *intelligence* and assume it has negative connotations, suggesting activity that is secretive, subversive and possibly illegal. There is an implication of dubious and immoral activity used to protect a police state. When the word is used in conjunction with the police, they fear the worst. However, intelligence-led policing actually develops data and information analysis into crime intelligence processes to the point where, 'as opposed to being a marginalised, subordinate activity, mythologically and furtively pursued by a caucus of officers, the collection and analysis of intelligence has become central to contemporary policing' (Christopher 2004: 117). When practised properly, intelligence-led policing provides an objective mechanism to formulate strategic policing priorities. The difficulty is that few outside law enforcement are aware of this broader interpretation of the term. As Grieve notes, 'The word intelligence needs to be reclaimed from the secret world, made less threatening to communities and used in their service' (2004: 26). Within the conceptual framework of intelligence-led policing, intelligence has a meaning more similar to competitive or business intelligence as commonly used in the business world.

For most of the history of policing, criminal intelligence was used to support individual, reactive investigations. Informants penetrated the organisational structure of criminal groups, and wiretaps and other forms of surveillance were employed against known, recidivist offenders. The aim was always to gather evidence to support a criminal prosecution. This is not the model of intelligence-led policing. Although achieving a prosecution against a serious repeat offender is rarely discounted, intelligence-led policing seeks to use crime intelligence for more than just individual cases. Intelligence-led policing uses crime intelligence for strategic planning and resource allocation, so that investigative action is used to target the right offenders and predict emerging areas of criminality. One of the unique aspects of intelligence-led policing is this use of crime intelligence – what was once a case-specific and myopic tool of crime control – as a strategic resource for better targeting and managerial decisions. In an intelligence-led policing model, crime intelligence drives operations rather than operations dictating intelligence-gathering priorities. This move from investigation-led intelligence to intelligence-led policing is revolutionary for modern policing.

The development from an investigative ethos to a strategic 'business model' (John and Maguire 2003: 38) to address a wide variety of policing problems provides police and analysts with a real opportunity to have a greater impact on crime. Instead of tackling crime one laborious investigation at a time, never truly having an impact on the more expansive criminal opportunity structure, the capacity to step back and place threats and risks into a holistic perspective that assesses the social harm of criminality may allow policing to prevent crime across a wide area rather than solve a single event that has already occurred. A further intriguing aspect of intelligence-led policing is the concentration on prolific and persistent offenders. This focus stems from the realisation that a relatively small percentage of the population is responsible for a significant percentage of crime (see Chapter 3). Intelligence-led policing is also a realisation of the need to better integrate the information systems available to police so that a wider array of data and information sources can be brought to bear when creating a picture of the criminal environment. As Osborne (2006) points out, some of the information analysts require is inaccessible not just because of technological failures or lack of computer literacy but also as a result of interjurisdictional rivalries or a simple lack of understanding by police management and analysts. While we are now operating in an information-rich environment, it is not necessarily easier to translate that information into action; we are, in effect, information-rich but knowledge-poor.

Intelligence-led policing is quite different from the meaning of intelligence common in a military or national security context. Unlike in the military, law enforcement analysts are rarely a recognised feature of the managerial sphere, and across policing there is a lack of understanding of the role and applicability of crime intelligence analysis to strategy. Crime intelligence techniques and applications are seldom institutionalised, even with the supposed introduction of intelligence-led policing to some jurisdictions. There is so little research in the area of crime analysis that even an agreed establishment of analysts to population ratio, sworn officer count, or crime rate does not exist. For example, Cope (2003) found that the ratio of analysts in different UK police forces varied considerably. In the US, while about three-quarters of police departments with more than 100 sworn personnel employ at least one person in a crime analysis function, only 23 per cent of smaller departments have a dedicated crime analysis person (O'Shea and Nicholls 2002). The large departments (100 or more sworn officers) range from employing no crime analysts to one department that makes use of over 10 per 100 sworn officers (O'Shea and Nicholls 2002: 13).

A holistic approach to crime control

Crime control has been the central tenet of most police models in recent times. Some have questioned the wisdom of the police returning to crime control or administration of justice as their dominant function, suggesting that the community or social components of policing remain the central focus. Tim Newburn and Rod Morgan have argued that a significant policy shift away from other activities that police perform towards crime-fighting as a way to prevent crime is a 'dangerous illusion' (Morgan and Newburn 1997: 9), and they advocate a balance between police functions:

> We do not doubt the value of 'intelligence-led policing'. On the contrary, we also think there is a powerful case for concentrating a good many police resources on identifying and bringing to book persistent offenders. However, we do not think this is a policing panacea. And the key question is: how many police resources are to be devoted to this as opposed to other, in our opinion, *equally important* police objectives? (Morgan and Newburn 1997: 203, emphasis in original)

Embracing the crime-fighting image may indeed threaten the legitimacy of the police, and it may see the police move away from what is perceived to be a more traditional service ethos. Yet, this crime-fighting role is precisely what police expect to do and why officers usually join the police, at least initially. Importantly, it is also the role that the public usually ascribe to them. If criminal intelligence really is, according to John Abbott – former

9

Director General of the National Criminal Intelligence Service – 'the future of policing' (Johnstone 2004: 409), then 'By effective use of analysed intelligence the traditional dichotomy between crime fighting and problem solving may be resolved to the benefit of the community' (Amey *et al.* 1996: 32-33). One potential solution, proposed elsewhere and in this book, is to move to a strategic social harm approach that integrates the benefits of objective analysis with a greater appreciation for risk as perceived by the community. A strategic social harm approach works to 'establish priorities for strategic criminal intelligence gathering and subsequent analysis based on notions of the social harm caused by different sorts of criminal activity' (Sheptycki and Ratcliffe 2004: 204).

While a number of police departments are experimenting with intelligence-led policing, some claims to be intelligence-led are rather dubious and often just based on the police department making arrests in a big case rather than demonstrating any proof that the case was a priority resulting from managerial decisions based on a strategic assessment of the criminal environment. Unfortunately, many such approaches tend to stress the *intelligence* aspect of *intelligence-led policing* rather than emphasising *policing*; in doing so, they relegate the value of crime intelligence to a sideshow rather than as central to forming organisational goals (Ratcliffe in press).

This book does not present the concepts of intelligence-led policing as a *fait accompli*. As Brian Flood explains, 'It has been a journey of adaptation: from the lingering, attractive certainties of the pre- and post-war years to the uncertain, information rich, intelligence-led, 21st century world of multi-agency law enforcement' (Flood 2004: 37). That process of adaptation continues today.

Are police leaders ready to be more flexible in their view of both the criminal environment and their own working environment? Are analysts able to conceptualise the organised crime world with a view to prevention? Are managers ready to allow civilian crime intelligence analysts to sit at the big table? How much are decision-makers prepared to allow risks identified in strategic documents to trump their personal biases, pressure from the media, and expectations from the rank and file? The answers to these questions may predict the future of intelligence-led policing.

Case study

Operation Nine Connect

To demonstrate how intelligence-led policing differs from traditional investigative approaches to crime control, consider the following case. A 2004 survey of law enforcement agencies in the US state of New Jersey found there were an estimated 148 gangs in the state, and nearly 30 gangs that had over 100 members (NJSP n.d.). Police leadership in the New Jersey State Police (NJSP) recognised that they did not possess sufficient resources to tackle all of these threats to public safety, so they triaged gangs by focusing on the most violent, entrenched and pervasive groups (NJSP 2005). In order to prepare a strategic assessment of the situation, NJSP analysts drew on a variety of data and information sources, including information from 300 intelligence reports, data from 177 municipal police departments, over 50 media articles, and covert information gathered from nearly 100 confidential informants. The resultant strategic assessment informed the leadership of the NJSP that, of all gangs in the state, the Bloods street gang were the major threat to public safety. More importantly, a subset of the Bloods, called the Nine Trey Gangsters, was identified as an emerging threat. Not only were they actively recruiting but, under the leadership of David 'Duke' Allen from his cell in Trenton State Prison, were attempting to coordinate Bloods' activities and crime across different counties and police jurisdictions. The strategic assessment therefore possessed many of the characteristics of an intelligence-led policing ethos. It was strategic, future oriented and targeted; it aimed to influence decision-makers; by focusing on violent gangs in the triage process it had a strategic social harm component; and the targets were prolific and serious offenders.

The strategic assessment quickly resulted in a large police operation (Operation Nine Connect) that aimed to disrupt gang activities through enforcement action. Operation Nine Connect resulted in the arrest of some 60 members of the gang on 25 July 2006, with at least 30 others being arrested subsequently (NJSP 2006b; Ratcliffe and Guidetti 2008). While much of the work conducted after the strategic decision to target the Nine Trey Gangsters was traditional investigative policing, the strategic targeting and resource decision – based on a social harm criterion and utilising a range of information sources to create an objective, future-oriented and targeted analysis product that influenced policy – was the key intelligence-led policing component.

The structure of this book

The chapters are laid out in the following manner. The first topic addressed is the level of confusion regarding the origins of intelligence-led policing. The rise to prominence of intelligence-led policing in post-9/11 America has left a residual belief that intelligence-led policing emerged as a result of a 2002 Criminal Intelligence Sharing Summit organised by the International Association of Chiefs of Police (Carter 2005). Readers from Kent Constabulary (the first practical application site of the intelligence-led policing model) might dispute the view that, 'traditionally, ILP has been viewed as a specialized police function targeted primarily at terrorism and homeland security' (McGarrell *et al.* 2007: 143). As Chapter 2 ('Origins of intelligence-led policing') will show, intelligence-led policing originated as a force-wide strategy to combat local and organised crime; the first arguments for this more proactive style of policing used the mundane examples of burglary (Audit Commission 1993) and stolen cars (NCIS 2000). Chapter 2 explains that the ideas and language of intelligence-led policing stretch back much farther than the recent fixation with counter-terrorism; intelligence-led policing has its origins in changing ideas about fiscal accountability and public sector management that predate 9/11.

To establish the need for intelligence-led policing, Chapter 3 ('The magnitude of the crime challenge') outlines the challenge facing the police and the criminal justice system. This is necessary in order to appreciate the aims of intelligence-led policing to tackle persistent, recidivist offenders and move away from a reactive model of crime control. How many crimes get reported to police? How many of these are detected and cleared by police? How many offenders arrested by police actually get a court appearance, and how many of those end up with a custodial sentence? The answers to these questions can be found in Chapter 3 with a quantification of what is called the *crime funnel*, a useful way to conceptualise the criminal justice system that will be returned to later in the book.

Wardlaw and Boughton (2006: 134) argue that 'the concept of intelligence-led policing is now widely espoused by police services as a fundamental part of the way they do business. But for such a widely talked about concept, there is remarkably little clarity about its definition and fundamental concepts.' Chapter 4 ('Defining intelligence-led policing') addresses this lack of clarity. This chapter compares intelligence-led policing with existing conceptual models of policing, explaining where intelligence-led policing is distinct from these other models, and showing where intelligence-led policing can work in a complementary manner with some of them (especially problem-oriented policing).

Establishing a definition of intelligence-led policing is not the same thing as seeing how it works in practice. This enters the realm of the relationship between crime intelligence analysts, the criminal environment, and decision-makers in the criminal justice system. Chapter 5 ('Analytical frameworks') explores some of the conceptual analytical models of policing: the intelligence cycle, SARA, and the British National Intelligence Model. These conceptual models are vital to understanding the business processes of analysis in the policing world. The chapter concludes with an outline of the 3-i model as a conceptual model for intelligence-led policing.

The 3-i model forms the basis for the three chapters that follow. Chapter 6 ('Interpreting the criminal environment') unpacks the role of the analyst in target selection. As Gill points out in regard to targeting processes, 'This is the mechanism by which law enforcement seeks to bridge the gulf between the large number of crime-like incidents or patterns to which it could theoretically respond and the much smaller number for which it is realistically resourced' (Gill 2000: 261). In an information-rich but knowledge-poor environment, analysts are increasingly influential in dictating the targets of police interdiction. To determine from the myriad crime problems which crime threats will be tackled carries a significant responsibility. As Gill continues, 'It is the enormity of this gulf that provides law enforcement with such extensive discretion and the potential for discrimination or unfairness if targeting practices go unchecked'. Chapter 6 also examines the subjects of information gathering and collation, and concludes with a look at analytical techniques and the importance of strategic analysis within intelligence-led policing.

Chapter 7 ('Influencing decision-makers') continues the 3-i model thread by looking at the vital interface between analysts and decision-makers. It first asks the rarely addressed question of who are the most appropriate decision-makers in the modern criminal justice system. Chapter 7 also explores how analysts can better understand the environment that various decision-makers work within and how to use that knowledge to maximise the analyst's influence.

Chapter 8 ('Having an impact on crime') completes the 3-i model by revisiting the crime funnel to make a case for crime prevention. It also looks at 'disruption', part of the lexicon of intelligence-led policing in many police organisations, a word that is ambiguous and not clearly defined by most agencies. Agencies designed to combat organised crime are growing to realise that traditional investigative policing is inefficient in controlling serious organised crime. As a result, 'disruption' has become a favoured term. Sheptycki argues that the perceived threat of transnational organised crime has 'provided a range of transnational platforms of governance... with tools to influence the development of national policing systems which are being progressively re-engineered around the "intelligence-led policing" paradigm' (Sheptycki 2005: 3). In better understanding this re-engineering, the chapter views the crime situation through the lens of a decision-maker's perspective.

While there have not been many quantitative or qualitative studies of intelligence-led policing as a crime-control strategy, there have been some. The penultimate chapter ('Evaluating intelligence-led policing') examines these studies by drawing together research from across the globe. In particular, Chapter 9 outlines Operation Anchorage, a burglary reduction operation that had all of the ingredients of an intelligence-led operation: informants and surveillance used to target recidivist offenders, and managerial decision-making used to direct resources and select targets.

The last chapter explores some of the challenges that intelligence-led policing may face in the future. Recent interest in intelligence-led policing, both from the community and from within policing, has provided opportunities and challenges. While there has been an increase in funding and enthusiasm for crime intelligence across the police and security field, this has also brought 'greater expectations of what can be delivered, as well as much greater scrutiny and accountability in relation to the performance of the intelligence community' (Keelty 2004: 1). The ethical and legal challenges of covert activity are discussed. Chapter 10 also explores the potential for intelligence-led policing to be the binding agent used to link local crime concerns with the widening security agenda at the national level. The chapter, and the book, concludes with a modest agenda for the future as a preliminary road map to consider where intelligence-led policing is now, and where it could be in the future.

2

Origins of intelligence-led policing

While there has been a flurry of interest in intelligence-driven approaches to crime control over the last few years, the origins of intelligence-led policing stretch back considerably further, and are a little indistinct (Gill 2000). This chapter begins by reviewing the environmental shifts and managerial changes within law enforcement that have created a landscape conducive to intelligence-led policing, and then explores the specific conditions in the UK and the US as illustrative of the influence that the local environment can have on police strategy.

Both universal and local influences have left one informed commentator to claim that law enforcement policy is attempting to return to a preventative model of policing through intelligence-led policing (Flood 2004). That remains to be seen; however, before getting to that point, it is worth remembering that public policing originally prioritised crime prevention. As the first officers of a modern police force walked out of (the old) Scotland Yard in September 1829, one of their first police commissioners wrote, 'The primary object of an efficient police is the prevention of crime: the next that of detection and punishment of offenders if crime is committed. To these ends all the efforts of police must be directed' (Mayne 1829). While preventative patrol remained a focus, the spotlight soon fell on Mayne's secondary objective, detection and punishment of offenders. In the early 1840s, the Metropolitan Police hired a number of plain-clothed 'intelligent men' to investigate and recover stolen jewellery from a robbery (Ross 2005). Within 30 years, there were formal detective divisions, and the emphasis began to slip away from crime prevention to crime detection.

Detectives did not have to wear a uniform, investigated the most serious crimes, made more arrests than the average copper on the street, and gained considerable influence within the police force. They knew all the local villains, were well connected, and seemed to be an autonomous clique within the police department. Not being answerable to the crime rate enabled detectives to thrive in a situation where the worse the crime, the better for a high-profile arrest. It is perhaps no wonder that crime prevention became a less attractive option, and young officers were often drawn to a career as a crime-fighting detective.

The introduction of police cars and the universal adoption of modern communication devices such as the telephone and the police radio advanced the crime-fighting model of policing and pushed prevention even further to the periphery. Now the public could call the police station, and with the miracle of the radio, patrolling officers could be contacted to rush to the scene of the crime within minutes. Dedicated emergency numbers like 911 (in the US) and 999 (in the UK) began to drive the day-to-day work of police officers, who were now more crime responders than crime preventers.

This reactive model of police work, where police respond to crime information from the public and investigate each offence, is still a popular one today, and has been termed the *standard model of policing* (Weisburd and Eck 2004). Although pervasive, the standard model has long been vulnerable to criticism resulting from internal and external drivers for change, drivers that have had significant impacts on the operational environment of many police departments.

Drivers for change

Policing has been traditionally perceived to be resistant to change; however, the modern policing situation is one of almost constant adaptation to pressures both internal and external. These pressures include complexity in policing and the performance culture, managing internal risk, the demand gap, limitations of the standard model of policing, organised and transnational crime, and changes in technology. These pressures and how they have driven a move towards intelligence-led policing are examined below.

Complexity in policing and the performance culture

The law enforcement world has grown increasingly complex, and this has been a driver for a better level of organisation of knowledge within policing. Increasing ability to use information to inform or evaluate decisions has driven a greater managerialism culture, a culture that has increased the bureaucratic load. Ericson and Haggerty's (1997) extensive study identified four ways that the paperwork burden alone has increased:

- Police administrators demand greater internal accountability.
- In the 'knowledge is power' culture, police overproduce information to retain in case it might be useful.

- An obsession with reporting drives internal audits and monitoring systems.
- Redundancy in retaining paper and electronic records creates duplication and drains resources.

Ironically, much of the crime-related knowledge and information that police departments create is rarely used internally but 'is disseminated to other institutions (for example, those concerned with health, insurance, public welfare, financial matters, and education) for their risk management needs, rather than used for criminal prosecution and punishment' (Ericson and Haggerty 1997: 5). Other agencies are now aware that police collect a mountain of criminal justice data, and expect the police not only to use this data to influence operational tactics, but also to make this data available to them. While these changes have occurred across most of policing, given the predominance of the detective in early policing, it is surprising that investigations is one area that has remained resistant to change, leading the authors of a major review of the investigative function to conclude:

> In many fundamental respects, the investigation process, though showing some advances, seems to have been relatively uninfluenced by significant changes in policing, the crime problem and technological advances made in the past thirty years. In the main, it is our view that progress in police criminal investigative efforts remains largely isolated from broader police efforts to respond more effectively, more efficiently and more resolutely to the crime problem in general. (Horvath *et al.* 2001: 9)

The development of intelligence-led policing is recognition that police executives require some form of process or methodology to devise more objectively priorities and strategies, to manage better the information that they now have at their fingertips, and to use this information for operational strategy decisions. The performance culture that has swept across many police services and is in part enabled by the increased reporting and digitisation of police activity has required greater analytical ability to make sense of this new (and often unwelcome) oversight. Since the inception of key performance measures for the British police services in the early 1990s (Davidoff 1996), what sought to achieve greater efficiency from the police has developed into an industry apparently fixated with the continual collection and monitoring of every aspect of police activity. The impact of this performance culture on policing is significant, and is a subject of discussion in Chapter 9.

The drive for greater efficiency is founded on the hope that with a strategic decision-making process in place, police strategies can be more easily articulated and justified internally and externally. This ability to communicate objective decisions helps address a second force for change, the increasing need to manage risk within law enforcement.

Managing risk

With greater access to information, police chiefs and executives in policing are now under far more scrutiny than before; as a result, their professional judgements and decisions are tempered by risk management (Flood 2004). This need to manage risk may be one of the most significant changes in law enforcement in recent years (Ericson and Haggerty 1997). Police departments now publish annual reports, address neighbourhood watch meetings, attend Safer Cities Initiative events, speak to the media far more than before, and address political bodies. The decisions made in a police department are now rarely confidential. This can be seen in the wealth of documents that were once for police use only, but that can now be examined in court or used in litigation against the department. As Brian Flood accurately (though a little cynically) surmises, 'In the face of an established social trend that seems to disallow honest mistakes, apportions blame and makes sure that someone "pays" whenever misfortune strikes, it is nothing more than common sense to ensure that police actions should be based, wherever possible, on rigorously evaluated intelligence of known provenance rather than on intuition, even where the latter may have its roots in long experience' (Flood 2004: 43). The difficulty with intuition, or 'the copper's instinct', is that not everyone in law enforcement has the same intuition or instincts, and given a set of similar crime problems, officers often respond in different ways.

The demand gap

A further problem faced by practitioners of the reactive, crime-fighting model of policing is the demand gap (Flood 2004). For much of the history of policing, the numbers of police were able to maintain a rough parity with the crime rate. However, the 1960s and 1970s saw an inexorable rise in crime. Factors for this increase in reported crime included greater levels of unemployment, increases in relative deprivation, and, more recently, the explosion in the availability of consumer items that are attractive, portable and easy to steal. For much of this period, the police were not held responsible for this increase in crime; people blamed the influence of social forces beyond the control of the police. The problem with arguing that police are neutral agents in the control of crime is that it is difficult to articulate for more resources. It is therefore a position that sits uneasily with the police. While many in law enforcement privately subscribe to the hypothesis that the police have little control over the larger social drivers that are believed to generate criminality within the general population,

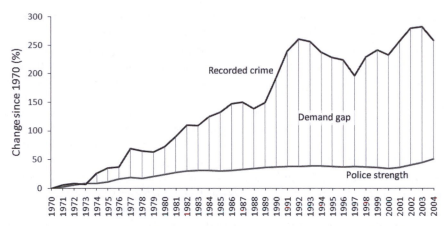

Figure 2.1 Change in UK police strength and recorded crime since 1970 (index year) showing the demand gap in resource availablity

they publicly echo calls for more resources and officers when crime rates increase. Either way, increases in personnel did not match the explosion in crime rates that occurred in many industrialised countries during the 1970s and 1980s.

Figure 2.1 shows that increases in police strength in England and Wales since 1970 (the index year for the chart) were unable to keep pace with the rapid increase in recorded indictable offences over the same period. While these figures have to be interpreted with caution (police recording practices have changed many times over the years), the gap between the lines (the demand gap) is broadly indicative of an increasing workload for the police that was not matched by increases in resources. While police strength increased by about 50 per cent, recorded crime increased by 250 per cent. In the US, the demand gap problems started in the late 1950s

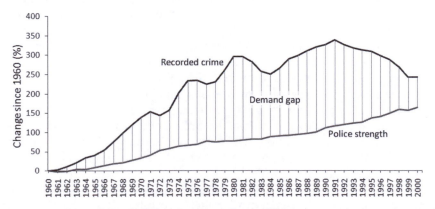

Figure 2.2 Change in US police strength and recorded index crime since 1960 (index year) showing the demand gap in resource availability

and early 1960s, and though accurate figures for this period are difficult to establish, Figure 2.2 shows a similar trend with an index year of 1960.[1]

The demand gap had direct consequences for operational policing. As a young police officer on H district in the East End of London in the 1980s, I recall coming on duty and, before my work day had even started, being handed a list of half a dozen burglaries I was required to attend and on which to write reports. Before my boots had hit the streets, any time for preventative patrol had been eroded by public demands for service. Preventative patrol – long thought to be the backbone of the police crime prevention function – needs police officers to have time that is not committed to other policing tasks. Yet, over time, as the gap between the numbers of police and the demands on the police increased, uncommitted time for preventative patrol became a scarcity for most officers.

As the paperwork mountain caused by more crime increased, police found themselves spending more and more time engaged in report-writing, counting crime, and creating statistical returns of crime that they did not use themselves but that were created for other agencies (Ericson and Haggerty 1997). By the 1980s, police in the UK, US and elsewhere found themselves in a situation where the increase in crime and demand for police services significantly outpaced any increases in the resources available to the police. The traditional tools of criminal investigation and preventative patrol that had pacified the public for many years were ineffective in containing rising criminality.

Limitations of the standard model of policing

Since 1829, modern policing functioned in the belief that there are some policing truisms whose worth it would be considered heretical even to question. Included in this list are activities that have collectively become known as the standard model of policing: random patrol across the entire geographic area of responsibility, rapid response, deployment of officers to crime investigation, and reliance on law enforcement and the legal system to suppress criminal activity (Weisburd and Eck 2004). These tactics are overwhelmingly reactive in nature, and are often uniformly applied by police departments irrespective of their size, the crime problems that they have to combat, and the nature of the area that they have to police. Tilley (2003a: 313) calls this 'fire brigade' policing, where once 'the fire is put out, the case is dealt with and then the police withdraw to await the next incident that requires attention. There is nothing strategic about response policing. There are no long term objectives. There is no purpose beyond coping with the here and now.'

Since the beginning of policing, there has been a universal acceptance of the preventative role that patrol policing fulfills. Everyone knew that offenders would be inhibited from committing crime because of the perceived threat of arrest from watchful officers. This view was more often than not shared by the public and the police alike, but a groundbreaking study changed all this. From October 1972 through 1973, the Kansas City Police Department varied their patrol strategy to test the hypothesis that differences in the number of police patrolling an area affect the crime rate. In five beats, the police only responded to crime (the 'reactive' beats) but kept out of the beat for the rest of the time. In another five beats (the 'proactive' beats), the police increased the number of patrolling officers by two or three times, and in five further beats, the police maintained the usual level of policing (the 'control' beats, usually one patrol car per beat) (Kelling *et al.* 1974). When the research team from the Police Foundation evaluated the levels of crime, traffic accidents and public perception of the police, they found some surprising results.

The different levels of patrol had no effect on burglaries, vehicle crime, robberies or vandalism; citizen fear of crime did not increase in the 'reactive' beats; the experiment had no impact on citizen perception of the police or police response times; and traffic accidents did not apparently increase in the areas with fewer police (Kelling *et al.* 1974: 2-3). Overall, it was clear that police patrol did not have the preventative effect that everyone thought it did. With the benefit of hindsight, there appear to be ways that police can perform more targeted patrols and affect crime levels (Sherman and Weisburd 1995), but the Kansas City preventative patrol experiment was important for two reasons; it dispelled the myth of random preventative patrol and it highlighted the value of research to improve policing practice.

Once the research door was opened, a plethora of policing strategies was studied. For example, Spelman and Brown (1981) discovered, through interviews with over 4,000 members of the public, that delays in citizen reporting time had a huge influence on the likelihood of making an on-scene arrest. When the public delay in calling the police, attempts to reduce response time have no impact on reducing overall crime rates. What is clear from this research period is the lack of evidence to support the standard policing strategies long held to be the backbone of effective policing. As David Weisburd and John Eck summarise:

> While [the standard method of policing] remains in many police agencies the dominant model for combating crime and disorder, we find little empirical evidence for the position that generally applied tactics that are based primarily on the law enforcement powers of the police are effective. Whether the strategy examined was generalized preventive patrol, efforts to reduce response time to citizen calls, increases in numbers of police officers, or the introduction of generalized follow-up investigations or undifferentiated intensive enforcement activities, studies fail to show consistent or meaningful

21

crime or disorder prevention benefits or evidence of reductions in citizen fear of crime. (Weisburd and Eck 2004: 57)

Organised and transnational crime

We have had organised crime since the days of high seas piracy (Hobbs 1997); however, the recent expansion in the number of organised and coordinated groups of criminals poses a particular challenge for law enforcement. These challenges are significant in two categories: organised crime and transnational crime. First, within a nation's borders, groups of offenders bond together for mutual support and mutual protection, and their tentacles spread across different types of criminal endeavour. Activities associated with organised crime groups include racketeering, political corruption, drug trafficking, and black market commodity transportation. Many groups are organised along racial or national lines. For example, the emergence since the 1970s of organised gangs from poor and socially disorganised neighbourhoods has been a particular problem in the US, where small, homogeneous neighbourhood groups have grown into nationwide organisations that commit a range of criminal activities and employ networks that are not necessarily severed when gang members are imprisoned. For example, recent estimates of gang membership in US correctional facilities range from just over 11 per cent of inmates of federal prisons to over 15 per cent in local jails (BJA 2005). Penetration of these groups by law enforcement is particularly challenging.

A second problem for police is caused by the growth of criminal opportunities resulting from globalisation. While organised crime has been discussed and perceived as a problem since the 1920s, the explosion in drug and people trafficking has propelled transnational organised crime into a problem that has been taken seriously only since the 1990s (Gill 2000). It has long been known that offenders take advantage of the administrative boundaries of police departments. In nineteenth-century London, offenders deliberately preyed on victims close to the borders between the two new police departments, the City of London Police and the Metropolitan Police (Mayhew 1862). However, the breakdown of national boundaries in the last century, coupled with the added complications of the end of the Cold War, has accelerated changes on an international level, with a corresponding increase in transnational crime. Sheptycki (2005), citing research by Bayley and others, notes that the threat of transnational organised crime was a driving force in the internationalisation of US law enforcement in the 1990s, and continues to be a significant driver for globalised policing in Europe. Sheptycki goes on to note that the threat of transnational organised crime was the primary motivating force behind attempts to enhance transnational policing, at least until the 9/11 terrorist attacks.

Federal intelligence agencies now have desks specifically to address groups such as South-East Asian organised crime and the Russian mafia, and there is a range of federal and national agencies that have mandates to interdict transnational organised crime organisations and to link domestic and international intelligence on these groups. In the US, agencies with an interest in organised and transnational crime, such as the Drug Enforcement Administration (DEA), Federal Bureau of Investigation (FBI), and the myriad other agencies under the Department of Homeland Security, are mirrored elsewhere by the Serious Organised Crime Agency (SOCA) in the UK, the Criminal Intelligence Service Canada (CISC), and the Australian Crime Commission (ACC). The Australian Federal Police have established liaison officers across the globe representing Australian interests in the fight against transnational crime, from international connections such as the UK and the US to regional interests such as Vanuatu and Myanmar. They have established Transnational Crime Units in places such as Papua New Guinea and Tonga, and set up the Pacific Transnational Crime Co-ordination Center in Fiji (Keelty 2006).

The recent change in the complexity of modern criminality has had local implications. Local police are now unable to isolate themselves and fixate on local issues. As offenders learn and adapt, and as their mobility increases and they cross jurisdictional boundaries to a greater extent now than at any time in history, the policing environment has become more complex and challenging.

Changes in technology

Traditional intelligence systems were not sophisticated. At many police stations, a room was dedicated to wall-to-wall card drawers filled with folders and card files related to local offenders. In the US, this file system was sometimes called the 'dossier system' (Carter 2004). The file system (it would be too generous to call it a real intelligence system by today's standards) was maintained by an officer known as the collator. Better collators would take an active interest in the upkeep of the files, cross-reference files for improved intelligence use, and provide information for briefings; however, the job of the collator (or, more recently, the local intelligence officer) did not traditionally attract the best candidates. The post was more commonly associated with people considered unfit for more important duty – 'the lame and the walking dead' (Maguire and John 1995: 19). As a result, the information in most collators' files was collated but never used in any meaningful manner.[2]

Since the 1980s, the rapid digitalisation of the rest of the world has not gone unnoticed within the sphere of policing, though adoption has been somewhat slower (for an exception to this, see Weisburd and Lum (2005) on the rapid adoption of crime-mapping technology). Computerised intelligence databases are now able to cross-reference information across numerous databases, search by name or keywords, and perform fuzzy searches of partial information, and new software can disseminate the results in a range of output formats such as link diagrams and maps. This has dramatically changed the nature of police intelligence practice by raising the volume of what can be accessed and integrated into an intelligence package.

Collectively, all of these drivers for change in the way that policing operates are relatively international. In other words, police services and departments around the world have all been affected to a greater or lesser degree by an environment that is more complex and accountability oriented, where demand outpaces resource availability, and where emerging threats to community safety present challenges for the traditional order of policing. However, there are also drivers for change that are specific to certain situations and nations. The next sections identify key drivers in the US and UK policing domains.

The US policing landscape

In the US, there are some facets of the law enforcement environment that help to explain further the growth of various new policing models. These include the fragmentation and overlap of police organisations in the country, a historical mistrust of any involvement of police with activities labelled with the word 'intelligence', and the growth of policing paradigms that were a response to problems not necessarily shared with the same vigour in other countries.

Fragmented and uncoordinated

Law enforcement in the US, given its historical and political origins, is fragmented and lacks both vertical and horizontal coordination, a management issue documented since the President's Commission on Law Enforcement and Administration of Justice in 1967. To get some scale of the fragmentation issue, consider the following. In October 2006, the

Table 2.1 US non-federal police agencies and officer totals, 2004

Type of agency	Number of agencies	Number of full-time sworn officers
Local police	12,766	446,974
Sheriff	3,067	175,018
State	49	58,190
Special jurisdiction	1,481	49,398
Constable/marshal	513	2,323

US population hit 300 million. At the same time the UK population was stable at about 60 million. The UK has 52 geographic police services (39 in England, four in Wales, one in Northern Ireland and eight in Scotland). If the US had the same ratio of agencies as the UK (using population as the denominator) it should have 260 police departments; however, in 2004, the US had 17,786 state and local police departments.[3] As Table 2.1 shows, the Bureau of Justice Statistics found that the majority of non-federal departments and sworn officers are employed in local municipal police departments. With an additional 104,884 officers employed in federal law enforcement, the US sworn officer community exceeds 800,000.

In this environment, sharing regional intelligence on crime patterns and offender activity is essential, because criminal endeavours and opportunities spanning local policing domains are particularly well suited to take advantage of weaknesses in a policing model dominated by local control and minimal regional cooperation (Sheptycki 2002). In terms of fighting the increasing complexity of the criminal world, the US system of local government and independence of law enforcement control actively militates against an organised response.

In response, the 1973 National Advisory Commission on Criminal Justice Standards and Goals argued that every law enforcement agency and state police should establish a capacity to gather and disseminate information on offenders, and that every state should provide a centralised clearing system. Furthermore, they argued that every police agency with 75 or more sworn employees should have an intelligence capability. In their nearly 70 recommendations and standards, they also called for additional planning at the metropolitan and regional levels (LEAA 1973).

A resultant development was the Regional Information Sharing Systems (RISS) network, used as the primary formal method of passing criminal intelligence between agencies. The Criminal Intelligence System Operating Policies (28 CFR (Code of Federal Regulations) Part 23) – perceived by many in the US as the main constraint on intelligence sharing – was written to apply primarily to the RISS centers (Peterson 2005). Since 9/11, the mantle of information-sharing hub appears to have been passed on. As the following viewpoint from Ray Guidetti demonstrates, the fragmented and uncoordinated nature of American policing creates particular challenges for information sharing, challenges that are starting to be tackled with the introduction across the US of fusion centers.

Viewpoint

Fragmented policing and the role of fusion centers

Ray Guidetti

The dreadful attacks of 9/11 and the subsequent approach to counterterrorism have drastically shaped the policies, strategies, and operations of law enforcement agencies across the US, and have thrust American policing into a new age. Practitioners have begun to view policing from a new paradigm that has been called the Homeland Security era. It is an age where conventional thinking expects intelligence and information-sharing to carry the day. Yet even with the imperative of growing terrorism and radical jihadism, organisational structures, perceptions, traditions, and cultural divides still daunt this mission. Police intelligence operations of the past, and the negative connotations associated with such practices, continue to demonize the tradecraft of criminal intelligence domestically. Moreover, lack of an official doctrine regarding domestic intelligence at the national level undermines our concerted efforts to adopt effective strategies.

One particular US problem that is not shared by other countries is the plethora of over 18,000 law enforcement agencies spread across federal, state, and local governments. Structurally this makes cooperation more challenging, and particularly so when police administrators have yet to reward information and intelligence sharing. Faced with these pitfalls, police professionals are turning to fusion centers to spearhead efforts to produce intelligence that drives policy, strategy, and operations at the state and local levels.

The New Jersey Regional Operations Intelligence Center (NJ ROIC), for example, sits between a mass of federal agencies, a few state agencies, and over 550 local police departments. The role of our center is to maintain state-wide situational awareness for response to current and future security issues concerning New Jersey. By collecting and analyzing information, the NJ ROIC seeks to craft finished intelligence products designed to interpret the patterns and trends of the criminal environment, and then provide predictive analysis to consumers. Nonetheless, the job is difficult in the absence of clarity from the federal government. 'Building the plane as we're flying it,' is the common mantra that echoes throughout this center.

By their very nature, fusion centers are designed to blend information from a variety of sources, an array of disciplines, and from every level of government. The challenge is intimidating and necessitates allied agencies to not only earmark liaison officers to carry out the fusion center mission, but construct changes to their existing policies and procedures that in the past may have obstructed information and intelligence sharing. Many of today's fusion centers concentrate solely on terrorism, while others adopt an 'all crimes, all hazards, all threats' approach. Regardless of their focus, each will have to confront the obstacles inherent to change: the fusion center is the first attempt at introducing the concepts of intelligence and intelligence-led policing to an undeveloped network of potential information collectors and intelligence producers and consumers.

Despite present-day thinking that increasingly recognizes the value of intelligence and intelligence-led policing, the acceptance among mainstream practitioners continues to be disheartening. This is particularly troubling in the wake of 9/11. It has, however, provided an inimitable opportunity for fusion centers to become collaborative information-sharing environments across Federal, state and local levels. These centers have the prospect of molding the concepts of intelligence into the operating domain, yet their success will undoubtedly rely on the creativity, leadership, and ingenuity of those leading them.

Lieutenant Ray Guidetti, a 15-year veteran of the New Jersey State Police and career intelligence officer, supervises the Analysis Element within New Jersey's fusion center.

Demonising intelligence

From the original 'dossier system' of the 1920s, police in the US had long kept information on suspect persons such as bootleggers and high-profile criminals. However, when the House Committee on Un-American Activities (formed in 1937) resumed in the period immediately following World War II, fuelled by the advocacy of Senator Joseph McCarthy, some US police departments began to use dossiers to catalogue the activities of people believed to be communists or communist sympathisers. These dossiers were still in use during the growth of the civil rights movement and in the protests surrounding US involvement in the Vietnam War (Carter 2004).

Serious questions began to emerge about the use of intelligence records and the intelligence activity of police departments when evidence came to light of the bugging by the FBI of Martin Luther King, Jr. When William C. Sullivan, former Assistant Director of the FBI's Domestic Intelligence Division, testified in 1975 before the Senate Select Committee to Study Governmental Operations with Respect to Intelligence Activities (the findings of which are also referred to as the Senate Select Committee on Intelligence Activities, or the Church Report), he explained that from 1963 to his assassination in 1968, Dr King had been 'the target of an intensive campaign by the FBI to neutralize him as an effective civil rights leader' (DOJ

1977: 1). As revealed by the Church Report, the FBI's counterintelligence programme (COINTELPRO), which ran from 1956 to 1971, rapidly moved from its original aims of targeting foreign intelligence agencies during the Cold War to spying on American citizens and dissident political bodies (Brodeur 1983). They even went as far as planting false information and rumours about American political leaders (White 2004).

The lack of governance of police intelligence units had a corollary outcome in a degree of abuse of the ethics of the intelligence process. Intelligence files were kept on people who were not criminals but merely politically active and vocal in their objections to government policy. As a result, a number of police departments, either through political pressure, voluntarily, or from court mandate, closed down their criminal intelligence units (Peterson 2005).

> Moving into the late 1960s and early 1970s, this movement of lawsuits reached toward law enforcement intelligence units. It was increasingly discovered that police agencies were keeping intelligence files on people for whom there was no evidence of criminality. The practice of keeping intelligence dossiers on a contingency basis was found to be improper, serving no compelling state interest and depriving those citizens of their constitutional rights. As a result, the courts repeatedly ordered intelligence files to be purged from police records and in many cases police agencies had to pay damage awards to plaintiffs. The decisions also permitted citizens to gain access to their own records. Many activists publicized their intelligence files as a badge of honor, often to the embarrassment of the police (Carter 2004: 25).

Coupled with the Watergate scandal, the focus of US intelligence management (both national security and criminal) became obsessed with the legality of its practices resulting in a raft of legislation that limited intelligence-gathering activities. In the minds of the public, police use of intelligence became viewed with suspicion, while within law enforcement it became seen as a liability that few were prepared to risk employing.

The repercussions of this phase in US law enforcement history are still being felt today. The National Institute of Justice – the research, development, and evaluation agency of the US Department of Justice – still avoids the term 'intelligence-led policing' in preference for a broader but less accurate term, 'information-led policing'. And a recent survey of over 800 police departments in the US found that only about 40 per cent of large departments (with more than 100 sworn officers) enter intelligence records onto a computerised system (O'Shea and Nicholls 2002: 17).

The community policing era

From the 1920s to the 1970s, American policing moved from being a political tool to the professional model of policing favoured by August Vollmer and articulated on a grand scale by Orlando Wilson. Focusing on serious crime, Wilson and his reformist colleagues emphasised the importance of bureaucratic autonomy, operational efficiency, and the use of command and control systems to ensure internal accountability (Kelling and Wycoff 2002). As in the UK, this standard model was dominated by rapid response, car patrols and criminal investigations.

However, at the same time as this model was attaining dominance, it was being undermined in the US by public concern regarding police actions they were witnessing for the first time. Although the police were not to blame for the social conditions that fuelled many of the urban riots of the 1960s, it was the activities of police on the streets that appeared to be the catalyst for many of the riots. The police response to often peaceful protestors demonstrating against the Vietnam War and for the civil rights movement brought unwanted attention to the doors of local police chiefs. The graphic television images of police with dogs and water cannon brought an unwelcome and unexpected reality into the homes of middle-class America.

President Lyndon Johnson's Crime Commission on Law Enforcement and the Administration of Justice, in operation after July 1965, produced their report titled 'The Challenge of Crime in a Free Society' in 1967. Like similar reports of the time, the commission noted the relationship between social factors, such as racism, the moral failings of offenders, social injustice and poverty, and the resultant violence and disorder. The commission recommended that the police work especially hard in minority communities, and that they make attempts to regain legitimacy and offset the unpopularity of the police through community relations programmes.

In these early days, officers assigned to such programmes were sometimes drawn from the 'empty holster crowd' – officers who were assigned to limited duties because of drinking problems or other issues that prevented their being issued with a firearm (Kelling and Wycoff 2002: Ch. 3: 2). But this was at least a beginning, and the community policing movement, although taking time to gain momentum, can trace its roots back to these tumultuous times of the 1960s and 1970s. The community policing industry, with its philosophical triumvirate of citizen involvement, problem solving and decentralisation (Skogan 2006b), was attractive to police managers rocked by falling public confidence, and political leaders looking to improve the standing of the police department and control public fear of crime.

The community policing era promoted the notion of public accountability for their response to crime to some police chiefs for the first time.

Furthermore, through the broad conceptual framework of community policing, problem-oriented policing was able to surface as a data-driven, objective crime-reduction strategy – important characteristics for the eventual emergence of intelligence-led policing.

Slow emergence of problem-oriented policing

Michael Scott, Director of the Center for Problem-Oriented Policing and a chronicler of the growth of problem-oriented policing, argues that problem-oriented policing is still in its relative infancy (Scott 2000). But there is still enough evidence from the last 25 years to trace the growth and development of problem-oriented policing as both an idea and a policing movement.

Madison, Wisconsin, was the first police department to adopt formally Herman Goldstein's problem-oriented policing approach when they tackled the problems of drunk driving and repeat sex offenders. Within a few years of the publication of an early article on the topic (Goldstein 1979), UK police services were also experimenting with problem-oriented policing (Leigh *et al.* 1996), and in the US the police in Baltimore County (Maryland) and Newport News (Virginia) were evaluating more formal experiments.

The nationwide accessibility of the report on problem-oriented policing in the Newport News Police Department was hugely influential in spreading the message and techniques to a large practitioner audience. John Eck and William Spelman (1987) introduced the SARA methodology to a huge audience of police officers looking for a way to have an impact on crime problems in their communities, and the SARA approach of *S*can, *A*nalyse, *R*espond and *A*ssess, has become one of the best-known acronyms in modern policing. Scott (2000) lists over 60 prominent police agencies now associated with problem-oriented policing, looking, in the words of Herman Goldstein, to draw 'the police away from the traditional preoccupation with creating an efficient organisation; from the heavy investment in standard, generic operating procedures for responding to calls and preventing crime; and from heavy dependence on criminal law as the primary means for getting their job done' (foreword in Scott 2000: vi).

Problem-oriented policing is important to the development of intelligence-led policing because it has opened the eyes of a whole generation of police managers to the possibilities of using crime analysis to form operational strategies and solve problems. Through the work of environmental criminologists and the development of areas such as situational crime prevention, new methods of strategic crime management that address long-term solutions to crime problems are increasingly possible.

Rapid emergence of Compstat

Not only were the 1980s and 1990s a period of innovation for problem and community-based crime control solutions, but they were also the period that saw the rapid emergence of Compstat as a crime-fighting strategy. The meaning of the word 'Compstat' is not very clear (Maple and Mitchell 1999). Most people claim that it is shorthand for 'computerised statistics' (Vito *et al.* 2005) or 'computer comparison statistics' (Walsh 2001), though it has recently been claimed to represent 'compare stats', the name of an original computer file used to store crime data (Silverman 2006). Either way, Compstat began in the Crime Control Strategy meetings of the New York City Police Department (NYPD) in January 1994. Police Commissioner William Bratton, newly hired from the city's Transit Police by Mayor Rudy Giuliani, created Compstat with the primary aim of establishing accountability among the city's 76 police commanders (Magers 2004). The much-publicised crime drop in New York around this time cemented the popular view that Compstat was responsible for making the city safer: major crime in the city fell by half from 1993 to 1998 (Walsh 2001).

In 1996, the prestigious Ford Foundation and John F. Kennedy School of Government awarded Compstat the Innovations in American Government Award, noting that although other police departments were using crime-mapping technology, the innovative component in New York was the organisational overhaul that brought commanders and managers together (Ford Foundation 1996: 31). Other awards followed, notably from then Vice President Al Gore, and considerable publicity propelled Compstat into the national spotlight. The mayor of Baltimore even uses a variant of Compstat (called CitiStat) as a management process for his city government (Silverman 2006).

However, as numerous researchers have argued, there may have been additional factors that explain the rapid spread of Compstat. David Weisburd and colleagues (2003) note that the problem-oriented policing movement had already demonstrated the benefit of a data-driven, decision-making platform to police managers; there was increased knowledge in regard to the effectiveness of responses to crime; Compstat coincided with the digital explosion that reduced computing costs; and, finally, police leaders were becoming more comfortable with professional management concepts. While limiting themselves to the effect of Compstat on homicide rates, Eck and Maguire's (2000) examination of various different strands of evidence resulted in the conclusion that 'there is little evidence to support the assertion that Compstat caused the decline in homicides' (p. 235). Erroneous or not, the reputation had nevertheless been established, and Compstat spread rapidly throughout the US and the rest of the world. Only five years after the NYPD started using Compstat, one-third of large US police departments had implemented it, and Weisburd and colleagues' survey predicted that Compstat would achieve 90 per cent saturation in large US police departments by 2006. A more in-depth description of the processes and conceptual structure of Compstat follows in Chapter 4.

9/11 and homeland security

One final driver for intelligence-led policing has been the move towards what has been called the Homeland Security era, an outcome of the events of 9/11. In the aftermath of the terrorist attacks, the Department of Homeland Security was formed and there were numerous calls for police agencies in the US to build global partnerships and increase information sharing in the domestic arena (McGarrell *et al.* 2007). By the spring of 2002, the IACP held a Criminal Intelligence Sharing Summit, from which the Global Justice Information Sharing Initiative (Global) Intelligence Working Group (GIWG) was formed. It subsequently created the National Criminal Intelligence Sharing Plan (GIWG 2003).

One of the implicit arguments of the National Criminal Intelligence Sharing Plan appears to be the assumption that, if greater information sharing had occurred prior to 9/11, the tragic events could have been prevented. Thus, a key theme that resonates throughout the plan is the need to overcome the 'long-standing and substantial barriers that hinder intelligence sharing' (GIWG 2003: iv). The response to this has been the creation of fusion centers and a greater awareness of the need for information sharing. The National Criminal Intelligence Sharing Plan's recommendations call for more funding for training and infrastructure, the creation and adoption of standards, the fostering of trust among law enforcement agencies, and calls to develop professional practice and make better use of new and existing resources.

Specifically how these recommendations will address the deep-seated and cultural obstacles that so effectively inhibit information sharing is unclear. At best, they provide excellent suggestions for ways to share information once these barriers have been overcome, though they do not address why the barriers exist. And this was not the first attempt at better coordination of American law enforcement activities. An evaluation of the HIDTAs (high-intensity drug trafficking areas) set up in the US to provide additional assistance to areas ravaged by drug crime found that the assumption that having officers from different agencies working together would improve law enforcement was not necessarily borne out (BOTEC 2001).

The vision of the GIWG has been to use the plan as both a representative intelligence-sharing plan, and as a 'mechanism to promote intelligence-led policing' (GIWG 2005: iv). It remains to be seen whether everyone in American policing visualises the conceptual framework of intelligence-led policing in the same way.

The British policing landscape

While European bureaucrats such as Eugène-François Vidocq (first head of the Paris Sûreté from 1812 to 1827) had employed card indices to maintain information on hundreds of criminals in the city, middle-class discomfort with this type of approach to policing delayed the introduction of criminal intelligence systems to the UK. This changed with the need to keep track of the Fenian uprising in the 1880s (John and Maguire 2007). However, even with the need to monitor spy networks during World War I and World War II, the use of criminal intelligence in the British police remained a peripheral activity and for over 150 years languished in the 'murky backwaters of policing' (Christopher 2004: 179).

A series of national studies in the 1970s and 1980s attempted to promote a greater enthusiasm and structure in criminal intelligence practice in the UK. The collection of Association of Chief Police Officers (ACPO) reports known as the Baumber, Pearce and Ratcliffe reports (ACPO 1975; 1978, ACPO 1986) identified a number of issues with the management and organisation of criminal intelligence, along with the lack of resources and status associated with intelligence, though with little apparent success in significantly improving matters. These reports did, however, provide a road map, and other drivers provided the necessary impetus.

New public managerialism and oversight

The demand gap, discussed earlier in this chapter, was a catalyst for a rethinking of police crime-control strategies. However, this took place during a time of increased demand for value for money from public agencies. The new public management movement in the UK began in the early 1980s with a focus on greater 'efficiency, effectiveness and economy' (Crawford 1997: 88). Increased fiscal constraints have not been restricted to the UK; the Royal Canadian Mounted Police (RCMP) had to cut 10 per cent of the workforce due to substantial budget cuts between 1994 and 1995 (Deukmedjian 2006). The British police were initially reluctant to yield to calls for greater local management responsibilities that threatened to shift power away from the central organisational hierarchies. There was also suspicion of the process of management by objectives with the allied threat of future resource allocations tied to greater perceived efficiency. As Silverman notes, 'while target-setting is the norm for the private sector, usually it is anathema for public organisations because it offers a yardstick against which performance can be more accurately measured and, if deficient, condemned' (2006: 280). But in the end, the police service could not remain immune to the wave sweeping across the rest of the public sector. While the 1993 Sheehy Inquiry into Police Responsibilities was largely resisted, the subsequent Police and Magistrates Courts Act brought the 'new public management' of the corporate world to policing (Gill 1998). The result was a considerable change in organisational structure and thinking.

Crime desks and crime management units began to appear in British police stations. At the crime desk (often staffed by a detective sergeant), every crime report was briefly reviewed and then a determination was made as to the value of further enquiries. A grading system was used to determine whether a detective would be assigned, and if not, processes were put in place to write letters to the victims of crime informing them that no further action would be taken – as in the majority of cases. In reality, the crime desk was more often simply an added level of bureaucracy to help cope with the explosion of paperwork associated with reported crime (Flood 2004).

The move to greater efficiency and effectiveness in policing did not necessarily receive universal approval. While a drive to greater efficiency within law enforcement was generally considered to be sensible and appropriate in times of financial constraint, it has also been argued that with a focus on internal organisational change and value for money, this results orientation makes it more difficult for agencies to work with other outside bodies because of the considerable degree of internal conflict caused by competition (Crawford 1997). However, internal competition for resources was matched by competition for resources externally, and police forces pointed to their crime-management systems as evidence of greater efficiency when arguing with other public agencies for their slice of the sparse public money pie.

Sporadic emergence of problem-oriented policing in the UK

The UK adoption of community policing never really took hold with the same pace as the US adoption, even though the UK did experience some of the problems that had precipitated the US move towards community policing. The Brixton riots of April 1981 (along with the subsequent summer of riots across other towns in the country) were probably the closest the UK got to the levels of public unrest and disorder that swept the US in the 1960s and 1970s. Some of the suggested responses echoed the US answer to their public disorder problems. The Scarman Report, published at the end of 1981, recommended that police work more closely with the community, focus on race relations training, actively recruit from ethnic minorities, weed out potentially racist recruits, and make policing more open to community scrutiny (such as the lay visitors scheme) (Scarman 1981). Scarman was also highly critical of the use of police stop and search powers. However, the response from the law enforcement apparatus was more of an organisational one than a philosophical shift in thinking about the business of policing. Lay schemes allowed approved members of the public to visit police stations unannounced so that they could check on the welfare of prisoners held in custody, stop and search powers were significantly curtailed by the Police and Criminal Evidence Act (PACE) 1984, and community consultation groups sprang up, but there was never the wholesale adoption of the community policing ethos that swept many police departments in the US. Fortunately, one offshoot from the community policing movement that did gain traction in the UK was problem-oriented policing.

Surrey Constabulary is credited as being the first UK force both to engage in problem-oriented policing (1982) and to implement some kind of programme on a force-wide basis (Leigh *et al.* 1996). Enthusiasm and levels of adoption varied considerably across the UK, influenced to a degree by the fact that some sites experienced considerable problems with implementation. Generating enthusiasm for problem-oriented policing and advertising success was difficult in the early days because not all of the early forces that ran problem-oriented policing projects (such as the Metropolitan Police, Northumbria and Thames Valley) built formal effectiveness evaluations into their projects, and the early formal evaluation in one part of Leicestershire was disappointing (Leigh *et al.* 1996). However, a number of drivers provided encouraging signs for the advantages of problem-oriented policing, some of which overlap with driving forces for intelligence-led policing. These included the demand gap, further research on the concentration of crime, a greater belief that community partnerships can help alleviate crime problems, and government support for community-centerd crime prevention (Leigh *et al.* 1998).

Problem-oriented policing has grown steadily in some forces, with some police forces (for example, Lancashire) faring particularly well at the annual Tilley Awards – an award funded by the Home Office (and modelled on the annual US Goldstein award) to recognise excellence in crime reduction by employing problem-oriented principles. However, the development in the UK has been sporadic: a number of forces paid lip service to the concepts of problem-oriented policing and preferred to develop their interest in intelligence-led policing.

The difficulty with a greater adoption of problem-oriented policing at this point in time might have been competition with intelligence-led policing. As Adrian Leigh and colleagues were publishing the second major government report on problem-oriented policing near the end of 1998, a number of forces were already moving towards an intelligence-led style of policing, research on intelligence-led policing was already being published (Gill 1998), and the National Criminal Intelligence Service was just over a year away from publishing and formalising the National Intelligence Model (NCIS 1999; 2000). In fact, the foundations for intelligence-led policing had been laid prior to the first Home Office reports on problem-oriented policing, with the Audit Commission report, *Helping with Enquiries: Tackling Crime Effectively*.

Helping with enquiries and policing with intelligence

In 1993, the Audit Commission published *Helping with Enquiries: Tackling Crime Effectively*. This management handbook was unlike most other governmental reports published in the UK. It was glossy, illustrated, and accessible. The cover even had an image from the inescapable British television police show, *The Bill*. Clearly, the Audit Commission wished to engage with practitioners and influence the manner of police operations.

The Audit Commission report addressed police effectiveness, and being an independent agency with a mandate to address the economic and effective management of public services, their recommendations sought to get the most value for money from the police in the fight against crime. *Helping with Enquiries* had three main points:

- Existing policing roles and the levels of accountability lacked integration and efficiency.

- The police were failing to make the best use of resources.

- Greater emphasis on tackling criminals would be more effective than focusing on crimes (Ratcliffe 2003).

The aim of the Audit Commission was to promote greater efficiency from the police by exhorting them to make better use of existing resources, because there was no promise of more money or personnel. This was attractive to a Conservative government trying to cut public expenditure. The Audit Commission did not explicitly define the term 'intelligence-led policing' but did strongly advocate proactive policing. *Helping with Enquiries* included a barrage of statistics to support the argument, statistics that were on the surface convincing. A few researchers considered these statistics in greater depth and questioned the validity of the apparently simple case proposed by the Audit Commission (see, for example, Dunnighan and Norris 1999, and a relevant paper by Townsley and Pease 2002); however, in the meantime, *Helping with Enquiries* was gathering vocal and enthusiastic supporters because it provided an argument for police to re-engage with what they considered to be core business, combating crime. Greater employment of intelligence against prolific offenders was a theme that proved highly popular. The Audit Commission (1993: 42) saw much that was wrong with focusing on crime not criminals, and attributed the cause of this as:

- insufficient interview training;
- forensic potential not utilised;
- scientific support under-resourced;
- pattern of activity highly reactive;
- intelligence work having low status and under-resourced;
- failure to exploit crime pattern analysis and informants.

This theme was taken up within a couple of years by another influential report from Her Majesty's Inspectorate of Constabulary (HMIC). From an operational police perspective, *Policing with Intelligence* (HMIC 1997) managed to hit all the right populist notes. Lined with quotations from Chinese military strategist Sun Tzu's *Art of War* (500 BC) *Policing with Intelligence* sought to build on the interest sparked by the Audit Commission report by propelling proactive tactics and management into the mainstream of British policing. Subtitled 'Criminal Intelligence – a Thematic Inspection on Good Practice', the report echoed the expectation of value for money from the first paragraph. The report further identified a number of key factors that HMIC considered to be vital in promoting intelligence-led policing:

- enthusiastic and energetic leadership that endorses intelligence-led policing and promotes it through a Director of Intelligence;
- a published strategy that sets the intelligence agenda for a force, as well as explains what is meant by 'proactivity';
- an integrated intelligence structure so that analysts can work at the hub of operational policing activities;
- criteria to measure performance to determine the effectiveness of the introduction of the crime intelligence function and the tasking of operational units;
- the forging of effective partnerships with local agencies that may be able to help police combat local crime and disorder problems (HMIC 1997: 1).

One should not underestimate the influence of both *Policing with Intelligence*, and the 'landmark' (Heaton 2000) report, *Helping with Enquiries: Tackling Crime Effectively*. These two documents pushed intelligence-led policing onto the radar of many in British policing, and cemented intelligence-led policing and proactive policing into the lexicon of law enforcement.

The National Intelligence Model

Flood (2004) argues that a significant driver for a better national capability in regard to criminal intelligence was coming from the operational level of police services. However, at the local level, the intelligence 'lacuna' (Christopher 2004) was still evident, though starting to be addressed. Beyond *Policing with Intelligence*, and *Helping with Enquiries*, Home Office-supported research was providing further indicators of the emerging enthusiasm for intelligence practices. On behalf of the Police Research Group (PRG), Mike Maguire and Tim John conducted a year-long examination of the value of criminal intelligence systems, surveillance and informants as local investigative strategies across eight police forces (Maguire and John 1995). They concluded that only those police services that had invested major organisational reforms had reaped any benefit from a move to greater proactivity in policing. They also concluded that:

- Major organisational reforms can be successfully implemented only if there is wholehearted commitment to them from the most senior officers in the force.

- Given the interdependence of different specialist roles within an integrated proactive system, it is clearly vital that all officers understand its overall purposes and expected benefits and their own contribution to it.

- The possible negative influence of broader 'cultural' factors should not be underestimated.

- Once the system is in operation, it needs to be continually monitored and reviewed.

- The key objectives and strategies of the system should also be reviewed at intervals, informed wherever possible by evaluations of outcomes.

- Access to resources, such as surveillance teams, which are supposed to be 'owned' by the whole force, should be seen to be equitable (Maguire and John 1995: 54–55).

A national model was clearly required. The Baumber and Pearce reports (ACPO 1975; 1978), while not necessarily being acted upon, had at least started a discussion about how to rescue criminal intelligence from the wilderness. Although police were too busy with the rapidly expanding crime problem, these documents suggested that better coordination of effort at the local and national level was necessary to achieve greater inroads into criminal activity. The accumulated effort of ACPO reports, the Audit Commission, HMIC thematic reports, and Home Office enthusiasm provided a fertile and receptive ground when the National Criminal

Intelligence Service, commissioned by ACPO, finally released the National Intelligence Model. The National Intelligence Model, with its tiers from serious and organised crime to regional and local levels, incorporates national priorities with the flexibility to adjust to local conditions. While notionally an intelligence model, the development team, especially Roger Gaspar and Brian Flood (Grieve 2004) recognised the value of the model as a generalized police management framework. Designed to professionalise intelligence practice across the country and to integrate criminal intelligence into the central framework of all police business and decision-making, this model is a key factor in the development of British intelligence-led policing.

Summary

The UK move towards intelligence-led policing might not have been matched by a similar level of enthusiasm from the US had it not been for the events of 11 September 2001. The realisation that some events such as a terrorist attack cannot be dealt with in a reactive fashion and that a proactive approach to crime prevention and disruption is necessary helped to propel the tenets of intelligence-led policing onto the international policing stage.

Table 2.2. Summary of main factors relevant to development of intelligence-led policing

Universal factors
Complexity in policing
Managing internal risk
The demand gap
Limitations of the standard model of policing
Organised and transnational crime
Changes in technology

Country-specific considerations

US policing landscape	UK policing landscape
Fragmented and uncoordinated	New public managerialism and oversight
Demonising 'intelligence'	Sporadic emergence of POP
Community policing era	*Helping with Enquiries* and *Policing with Intelligence*
Slow emergence of POP	The NIM
Rapid emergence of Compstat	
9/11 and homeland security	

NIM: National Intelligence Model; POP: problem-oriented policing.

When the International Association of Chiefs of Police (IACP) held a Criminal Intelligence Sharing Summit at Alexandria, Virginia, in the spring of 2002, they addressed a call from President George W. Bush to improve criminal intelligence data sharing among agencies at all levels of government. The experts brought together for the summit called for a National Intelligence Plan and a Criminal Intelligence Coordinating Council, and made a number of further recommendations. The first of their recommendations was to 'promote intelligence-led policing through a common understanding of criminal intelligence and its usefulness' (IACP 2002: v). Now US police chiefs from around the country are calling for greater development of intelligence-led policing (for example, Bratton 2007; Kerlikowske 2007).

The rhetoric of intelligence-led policing has spread to every state police service in Australia (Ratcliffe 2003) and the Australian Federal Police (Wardlaw and Boughton 2006); to the New Zealand Police (where it is called intelligence-based policing; NZP 2002); and to Canada, where the Royal Canadian Mounted Police adopted intelligence-led policing as far back as December 2000 (Deukmedjian 2006) and the Director General of Criminal Intelligence Service Canada (CISC) said that 'we know that intelligence-led policing is the most effective way to combat organized crime' (CISC 2006b).

It has been argued in this chapter that some universal drivers have pushed police towards a more objective, intelligence-driven approach to their work. These drivers are listed at the top of Table 2.2. The universality of these factors in affecting police services in most of the industrialised countries and beyond suggests that a unified response would flow. However, countries have different historical structures of policing, different organisational complexities, and different national psyches in regard to the role of police in a democratic society. As a result, national idiosyncrasies go some way to explain the development of different responses to problems that have plagued many countries. This chapter focused on the US and the UK, given that these countries have been responsible for originating many of the conceptual frameworks of modern policing. These national factors are listed in the lower part of Table 2.2.

While there appears to be a clear enthusiasm for intelligence-led policing, is there a quantifiable need for intelligence-led policing based on the nature of crime? The next chapter addresses this issue by exploring the magnitude of the crime challenge.

Notes

1 US crime rate sourced from the Bureau of Justice Statistics, at bjsdata.ojp.usdoj.gov/dataonline/Search/Crime/State/statebystaterun.cfm?stateid=52. Accessed

December 2006. Police strength sourced from *Uniform Crime Reports*, 1960 to 2000.

2 In many cases, the collator's files were a self-service affair. As a young constable, I made an off-duty (and unarmed!) arrest of a man wanted for murder by recognising him from a photograph in a collator's file. I found the photograph tucked away in the back of the collator's record, and I recognised the man while he was drinking outside an East London pub. Prior to his arrest, the photograph was never disseminated around the police station or shown to patrol officers such as myself, and it was not widely known that we had a wanted murderer in the area.

3 Source: Bureau of Justice Statistics, Law Enforcement Statistics: summary findings, http://www.ojp.usdoj.gov/bjs/lawenf.htm, accessed 17 September 2006.

3

The magnitude of the crime challenge

Why do we need intelligence-led policing? The answer lies in the nature of crime. In this chapter, I will show why a data-driven, offender orientation is necessary to combat the threat of crime, and why a reactive response to crime events – often through unfocused investigative action – is a recipe for failure. To understand the need for intelligence-led policing, some quantification is necessary. How big is the crime challenge facing the police? How much crime gets reported to police? How much of this is detected, and how many of these offenders get jailed? Is there a hard core of offenders committing most of the crime in our society? The answers to these questions have been a driving force for intelligence-led policing and have been used as evidence to drive a proactive approach. For example, as stated in the previous chapter, *Helping with Enquiries* – the Audit Commission report that advocated a move towards proactive policing and brought the concept of intelligence-led policing to a wider audience – argued for the police to focus on prolific and serious offenders and for an increase in the use of criminal intelligence. The report made a number of claims to support this approach, saying a small minority of offenders commit most of the crime, and that tackling the criminal, and not the crime, is the most efficient way for police to reduce crime. This chapter looks at the crime and offender data and considers whether these figures provide evidence to advocate an intelligence-led model of policing.

The crime funnel is a simple way to summarise the workings of the criminal justice system. It traces the 'wastage' of criminal activity from the original incidents down through the process of police recording, court practice and sentencing likelihood. In other words, how cases funnel down through the system and either get dropped or proceed to the next level. It is a useful exercise in understanding the way that the criminal justice system works (or does not!) and how the various stages of the system can help or hinder the development of intelligence-led policing. The first part of the chapter examines each stage in detail so we can begin to construct a model of the crime funnel.

The crime funnel

To estimate the crime funnel, we must utilise a variety of sources. Most of them are official records from the criminal justice system, but not all crime that occurs makes it into the official records. We therefore have to start by getting a measure of how much crime takes place and how much of this is actually reported to the police.

How much crime gets reported?

For the police to tackle crime and disorder, they have to know how much crime there is so that they can decide what offences to concentrate on. This has traditionally been a difficult area for researchers. For much of the history of criminology, official figures from the police and courts were the only records available to students of the criminal justice system. Because everyone knew that not all crime gets reported, many countries started to conduct surveys to ask people whether they have been the victim of a crime and whether they reported the offence to the police.

In the US, the biggest is the National Crime Victimization Survey (NCVS). Every year since 1973, researchers have surveyed householders and asked a series of questions about the crime they have been a victim of and how they responded. The most recent survey interviewed over 75,000 households. From this, the Bureau of Justice Statistics is able to estimate the likelihood of victimisation for most of the serious crime categories (rape, sexual assault, robbery, assault, theft, household burglary, and motor vehicle theft). They can then estimate the chances of being a victim of crime for the whole population as well as for segments of the population such as women, the elderly, members of various racial groups, city dwellers, or other groups. The annual British Crime Survey (BCS) similarly uses extensive survey information to elicit a more realistic estimation of national crime and discover more about the 'dark figure of crime' (Hough and Lewis 1989; Flood 2004) – the amount of crime that remains unreported. Like the NCVS, the BCS asks a large representative sample of the general public about their experience as victims of household and personal crime in the previous year. Each year, they interview over 50,000 people over the age of 16.

Both surveys aim to provide a count of crime that includes incidents not reported to the police. In this way, researchers and policymakers can estimate the real level of crime in a manner unaffected by changes in the way police record crime (Bottomley and Coleman 1976; McCabe and Sutcliffe 1978). For the offences the surveys cover, they provide a more complete picture of the national extent of crime than police figures. It also gives a better measure of the trends in crime, as willingness to report crimes to the police varies over time. Table 3.1 shows that both the US and UK have similar reporting rates for many offences, though the British appear to report fewer violent crimes and Americans report fewer burglaries.

Table 3.1 Crime reporting rates in the US and UK for selected offences.
Sources: British Crime Survey 2006/07, and US National Crime Victimization Survey 2004

Crime	US reporting rate (%)	UK reporting rate (%)
Motor vehicle theft	95	93
Burglary	53	66
Aggravated assault/wounding	64	58
Robbery	61	47
Assault without injury	40	36
Theft from the person	40	35
All violent offences	49	43
All crime	41	41

Given the reporting gaps apparent from Table 3.1, analyses based on police statistics do not necessarily reflect the real, underlying level of crime. Many offences are not reported for personal reasons: sexual offences may cause embarrassment to the victim; victims wanted by the police rarely contact the police for fear of being taken into custody; and shoplifters may simply have the stolen goods confiscated without the police being called. Other reasons for not reporting include apathy, the notion that the police are either too busy or not interested, and belief that the offence is not serious enough to warrant the involvement of the authorities, or that it is too inconvenient for the victim to contact the police. Worse, some crimes are not even noticed by these victimisation surveys. Some crimes of an ingenious nature such as tax evasion, computer crime and subtle cases of arson are not detected by the public or police and escape reporting altogether.

The BCS and the NCVS ask slightly different questions, but, as you can see from Tables 3.2 and 3.3, there are different reasons why people do not report crime. The public often make a conscious decision that the crime is not significant enough to make an official record. However, this causes problems when police try to make operational decisions based on an information source that is not complete. If police allocate resources on the basis of recorded crime alone, then variations in reporting rates may affect the distribution of crime reports. For example, fraud has a relatively low reporting rate because some people either do not know or are embarrassed that they have been tricked out of money, and some businesses do not report fraud losses for fear of appearing vulnerable to their customers or competition. Because the level of reporting fraud is low, there is the possibility that police pay less attention to this financially devastating crime. We can see from Table 3.2 and 3.3 that there is variation in reporting rate for crime types, but is there variation in how people report crime in different places?

Table 3.2 Reasons for not reporting crime to the police (UK percentages shown). *Source*: Crime in England and Wales 2006/07

Reason for not reporting	Vandalism	Burglary	Violence
Trivial/no loss/police would not/could not do anything	83	70	46
Private/dealt with ourselves	10	17	34
Inconvenient to report	5	6	4
Reported to other authorities	2	2	8
Common occurrence	3	2	4
Fear of reprisal	3	4	7
Dislike or fear of the police/previous bad experience with the police or courts	2	2	2
Other	3	9	10

Table 3.3 Reasons for not reporting crime (US percentages shown). *Source*: National Crime Victimization Survey, 2004

Type of crime	Crimes of violence	Robbery	Household burglary
Object recovered; offender unsuccessful	20	15	23
Reported to another official	14	5	4
Private or personal matter	19	8	7
Not important enough	7	6	4
Insurance would not cover	0.1	0	3

One of the few studies to look at local spatial variation in crime reporting comes from the Netherlands. Heike Goudriaan and colleagues (2006) merged four large questionnaires on crime and public safety from the Dutch Police Population Monitor surveys and compared the crime reporting rates across different neighbourhoods in the country. By merging the surveys from four years, they were able to analyse responses from over 300,000 respondents, of whom 110,950 had been victims of crime. Forty-three per cent of the respondents had reported the crime to the police (close to the UK and US rates), and the reporting rates for different crime types varied as we might expect, from 97 per cent for car theft down to 21 per cent for vandalism. They were also able to use population data to estimate reporting rates for different neighbourhoods, and distinguish between individual factors and the effects of living in different types of neighbourhood. They found that in neighbourhoods with high socio-economic status and close bonds between neighbours (social cohesion), the probability of a crime being reported is 46 per cent; however, for neighbourhoods where the social cohesion is weak, the reporting rate drops as low as 32 per cent (Goudriaan *et al.* 2006: 736).

One interesting new finding comes from Northern Ireland, where an increase in reported crime appears to be simply a greater willingness of people to report crime in regions of the province not traditionally supportive of the police. The recent inroads the Police Service of Northern Ireland (PSNI) have made with communities on both sides of the divide appear to be reflected in greater crime reporting from Republican areas of the province (Ipsos MORI 2007). It is thus ironic that a decrease in paramilitary activity and greater confidence in the PSNI will manifest itself as an increase in reported crime in mainly Catholic areas, even though the actual level of crime is unlikely to have changed significantly.

The uncoordinated and disorganised structure of the US criminal justice system does not easily translate to understanding national patterns. However, national reporting mechanisms in England and Wales can be used to show a broad trend. The BCS does not ask questions about crimes against or involving children, nor crimes that involve businesses, nor a range of other crimes (drug offences, fraud and so on), so to compare how much crime the public are a victim of, compared with how much is recorded by police, it is necessary to use a comparable subset of offences:

- burglary;
- robbery;
- vehicle-related theft;
- theft from the person;
- wounding;
- common assault;
- bicycle theft;
- vandalism.

The 2006/07 BCS reports that only 41 per cent of these incidents are reported to the police. This means that the majority of crime suffered by the public is never heard about by the police (57 per cent non-reporting rate). Therefore, for the first part of the crime funnel, we can generalise that for every 1,000 crimes, only 410 are reported to police (Nicholas *et al.* 2007).

Once a crime is reported to police, there is no guarantee that they will complete a crime report. There are many reasons why this might be. In some cases, the police misunderstand the public and fail to recognise that a crime has occurred. Also, the police are not required to record incidents where there is credible evidence to indicate that a crime did not take place, therefore not all crime that is reported to the police is recorded in official figures. Even in the worst crime areas, police activity, while appearing to be crime related, is more oriented to providing a social service, as the following case study from the city of Camden, New Jersey (USA) demonstrates.

Case study

Calls for service in America's most dangerous city

In November 2005, the publication of *City Crime Rankings*, an annual reference book from Morgan Quitno Press, labelled Camden, New Jersey, as America's most dangerous city. This dubious award, based on a combination of population statistics and crime counts, was an 'accolade' the city had also received the previous year.

Located across the Ben Franklin Bridge from Philadelphia, Pennsylvania, the city has about 80,000 residents and close to 500 police officers (with the inclusion of assistance from federal and state law enforcement officers). While a regeneration programme has attracted new businesses and tourism activities (an aquarium and a floating attraction, the decommissioned battleship *New Jersey*), the city still has a reputation for prolific drug markets, poverty and rampant crime. Less than half the city's residents have a high school diploma, nearly half of the city live at or below the poverty line, a quarter of the city's households have an annual income of less than $10,000, the homicide rate is 10 times that of the rest of the US, and one magazine said, 'If the Grim Reaper had a favourite vacation spot, it would be Camden, New Jersey' (Maxim 2006). Under these circumstances, it would be reasonable to assume that the city's police department is deluged by calls for service about crime.

In 2005, the CAD (computer-aided dispatch) system of the Camden Police Department logged 120,487 activities and calls. A number of these calls can be considered as being internal police activity, a category that includes service assignments to help with police administration, when officers report going on break or to conduct administrative activity away from their patrol area. Exactly 8.8 per cent of the CAD activity was internal police activity. 10.6 per cent of CAD activity involved directly performing a *social service*: missing person enquiries, checking buildings, being called to deceased persons or open hydrants, and dealing with traffic complaints and accidents.

The remaining four-fifths of calls (80.6%) in the Camden police CAD system related to crime. Some 13.9 per cent documented proactive work, a category that covers officers making arrests, executing warrants and conducting traffic stops. The remaining incidents logged on the CAD system were calls from the public that indicated potential criminal activity. This *potential crime* category includes report of a crime, person with a firearm, domestic complaints, and fights.

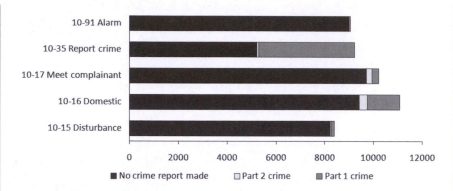

Figure 3.1 Top five potential crime calls for service, Camden NJ, 2005. Part 1 crime incidents include both violent and property crimes: homicide, rape, robbery, assault, larceny, auto theft and arson. The part 2 list includes weapon possession, prostitution, vandalism, fraud, sex and drug offences, disorderly conduct, and other miscellaneous offences

These calls constituted two-thirds of the calls in the Camden police CAD system (66.7 per cent). Sixty per cent of all *potential crime* calls come from just five categories of incident, making up 40 per cent of all CAD incidents. Figure 3.1 shows these top five calls for service. In 2005, the Camden police department received 48,622 calls in just these five call types. However, overall, as Figure 3.1 and Table 3.4 show, most calls do not end up with a police officer taking a crime report.

What can be seen from Figure 3.2 (and Table 3.4) is that while the bulk of activity relates to crime-fighting police work, the vast majority of incidents do not result in a crime report. One officer gave me a simple example of this. He recalled being summoned to a house to take a report of a stolen bicycle. In fact, the 'victim' simply wanted police to go across the road and tell the neighbour who had legitimately borrowed the bicycle to return it. Such is the nature of

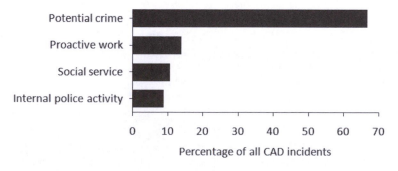

Figure 3.2 CAD incidents, Camden (NJ) 2005

Table 3.4 CAD incidents by response to each incident, Camden (NJ) 2005. Part 1 crime incidents include both violent and property crimes; homicide, rape, robbery, assault, larceny, auto theft and arson. The part 2 list includes weapon possession, prostitution, vandalism, fraud, sex and drug offences, disorderly conduct, and other miscellaneous offences

	Part 1 crime (% of category)	Part 2 crime (% of category)	No crime created (% of category)
Internal police activity	0.2	0.1	99.7
Social service	0.5	2.4	97.1
Proactive work	1.8	6.6	91.6
Potential crime	9.6	3.5	86.8

much policing in Camden. In fact, while 80 per cent of CAD incidents in Camden appear to relate to crime, over 80 per cent of these same incidents do not result in a crime report and have little to do with crime. They have more to do with the underlying poverty and lack of social cohesion across parts of the city. This case study shows that even in one of the most dangerous and violent cities in America, the workload of police is dominated by calls for service and activity that is characterised by social work rather than crime-fighting.

Crime-prone places

Not only are a minority of crime events reported to police, but also these events are usually highly clustered geographically. From early studies in Europe (Guerry 1833; Quetelet 1842) to research mapping offender residences in the large American cities (Burgess 1916, 1925; Shaw and McKay 1942), a whole field of criminology has evolved in recognition of the criminogenic nature of some places. Environmental criminology has become a major discipline with specific theories that are key to understanding the relationship between offending and place, theories that have a strong practical value in crime prevention and offender targeting (Eck and Weisburd 1995). Areas related to environmental criminology, such as situational crime prevention, crime prevention through environmental design, and crime science are also immensely useful to crime reduction practitioners (Brantingham and Brantingham 1990; Clark 1992, 2004, Felson 1998; Laycock 2001b; for an overview, see Wortley *et al.* in press). The use of geographical information systems to map and understand crime patterns has revolutionised crime analysis and has been widely embraced by researchers and police alike (Chainey and Ratcliffe 2005).

The strategic intelligence that has come from this research has been

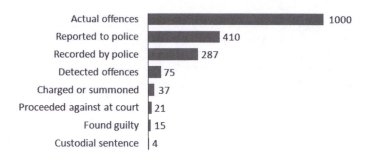

Figure 3.3 The crime funnel

illuminating for practitioners of crime prevention and intelligence-led policing. For example, analysis of calls for service in Minneapolis over one year found that a few hotspots produce most of the crime activity: only 3 per cent of the addresses in the city produced 50 per cent of all calls to the police (Sherman *et al.* 1989). In Seattle, it was found that a tiny percentage of the city's blocks (4–5 per cent) accounted for 50 per cent of the incidents reported to police, and this relationship lasted for years. Even though there was a citywide decline in crime, 84 per cent of street blocks had a stable trajectory maintaining about the same level of crime over 14 years (Weisburd *et al.* 2004).

The importance of crime hot spots as a targeting mechanism for intelligence-led policing has been recognised within the framework of the National Intelligence Model; one of the four elements of the tactical menu is the management of crime and disorder hot spots (NCIS 2000). Considerable effort has been made in the academic community to help analysts better define crime hot spots (Chainey *et al.* 2003; Eck *et al.* 2005), understand the temporal pattern of hot spots (Ratcliffe 2002a), and explore how this information can be used to combat crime (Ratcliffe and McCullagh 1998; Ratcliffe 2002a). This overall endeavour is particularly important given there is some evidence that police officers do not necessarily know intuitively where some crime problems are concentrated. Research in a police subdivision in Nottingham found that while police officers had excellent knowledge of the locations of residential burglary concentrations, they were less accurate when estimating vehicle crime and non-residential burglary hot spots (Ratcliffe and McCullagh 2001).

Completing the crime funnel

British national figures suggest that police record about 70 per cent of the crime that is reported to them. The recording rate varies from over 90 per cent for vehicle-related crime to only 36 per cent for bicycle theft (Nicholas *et al.* 2007: 47). We can use the general figure of 70 per cent in the crime funnel. From the original 1,000 crimes, 410 are reported to police, and police record 70 per cent of those, leaving 287 offences in the crime funnel.

Not all of these 287 crimes are solved. If a crime is counted as 'cleared up' by the police, then the police must have been able to identify a suspect and there must have been sufficient evidence to charge the suspect with the crime. If the offender is charged or summoned to appear at court, or if the offender is cautioned in some manner, has an offence taken into consideration, or receives a formal warning or penalty notice, then the clearance is called a sanctioned detection. Non-sanctioned detections are clearances where the offender has died or is seriously ill, the victim refuses to cooperate with police, or there is little point in prosecuting the case (perhaps the offender is too young). These classifications are similar to the system used by US agencies, where a case is cleared (similar to a sanctioned detection), not cleared, exceptionally cleared (similar to a non-sanctioned detection), or unfounded.

In 2006/07, the UK had an overall detection rate of 27 per cent (Nicholas *et al.* 2007). Our crime funnel offences have now shrunk from 287 reported crimes to 75 detected offences. However, slightly less than half receive a charge or summons and have a chance of appearing in court; therefore, of the 75 detected offences, only 37 proceed to a formal charge (Home Office 2006a: 3).

Home Office figures show that not all cases that receive a charge or summons appear in court, as the prosecution service can decide not to proceed once they receive the case. Overall, the majority of cases do proceed to court, with a little more than half the available cases prosecuted (Home Office 2006a: 3). About 73 per cent of offenders are found guilty after an appearance at either Magistrates or Crown court. Therefore, in the crime funnel, of the 37 that are cases that are charged, 21 make it to a court appearance, and 15 have guilty findings against them.

The final stage is the sentencing phase. The courts have a number of options available. They can fine the offender, subject them to a community sentence, jail the offender (a custodial sentence), or find some other outcome. In 25 per cent of cases, the offender is incarcerated. This means that of our final 15 remaining crimes, in only four cases will an offender receive a custodial sentence (Home Office 2006a). The final crime funnel is shown in Figure 3.3. These aggregate figures need to be interpreted with some caution. To understand a large criminal justice system, such as exists in most countries, some latitude is necessary when interpreting the crime funnel. However, these figures are useful to indicate a broad trend in the criminal justice system.

The crime funnel still over-estimates the number of arrests and convictions, because corporate crime, organised crime, and drug and prostitution offences are rarely recorded in surveys. Even with that caveat, what the crime funnel shows is the limitation of relying on the criminal justice system as a broad, unfocused tool to solve the crime problems of today. For example, even if everyone found guilty received a custodial sentence and we moved to a 100 per cent imprisonment rate, we would still only jail offenders for 15 of 1,000 crimes. Similarly, if every detected offender was forced to appear at court, that would still only send 75 cases for every 1,000 to court instead of the current 37. We are unable to demand such draconian rates from any part of the criminal justice system, and therefore relying on a purely criminal justice approach to crime control is unlikely to be successful in significantly reducing crime. The challenge for crime prevention practitioners is to have an impact on the 1,000 offences that the public are the victim of, rather than trying to improve the efficiency of the system further down the funnel and squeeze more benefit from a fairly inefficient system. For example, a 10 per cent improvement in prosecutions to secure more guilty pleas or findings would be a significant challenge, but would also have a minimal impact on the broader levels of crime. For every 1,000 crimes, this would increase the guilty findings from 15 to fewer than 17 – hardly dramatic when the source for these offences still numbers 1,000. I explore different scenarios using the crime funnel later in Chapter 8, but for now it is useful as a frame of reference to the discussions that follow.

The offender problem

The crime funnel shows that the criminal justice system is not well placed to respond to the crime problem. For every 1,000 crimes, less than 8 per cent are detected, and less than 1 per cent of these crimes result in a prison sentence. This is hardly a model of efficiency. So would a strategy that targeted specific prolific offenders be more worthwhile? This section explores the assumption that a few offenders are responsible for the majority of the crime, and, if so, whether it is possible to identify and arrest them.

Studies of the criminal careers of offenders give us an insight into the offending behaviour of people, such as when they start committing crime and how much crime they commit. The term 'career' should not be taken to mean that they make a living from their activity or that they commit crime as a full-time job. Quite the contrary: only a tiny minority of offenders can actually sustain themselves through crime alone. The word 'career' is used to indicate an activity that has a start time (called an 'onset'), a duration (the length of time an offender commits crime, usually measured in years), and a termination – when they finally give up a life of crime.

Much of the information about criminal careers comes from official records, such as police arrest logs and court records. The difficulty is that arrest logs only have a notification of offences for which the criminal is arrested or confesses, and the previous section showed that clearance rates are fairly low. So, as an alternative source of data, some criminal justice researchers interview offenders and ask them about their offending activity. This approach also has some limitations. For example, it is vulnerable to the ability of offenders to recall crimes they have committed, and offenders may decide to conceal a crime from the researcher or later deny an offence that they had earlier in their life reported to an interviewer (Farrington 1992). This type of research is also time-consuming and expensive because some studies take years to complete, requiring researchers to interview offenders at various stages in their lives. As a result, few criminal career studies of any size and significance have been completed, though a couple of influential studies do tell us a great deal about individual patterns of offending. The next sections examine the level of prolific offending, whether we are able to predict who these offenders will be, and whether the police can identify prolific offenders for targeting.

Individual offending and recidivism

Many people commit a crime at some point in their lives. For example, the Youth Lifestyles Survey, a survey of self-reported offending by 4,848 people between ages 12 and 30, found that 57 per cent of males and 37 per cent of females had committed an offence at some point in their life, and that nearly 20 per cent of them had done so in the previous 12 months (Flood-Page et al. 2000). Eighteen per cent of the crimes they committed were violent offences, and 55 per cent property crimes (criminal damage and fraud making up the majority of the remainder).

Illicit drug and alcohol use is prevalent among young people. More than half of US high-school seniors reported using illegal drugs at some point, over 5 per cent having used cocaine and 10 per cent amphetamines in the preceding year. Nearly three-quarters had consumed alcohol (Johnston et al. 2005).

While many people commit a crime, most people who get caught and have a run-in with the law only do so once. However, there are a small minority of offenders who commit significant amounts of crime, and in an intelligence-led policing environment, their identification and targeting are a central strategy. But how small or large is this group of prolific and persistent offenders, how much crime do they commit, and are there any risk factors that can be used to identify them early enough in their criminal careers to intervene?

The Cambridge Study in Delinquent Development was a longitudinal research project that has made a significant contribution to understanding criminal careers. In the early 1960s, researchers interviewed 411 boys from six primary schools in London when the boys were 8 or 9 years old.

The boys were then interviewed at ages 16, 18, 21 and 24, and finally interviewed again in their early thirties. Their names were also submitted to the Criminal Record Office (now the Criminal Records Bureau) to see whether, and when, they had been convicted of any of a range of offences, including theft, burglary, vehicle crime, handling stolen goods, sex offences, and drug use (a group of crimes termed notifiable offences). By the time the study group had reached their 25th birthday, one-third had been convicted of a notifiable offence (Barnett *et al.* 1987). This appears to be similar to estimates based on data from the US and other countries.

Using mathematical models based on the official conviction data for the 136 boys, the Cambridge team were also able to calculate the boys' conviction rate and length of criminal career, and estimate a rate at which the boys gave up crime (at least until their 25th birthday). To increase the accuracy of the models, they split the boys into two groups; the *frequents* (43 per cent of the offenders) had a higher conviction rate than boys estimated to commit less crime, a group they called the *occasionals* (obviously, the *innocents*, who had not been convicted of any crime, were excluded from this part of the study). The *frequents* had a conviction rate of 1.14 per year, meaning that they were convicted just over once a year, while the *occasionals* had a lower conviction rate of 0.41 per year. Of value from the mathematical models was the realisation that the *frequents* had a relatively low likelihood of desisting their criminal careers after each conviction of only 10 per cent, while there was a 33 per cent chance that an *occasional* would stop his criminal career after a conviction. Clearly, the *frequents* were less likely to be dissuaded from a life of crime by their experience with the criminal justice system.

The classic study of criminal careers was completed by Marvin Wolfgang and his associates, and followed about 10,000 boys born in the city of Philadelphia in 1945. Of this group, 35 per cent had convictions by the time they were 18 years old, a result very similar to the London cohort from the Cambridge study. Wolfgang's group categorised their offenders into one-time offenders, non-chronic recidivists (who had committed more than one offence but less than five), and chronic recidivists (five or more offences). The *chronics* were similar to the Cambridge study's *frequents*. Nearly half (46 per cent) of all the offenders were one-time offenders, while only 18 per cent were chronic recidivists. The 627 *chronics* constituted only 6.3 per cent of the whole cohort of 9,945 boys. However, this tiny percentage of chronic offenders were responsible for 52 per cent of all offences recorded against the entire cohort (Wolfgang *et al.* 1972: 89).

Probably the largest study has been carried out by the UK Home Office, which tracked the conviction record of every person born in the UK during four selected weeks in 1953, 1958, and 1963 (HOSB 1989). This research has revealed a wealth of information about criminal careers, mainly in regard to the 1953 cohort of 51,441 children. For example, one-third of men born in 1953 had a criminal conviction for a serious crime by their 31st birthday (a prevalence rate of 33 per cent), while the prevalence rate for females was only 7 per cent. Seven per cent of the men born in 1953 had six or more convictions before their 31st birthday, and this group accounted for 65 per cent of all the convictions for the whole cohort. The most likely age to commit an offence was 17 (Figure 3.4); however, men convicted earlier tended to have longer criminal careers, a finding replicated in the Cambridge Study in Delinquent Development.

In a review of a number of major studies, Petersilia (1980) concluded that the earlier a criminal career started, the longer it tended to continue. She also found that offenders tend towards generalisation, few offenders specialising in a particular category of crime. Offending rates varied; drug dealers committing more offences than burglars, who in turn committed more offences than robbers. She also found evidence that criminal careers are not marked by increasing sophistication as time goes on, nor of increased income.

The Cambridge Study in Delinquent Development found that both occasionals and frequents had criminal careers that averaged between 7 and 9 years (more so for prolific offenders), so, from an intelligence-led policing perspective that emphasises the targeting of prolific and recidivist offenders, the early identification of the frequent or chronic group members may be of considerable value.

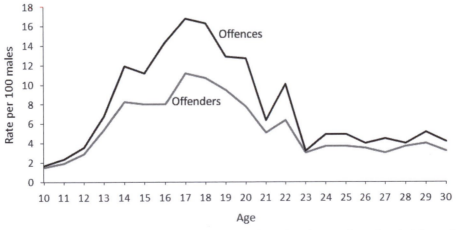

Figure 3.4 Prevalence of offenders per 100 males (based on the London cohort). Adapted from Farrington, D.P. (1992) 'Criminal career research in the United Kingdom', *British Journal of Criminology*, 32(4): 525

Predicting prolific offenders

David Farrington has pointed out that our knowledge of offending patterns is such that 'potential offenders can be identified at an early age with a reasonable degree of accuracy' (1990: 105–106). He estimated that the best predictors in 10-year-olds of having a criminal conviction later in life are socio-economic deprivation, antisocial parents and siblings, poor parental supervision and child rearing, coming from broken homes, low intelligence and a poor school record. However, many of these variables are unlikely to be available to police departments, so this information has little value from an intelligence-led policing perspective. After all, the public would most likely get upset if police started visiting schools and studying the personality traits of every child! What may be more useful is to identify variables from official records that might help to predict recidivism.

One factor is definitely previous convictions. In her analysis of 33,900 juvenile offenders brought before the New South Wales Children's Court between 1982 and 1986, Christine Coumarelos found that nearly 70 per cent of children appeared before the court and were convicted only once, and just 10 per cent had more than three appearances. In fact, over one-third of the time of the court was spent dealing with this small group (Coumarelos 1994). Coumarelos found that when a long enough study period is used, the age of first appearance in court can be used as a predictor of recidivism. The younger children are on first appearance and conviction, the more likely they will reappear before the court over subsequent years. Unfortunately, criminal convictions at an early age alone may not be sufficient to predict recidivism, due to the high number of false positives; that is, the large

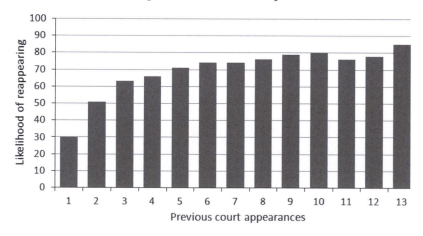

Figure 3.5 Risk of reoffending increases with court appearances.
Source: Coumarelos, C. (1994) 'Juvenile offending: predicting persistence and determining the cost-effectiveness of interventions' (Sydney: NSW Bureau of Crime Statistics and Research), p. 20

number of people who are convicted at a young age who do *not* go on to criminal careers. Farrington notes that while 61 per cent of the chronics in Wolfgang's Philadelphia cohort had a conviction by the age of 13, only 41 per cent of Philadelphia boys convicted by that age went on to become chronics (Farrington 1987). Other clues are therefore required for better target intervention tactics.

Coumarelos found that there was a greater likelihood of offenders reappearing before the court if, on their first court appearance, they were convicted of robbery or vehicle theft. A re-analysis of the Philadelphia cohort study suggested that a history of theft or criminal damage offences was a good predictor of recidivism (Clarke 1975). Unfortunately, involvement with the criminal justice system does not act as a good deterrent, but merely as a predictor. As shown in Figure 3.5, the likelihood of reappearing actually *increases* with the number of court appearances. While there is a 30 per cent chance youths will appear before the court after their first conviction, when they have appeared before the court 13 times, the chance of their appearing for a fourteenth time is 85 per cent.

While studying the personality traits of 10-year-old children is probably out of the question, local intelligence gathering can detect overt signs of behaviour that can predict recidivism. For example, the Youth Lifestyles Survey found that boys (12-17 years old) who used drugs were nearly five times more likely to be offenders. Other risk factors included being truant from school, lack of parental supervision, hanging around in public, and having delinquent friends. For men, the risk predictors for offending included drug use and having delinquent friends (as for the youths), and also included excessive drinking, leaving school without qualifications, or being excluded from school. While just 1 per cent of men had at least four of these risk factors, all of these men had committed a crime at some point and the majority of them were serious and/or persistent offenders (Flood-Page *et al.* 2000).

As children grow up and are exposed to different situations and conditions, we might expect that predictive factors for offending change. Researchers from the Home Office recently reported results from the 2005 Offending, Crime and Justice Survey, a survey that interviewed just under 5,000 10–25-year-olds. Identifying factors that individually (independently of the influence of other factors) predict offending, they found that the factors with the best chance (highest odds ratio) of predicting offending for 10–15-year-olds were being a victim of personal crime themselves, committing antisocial behaviour, taking drugs, and being regularly drunk (at least once a month). If we add being more likely to agree that criminal acts are acceptable, then the same factors predict offending for 16–25-year-olds (Wilson *et al.* 2006: 35-36). The stability of these risk factors throughout the development of children into adulthood provides significant opportunities to identify future prolific offenders.

Table 3.5. Background and systemic identifiable risk factors for prolific offenders

Background risk factors	Systemic identifiable risk factors
Socio-economically deprived	Early age of first conviction
Antisocial parents and siblings	History of court appearances
Received poor rearing as a child	History of drug usage
Coming from broken homes	Hanging around in public
Low intelligence	Having delinquent friends
Poor school record	Excessive drinking
Being truant or excluded from school	Being a victim of personal crime
Lack of parental supervision	Antisocial behaviour

We can therefore say that risk factors for predicting recidivism appear to include criminal convictions at an early age, drug (and alcohol) use, school problems and truancy, being a victim of personal crime, and delinquent peers. And some Australian research suggests that involvement in robbery or vehicle theft increases the chance of recidivism, though there is definitely a need for more research in this area. Previous convictions are also an excellent predictor of likely future offending. The key risk factors from this section are summarised in Table 3.5.

Can the police identify prolific offenders?

Most cops will tell you that they know the worst offenders in their patch, but beyond the anecdotal there is little research addressing this issue. And given the number of prolific offenders in society, the magnitude of the problem is substantial. For example, even if only a tiny percentage of boys are chronic offenders by the age of 18, as the Philadelphia cohort study found, a city such as Philadelphia has its hands full. In the 2000 census there were 124,475 males between 10 and 20 (some of the most prolific crime-active years), and if the percentage of 'chronics' has not changed since the Philadelphia cohort study, it means that the Philadelphia police department has to chase over 7,800 chronic offenders. And this conservative estimate does not include female offenders, criminals under the age of 10 or over 20, or guests coming to commit crime from outside the city. Nor, of course, does it include any of the occasional offenders who commit the other 50 per cent of the crime not committed by persistent offenders. Even if the police just concentrate on chronic male offenders aged 10–20, this prolific criminal group still outnumber the number of police officers in the city.

Knowing that persistent, recidivist offenders commit much of the crime is not the same as knowing and targeting these individuals, yet offenders do help by bringing themselves to notice, a process called offender self-selection (Wellsmith and Guille 2005). There is more on offender self-selection in Chapter 6. Results from a self-report study of offending seem to suggest that the police know who the recidivist offenders are. As Flood-Page and colleagues report, 'The police had some contact with the majority of offenders. Two-thirds (68 per cent) of persistent offenders had been stopped, told to move on or been visited at home by the police in the past year' (Flood-Page *et al.* 2000: vi). When the Australian Federal Police launched Operation Anchorage, a burglary crackdown in Canberra, they succeeded in targeting prolific property offenders (see the Operation Anchorage case study in Chapter 9). Seventy-seven per cent of the people arrested in the operation had at least one previous conviction, and these 225 offenders were responsible for a whopping 1,748 previous offences. Eighteen per cent of the offenders arrested during Operation Anchorage had 15 or more previous convictions and were responsible for 62 per cent of all of the previous convictions from the Anchorage arrestees (Makkai *et al.* 2004). So successes are possible, but the challenges are significant.

As Townsley and Pease (2002) note, knowing that a few offenders target a few victims in a few, select locations is only useful in an operational context if the links between these assertions can be tied together. Furthermore, there are a number of reasons why the practice of targeting recidivists may not be exactly perfect. The targeted individual may not be a recidivist, may be a recidivist but not at that particular time, or may work with co-offenders who keep committing crime even when the recidivist is arrested. Identifying and targeting repeat offenders is, however, something that the police may be ideally suited to do, and it may be one of the most effective ways to use police resources. More research into targeting strategies and the selection of suitable offenders is clearly necessary.

Organised crime

One feature that is not possible to include in the crime funnel is the impact of organised crime. The perception over recent years is that organised crime is a rapidly expanding threat to the security of modern society. Organised and transnational crime groups are generally associated with people trafficking (in some cases for economic migration but often associated with sexual exploitation), drug trafficking, offences against children, corruption and terrorism. Organised crime groups pose not only a challenge to law enforcement but also a particular threat to the hegemonic status of governments, not just in terms of controlling crime but also in respect to legitimacy, as demonstrated by the EU Organised Crime Threat Assessment:

> The main threatening aspects of OC [organised crime] groups are, first, the overwhelming obstacles in dismantling them because of

their international dimension or influence, and second, their level of infiltration in society and economy. The first aspect gives them a sort of impunity and perpetuity that counteracts law enforcement efforts. The second aspect makes them mingled with the legal world, negatively affecting the willingness to attack these OC groups, the level of corruption and democratic dynamics. Also, the more an OC group is established and has infiltrated society, the more the upper level can gain a layer of respectability and become more difficult to bring to justice. (EUROPOL 2006: 5)

Of course, a significant challenge with measuring the impact of organised crime is first to define it, and then determine how organised it is. Defining organised crime is difficult because of the vast range of crime activities that require some sort of collective organisation. Criminal groups vary in scope and degree of organisation, ranging from long-term, hierarchically structured teams, to 'loose networks of career criminals, who come together for specific criminal ventures and dissolve once these are over' (SOCA 2006: 14). This means that the term *organised crime* is loosely applied to amorphous groups of offenders committing offence types that are believed to require some sort of organisation, as well as to mafia or triad-type syndicates (Stelfox 1998).

In the UK, the Serious Organised Crime Agency estimates that both the economic and social costs of organised crime, as well as the costs incurred by the law enforcement system in attempting to curtail organised crime, place a burden on British society of upwards of £20 billion every year (SOCA 2006). While some crime groups have specialities in terms of the crime they commit, significant numbers are diversifying into multiple types of criminal activity. As SOCA points out, law enforcement is structured for bureaucratic efficiency; however, organised crime groups rarely 'think in terms of discrete crime sectors. Instead, they will see opportunities for making money which they are likely to take if they have the criminal capability' (SOCA 2006: 15).

One might think that sectoring or compartmentalising our thinking about organised crime would help establish some baseline measurements. For example, most of the larger groups are involved in money laundering at some point in their criminal activities in order to keep their profits out of the hands of police. Again, however, estimates of the extent of money laundering are difficult to establish. While estimates of the yearly global sums laundered can range from US$500 billion to US$1.5 trillion (Brooks 2001), the estimates that do exist have 'little evidence to justify them' (Levi 2002: 184).

Organised crime and the offences that are associated with it are thus another constituent of the huge 'dark figure' (Biderman and Reiss 1967; Coleman and Moynihan 1996) of crime that official figures do not reflect.

As the following viewpoint by Rob Fahlman indicates, this knowledge gap has not gone unnoticed, and threat and harm measurement tools are currently being developed for better assessment of the extent of organised crime.

Viewpoint

Threat measurement techniques for organised crime

Rob Fahlman

Taking organised and other serious crime out of the murky shadows and analyzing it to better understand its complex and evolving nature, will shed light on how to more effectively and efficiently tackle this pervasive hydra. The international crime industry cannot be successfully tackled with yesterday's solutions. As Jack Straw, former British Home Secretary, said, 'we should not be fighting the crimes of the 21st Century with the tools of the 19th'.

The law enforcement community is now striving to deal more effectively with the threats and harms posed by organized crime (OC) and other serious criminality. From basic information to more sophisticated intelligence systems designed to combat criminal networks as well as individual criminals, there has been a growing awareness in recent years of the importance of gaining early warnings of relative threat levels and shifts in criminal markets. This strategic intelligence should be regarded as an essential service in the provision of knowledge to both strategic and operational decision-makers across a continuum of strategies to more effectively control, reduce and prevent organised and serious crime.

Recognizing the clear value of a robust strategic intelligence capability, Criminal Intelligence Service Canada (CISC) follows the principles of intelligence-led policing. CISC is Canada's criminal intelligence network, comprising some 380 member agencies at the local, provincial, regional and national levels. In 2003, CISC embarked on a process to develop an integrated threat assessment model for organised and serious crime affecting Canada. This model included building a capacity to prepare annual integrated OC threat assessments at both the provincial and national levels. Key to this threat assessment model is the full employment of an analytical technique developed by the Royal Canadian Mounted Police (RCMP) known as Sleipnir.

This threat measurement technique uses a rank-ordered set of 19 criminogenic attributes (including for example, ability to corrupt, sophistication, scope, monopoly, and links to other OC groups and criminal extremists/terrorist groups) as the basis of a comprehensive, structured and reliable method of comparing OC groups. This structured comparison assesses the relative threat posed by OC groups to Canadian society, thus allowing the development of an inventory of groups by relative threat level. This ranking is used to support target prioritisation, further intelligence gathering and crime reduction strategies.

More recently, it has been recognized that in addition to threat level measurement indicators, there is a need for developing harm-based measurement tools to assess the adverse consequences of criminal activities. These consequences may be direct and tangible with effects that can be quantified in terms of monetary loss, such as fraud or thefts, or intangible effects more difficult to quantify such as the loss of quality of life caused by crime or the fear of crime in a neighbourhood. Within the Canadian criminal intelligence community, CISC is working with the RCMP and their Harm Prioritisation Scale methodology with the aim of ranking the relative harms (social, political, economic) caused by specific OC groups. This additional layer of analysis will complement the Sleipnir threat assessment technique within the integrated threat assessment model. These intelligence-led policing management tools provide a solid foundation to help focus investigative resources for optimal impact on crime reduction and, more importantly, crime prevention.

Robert C. Fahlman, former Interpol General Secretariat Assistant Director responsible for Interpol's global Criminal Intelligence Program, is a career professional intelligence officer with the Royal Canadian Mounted Police. Since 2002, he has been attached to Criminal Intelligence Service Canada where he is currently acting Director General.

Summary

Understanding the where, when and who of crime is a fundamental step before deciding what to do to reduce it. Calls for service are not a strong indicator of the crime level, as probably most cities, including high-crime ones like Camden, New Jersey, are hampered by a flood of calls to the police that are not related to crime at all. As this chapter has shown, even when there is a crime, variations in the reporting rate, crime type and even geography hamper attempts to get a true measure of the impact of crime on society. Police record management systems finally record only about three in every ten offences.

The crime funnel paints a fairly bleak picture of the criminal justice system. For every 1,000 crimes, only 75 get detected, and from this only four cases result in a custodial sentence. This is compelling evidence that a broad-brush reliance on the legal and criminal justice system to impact positively on the crime rate is a flawed strategy. This does not necessarily suggest that other strategies will work; however, crime prevention and crime disruption activities, when effective, work higher up the funnel and prevent offences falling into it. Sir Richard Mayne, one of the first commissioners of London's Metropolitan Police, seemed to understand this when he said that 'the primary object of an efficient police is the prevention of crime: the next that of detection and punishment of offenders if crime is committed' (Mayne 1829).

Targeting offenders may be the best way to use our scarce police resources in the most effective way, as an intelligence-led policing model suggests. But the challenges are significant, given the numbers involved. The criminal careers research can best be summarised as 6 per cent of the population commit about 60 per cent of the crime. However, this assertion still leaves (1) a large number of prolific offenders to be disrupted or incapacitated, and (2) a significant minority of the crime being committed by occasional offenders who may not come to notice. Academic studies that can identify likely offenders at a young age through personality traits are all well and good, but some children possessing many of the risk signs of criminality do not grow up to be arch-villains, and so targeting young people on the basis of traits they might grow out of is highly unethical. These studies have little practical benefit to offer police officers responsible to the community on a day-to-day basis.

An integrated strategy that combines some of the benefits of problem-oriented policing with the targeted and objective approach of pro-active policing seems to be the direction in which proponents of intelligence-led policing are heading. In talking about a combination of problem-oriented policing and intelligence-led policing through the National Intelligence Model, Clarke and Eck (2003) write:

> The one provides a standard methodology for tackling specific recurring crime and disorder problems harming a community. The other is a standard approach to the collection, analysis and dissemination of intelligence that will ensure uniform practice across the country. Both models put the crime analyst at centre stage because they take it as given that policing must be evidence-led. (p. 11)

The vision of intelligence-led policing and problem-oriented policing acting in a complementary fashion is timely. The next chapter explores the distinctions between intelligence-led policing and other conceptual models of policing, such as problem-oriented policing, Compstat and community policing.

4

Defining intelligence-led policing

The Audit Commission never defined intelligence-led policing, nor did the National Criminal Intelligence Service when they issued the first public documents on the National Intelligence Model (NIM). Indeed, definitions of intelligence-led policing are hard to find, and most publications tend to discuss the challenges and merits of intelligence-led policing without actually defining it (for example, see IACP 2002). The situation appears to be analogous to the statement by US Supreme Court Associate Justice Potter Stewart, who, in a 1964 ruling regarding hard-core pornography, wrote, 'I shall not today attempt further to define the kinds of material I understand to be embraced within that shorthand description; and perhaps I could never succeed in intelligibly doing so. But I know it when I see it.' There appears to be an unwritten assumption that police officers and crime intelligence analysts may not be able to define intelligence-led policing, but they know it when they see it. Yet, without care and clarification, the term intelligence-led policing could become 'trite and jargonistic' (Keelty 2004: 6).

This chapter aims to demystify intelligence-led policing and approach a definition in order to provide the conceptual apparatus for the rest of the book. However, in the process, I will also argue that intelligence-led policing is an evolving concept and the tenets of intelligence-led policing have shifted over time. Comparisons will be drawn with other significant frameworks for policing to determine better the similarities and differences with other styles of law enforcement management. The chapter concludes with an attempt at a definition of intelligence-led policing, in addition to identifying where it varies conceptually from the main current policing paradigms.

To distinguish intelligence-led policing from other models, the chapter takes the rather challenging approach of attempting to identify the central precepts of community policing, Compstat and problem-oriented policing for the purposes of comparison with intelligence-led policing. Such a venture is fraught with contention given that these concepts are sometimes interpreted differently by an audience passionate about policing and the conceptual models they advocate. It is not my intention to make the definitive statement of these other conceptual models; I leave that to others more versed in, and more articulate about, these paradigms. As Tilley (2003a) points out, any attempt to highlight the distinctive components of each policing model inevitably creates contrasts that are more stark than they often are on the ground. The aim here is to present the distinguishing characteristics of intelligence-led policing. In the process, I ask that the reader recognise that this requires both a considerable degree of generalisation and some latitude to attempt to distil into a few paragraphs the varying policing models employed across hundreds of different police departments in many countries.

Related policing frameworks

Intelligence-led policing did not originate out of thin air as a new conceptual way of conducting the business of policing. It built on experiences from the past, the organisational climate of the time, and the aspirations of its architects. As such, it is influenced by the existing policing models of the time. A paradigm shift involves a change in the basic assumptions about a process (Kuhn 1962) and it is difficult to identify those current policing movements that constitute a paradigm shift from the existing mode of policing at the time. It is much easier to define the original model from which the approaches in this chapter have their genesis.

As stated in Chapter 2, the standard model of policing traditionally comprises random patrol, rapid uniformed response, deployment of officers to crime investigation once an offence has been detected, and reliance on law enforcement and the legal system as the primary means of trying to reduce crime (Weisburd and Eck 2004). Defined by a faith in the traditional hierarchical system, an aim of solving reported crime, and the practice in which police management organise units within police administrative boundaries in an attempt to improve police efficiency, the model has been the subject of extended criticism. This model, summarised later in the chapter in the first column of Table 4.1, will be the benchmark against which more recent conceptual frameworks for policing are measured.

In this section, I will discuss community policing, problem-oriented policing, and Compstat. Whether these frameworks constitute paradigm shifts or more modest variations to an earlier style of policing is a point for discussion; however, it is clear that they are significant movements in the current policing environment. Furthermore, they are all part of a reform movement in policing, one that sees the need for change due to the failings of more traditional methods of policing (Tilley 2003a). Each recognises that policing needs to be less reactive, but they differ in their conceptual philosophy as well as the tactics that emanate from each model.

Of course, there are differences between policing tactics and conceptual frameworks (or models) of policing. For example, increasing foot patrols, where officers spend more time out of their cars and more time engaging with the community on walking beats, is a tactic. Moving to a community policing ethos that emphasises foot patrol as one of its approaches is the adoption of a conceptual framework. Conducting surveillance of a suspect is a tactic. Moving to an intelligence-led policing philosophy that (among other things) emphasises greater use of surveillance to target prolific offenders identified and prioritised through a strategic assessment is adoption of a conceptual framework. While I address some of the main conceptual models, there are other approaches to crime reduction that have not reached the widespread diffusion of community policing or Compstat but nevertheless are potentially significant players in the way that we will police in the future. Examples include evidence-based policing (Sherman 2002), hot spot policing (Weisburd and Braga 2006a), broken windows theory (Wilson and Kelling 1982; Taylor 2001; Sousa and Kelling 2006), and third-party policing (Buerger 1998; Buerger and Green-Mazerolle 1998). There is not the space in this book to examine these additional strategies, though a recent book provides a useful overview (*Police Innovation: Contrasting Perspectives*, edited by Weisburd and Braga 2006b). These models conceptually differ, but the tactics they advocate (such as saturation patrols or greater use of civil enforcement) can be incorporated within broader frameworks such as problem-oriented policing. As the next sections show, there are some challenges in trying to decipher this 'terminological mess' (Ponsaers 2001: 271)!

Community policing

The origins of community policing have been described in Chapter 2. This section seeks to identify the key ingredients of a community policing style, a task that is not as easy as it sounds. Community policing defies definition. Some academics and practitioners see it as a policing philosophy, while others define community policing by the programmes that are associated with it. For example, neighbourhood mini-stations, customer satisfaction surveys, foot patrols, school visits, the Drug Abuse Resistance Education (DARE) programme, local newsletters and Neighbourhood Watch are all programmes that are commonly associated with community policing. However, these programmes do not articulate its vision. While rarely articulated explicitly, the core purpose of community policing has been to increase police legitimacy in neighbourhoods that have lost confidence in the police (see Chapter 2). A central aim of community policing is to increase the legitimacy of formal governance and improve community satisfaction in policing services. For example, Deukmedjian and de Lint (2007) recount the difficulties the RCMP had in getting information from the East Indian

Punjabi community in British Columbia in the wake of the 1985 terrorist bombing of Air India flight 182 while it was over the Atlantic. Suspecting the bomb originated in Vancouver but lacking suitable linguists, the RCMP investigation was hampered by inability to access information from the Punjabi community. The subsequent prosecution, the most extensive in RCMP history, resulted in not-guilty verdicts against the chief suspects. For a brief time, the RCMP – as with many police departments – looked to community policing to help them regain legitimacy and restore this community connection.

Community policing can be defined extremely loosely as, for example, 'a collaboration between the police and the community that identifies and solves community problems' (CPC 1994). Alternatively, community policing can be conceptualised as 'an organisational strategy that leaves setting priorities and the means of achieving them largely to residents and the police who serve in their neighbourhoods' (Skogan 2006b: 27–28). Some authors are more descriptive:

> The main elements of a community policing philosophy might be summarized in a single sentence as a belief or intention held by the police that they should consult with and take account of the wishes of the public in determining and evaluating operational policing and that they should collaborate with the public in identifying and solving local problems. (Bennett 1994: 229)

Although it is tempting to determine that community policing is happening because there are Neighbourhood Watch meetings and foot patrols, this relegates community policing to a suite of tactics designed to address particular problems. Wesley Skogan, who has dedicated many years of research to community policing programmes, argues that community policing cannot be defined by the specific programmes that are often the most visible component of the model, because these programmes can change depending on the needs of the community (Skogan 2006b). Community policing is therefore a moving target that, if it is being followed in the manner suggested, continually changes with the whims of the public in line with their concerns regarding community safety, concerns that are not necessarily the same as those of the police department and are not necessarily even measured by traditional police data sources. It is the fluid and diverse nature of the definition of community policing that makes it so widely applicable. Indeed, a definition may not be possible. It may be the case that

> Different elements of community policing appeal to different audiences, and it has led to fruitless debates over what community policing 'really' means. In fact, it is this ambiguity and flexibility that

gives community policing its all-things-to-all-people character and has contributed to its political viability over two decades, embraced by public leaders across the political spectrum. (Mastrofski 2006: 44)

And embraced it has been. This style of policing 'has become so much a catch-phrase in modern policing throughout the world, that hardly any policing organisation wants to be seen as not participating' (Edwards 1999: 76). Community policing has become a truly international phenomenon. The 2006 Community Policing conference in Washington, DC, attracted over 1,300 participants from as far afield as Australia, Indonesia and Pakistan. But while universally popular, community policing appears to be something that is easier to say you are doing than to define what it is you do.

There is significant disagreement about what constitutes community policing; however, Taylor's (2006) review of a range of studies found some commonalities in the majority of definitions, such as organisational decentralisation, more autonomy to local officers, greater responsiveness to citizen input, and commitment to problem-solving and the building of local capacity to resist crime. Generally, from this and many other studies, we can summarise that the community policing model:

- increases the interaction between the police and the community, either directly through collaboration or simply through consultation;

- attempts to provide named and accountable officers who know their area;

- gives communities a greater hand in driving police priorities;

- enhances decision-making at the lowest ranks of the police service;

- regains the legitimacy of police in the eyes of the public;

- allows a social service ethos to predominate, in which perceptions of community safety take priority;

- gives precedence to solving community problems over reactive law enforcement.

Evaluations of community policing are themselves difficult to evaluate, in view of the difficulty in reaching agreement among scholars and practitioners as to whether a programme is a true community policing one:

The success of community policing will never be evaluated. The reason is simple. Community policing means too many things to different people. Its practices are so varied that any evaluation will be partial or challengeable as not being authentic 'community policing'. (Bayley 1994a: 278)

Though it should be possible to measure (through surveys, for example) changes in community satisfaction with the police if increased legitimacy is the aim, most attempts at community policing have been implemented without a clear set of aims and objectives. This often results in failure. It has been argued that the RCMP were unable to integrate the community into their community policing alignment strategy and create an empowerment ethos within the organisation, and 'the shift in executive discourse toward intelligence-led policing was an outcome of irreconcilable failures perceived during adoption of community policing' (Deukmedjian 2006: 536).

We can examine community policing on two scales. First – in regard to the breadth of crime and disorder problems that the approach is targeted to resolve – community policing is philosophically empowered to tackle a wide array of problems. Thus, on a problem focus scale that runs from *narrow* (perhaps just a focus on specific types of organised crime) to *broad* (that encompasses a whole gamut from violence to public nuisance abatement, for example), community policing has broad application. Indeed, this array of application areas is so broad that some problems fall beyond what most police officers would consider to be issues for the police at all. As Trojanowicz noted, 'community officers are so well received that they often find themselves inundated with requests that go beyond the scope of traditional law enforcement' (1994: 259). Secondly – on a continuum that explores the target of police operations that runs from crime events to offenders – it is more closely aligned to addressing crime and disorder events. Indeed, a focus on offenders might bring the police into conflict with some parts of the community and, as a result, risk losing the legitimacy

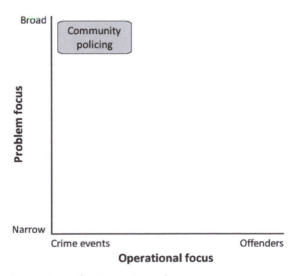

Figure 4.1 Two dimensions of community policing

that community policing seeks to regain. Figure 4.1 graphically shows the conceptual location of community policing on these continuums.

In summary, given the broad nature of community policing initiatives, community policing is difficult to define. However, this also means that it is easy to adopt, at least at a nominal level: true community policing may be a significant challenge. With a strong community focus, it is oriented towards neighbourhoods as the primary scale of activity, and has a bottom-up focus due to the discretion and autonomy given to patrol officers. It addresses a broad range of community issues (not just crime and disorder), and while the criteria for success are unclear and the subject of much discussion (see, for example, Mastrofski 2006; Skogan 2006b), a 'satisfied community' (Tilley 2003a: 326) and the expected outcome of an increase in perceived legitimacy of the police appear to be central aims. I have attempted to summarise these characteristics in Table 4.1.

Problem-oriented policing

Problem-oriented policing (POP) is considerably easier to define than community policing. The originator of problem-oriented policing, Professor Herman Goldstein, wrote that

> The emphasis in problem-oriented policing is on directing attention to the broad range of problems the community expects the police to handle – the problems that constitute the business of the police – and on how police can be more effective in dealing with them. ... It recognizes that the ultimate goal of the police is not simply to enforce the law, but to deal with problems effectively – ideally, by preventing them from occurring in the first place. It therefore plunges the police into an in-depth study of the specific problems they confront. It invites consideration of a wide range of alternatives, in addition to criminal law, for responding to each specific problem. ... It looks to increased knowledge and thinking about the specific problems police confront as the driving force in fashioning police services. (Foreword, in Scott 2000: vi)

Some researchers suggest that problem-oriented policing is integral to definitions of community policing (Oliver and Bartgis 1998), and community and POP have often been bracketed together. In the US, the availability of funds from the federal government with which to conduct problem-oriented policing through community policing grants helped to establish problem-oriented policing, but it also caused some problems for POP's proponents. As Scott (2000: 1) writes, 'While the link between problem-solving and community policing in this large federal funding program has yielded many benefits, the linkage has also blurred the distinction between problem-oriented policing and community policing'. This section builds on the brief history of the development of problem-oriented policing from Chapter 2, and aims to clarify the similarities and distinct differences between problem-oriented policing and community policing in particular (also see Weisburd and Eck (2004) for an excellent review).

Problem-oriented policing is a conceptual approach that can address a vast array of policing issues. Problem-oriented policing requires police to delve deeper into the underlying problems that affect the safety and security of the community they serve. This requires police to be able to scan the broad array of information sources they have access to, including calls for service, recorded crime, informants and the community, and to reclassify these requests for assistance or action into aggregations not based on bureaucratic categories but as items associated with an underlying problem. The hope is that by attacking and resolving the underlying cause of an issue, the police can establish long-term solutions to problems, problems that plague communities and cause significant workload drains on the police department.

For better understanding of a problem when it is initially identified, police have to conduct a thorough analysis so that all potentially useful avenues of enquiry are covered. Often, but not always, this results in the identification of a solution that lies outside the direct policing domain. Law enforcement can be highly effective in reducing crime in the short term: for a simple example, consider static patrols by uniformed officers at crime hot spots. Static police patrols at a street corner drug market will reduce crime in the immediate vicinity of the location and can reduce both drug and violent crime (Lawton *et al.* 2005). However, it comes at a significant financial cost and is thus a short-term fix. When the cops leave, the underlying cause of why that street corner was a good location for drug dealing has not been addressed, and it is often easy for the site to return quickly to being a lucrative drug location (Rengert *et al.* 2005).

The central tenets of problem-oriented policing (see also www.popcenter. org) are as follows:

- Require officers and crime analysts to identify crime and disorder problems, and issues that cause harm to the community.

- Seek a thorough and detailed analysis of a problem before determining a possible solution.

- Allow that potential solutions to crime problems do not exclude the possibility of enforcement action by police, but often seek a long-term resolution that does not involve arrests.

- Resolution of the underlying issue is at least as important as alleviation of the harmful consequences of the problem.

Table 4.1 Some generalised characteristics of five policing models

	Standard model of policing	Community policing	Problem-oriented policing	Compstat	Intelligence-led policing
Easily defined?	Yes	No	Fairly easy	Yes	Fairly easy, but still evolving
Easily adopted?	Yes	Superficially	Difficult	At the technical level, but managerially challenging	Managerially challenging
Orientation?	Police administrative units	Neighbourhoods	Problems	Police administrative units	Criminal groups, prolific and serious offenders
Hierarchical focus?	Top down	Bottom-up	As appropriate for the problem	Top down	Top down
Who determines priorities?	Police management	Community concerns/demands	Sometimes crime analysis, but varies from problem to problem	Police management from crime analysis	Police management from crime intelligence analysis

	Standard model of policing	Community policing	Problem-oriented policing	Compstat	Intelligence-led policing
Target?	Offence detection	Unclear	Crime and disorder problems, and other areas of concern for police	Crime and disorder hot spots	Prolific offenders and crime problems, and other areas of concern for police
Criteria for success?	Increased detections and arrests	Satisfied community	Reduction of problem	Lower crime rates	Detection, reduction or disruption of criminal activity or problem
Expected benefit?	Increased efficiency	Increased police legitimacy	Reduced crime and other problems	Reduced crime (sometimes other problems)	Reduced crime and other problems

- Greater decision-making and problem-solving freedom should be given to officers.

- Evaluation of the outcome of a solution is required in order to determine success.

Many problem-oriented policing practitioners used the SARA methodology to work through problem-solving. SARA involves:

- scanning: identifying recurring problems and how the ensuing consequences affect community safety;

- analysis: collecting and analysing all relevant data on the problem, with the objective of revealing ways to alter the causes of the problem;

- response: seeking out responses that might have worked elsewhere, identifying a range of local options, and then selecting and implementing specific activities that will resolve the problem;

- assessment: testing data collected before and after the response phase in order to determine whether the response reduced the problem and, if not, to identify new strategies that might work.

There are also variations based on SARA. For example, the RCMP used the acronym 'CAPRA' to signify Clients Acquiring and analysing information, Partnership, Response, and Assessment (Deukmedjian 2006).

As stated in Chapter 2, the adoption of problem-oriented policing has been at best a relatively slow emergence, and 'despite problem-oriented policing's wide appeal amongst senior officers, its implementation appears piecemeal in extent and halting in pace. The widespread transformation of problem-oriented policing rhetoric into practice cannot be expected anytime soon' (Townsley *et al.* 2003: 184). Braga and Weisburd (2006) go further by citing numerous studies that have identified a real disconnect with the aims of problem-oriented policing as articulated by Herman Goldstein (1979; 1990), yet contend that 'shallow' problem-solving responses can still be effective in crime control, and perhaps a less rigorous approach to the concept of problem-oriented policing is warranted.

One cause of the problem has been the inability to engage street-level officers in problem-solving. This does cause some difficulties for POP because it is sometimes (though not always) a bottom-up approach to crime control, resting greater responsibility in the lower ranks of the police service. Unfortunately, these same officers often defer to management for the identification and selection of problems; as happened when the RCMP attempted to implement a bottom-up style of community engagement (Deukmedjian and de Lint 2007). Furthermore, these officers usually have least control over resources. This lack of resources, or a mechanism to ask for them, resulting from the shift of emphasis from management to the front line, is seen as a 'structural difficulty' with problem-oriented policing (John and Maguire 2003: 65). It seems likely that it also influences priorities. Gundhus (2005) found that one Norwegian police station with a problem-solving preference was focused on low-level crime and public disorder concerns, whereas an organised crime unit with an intelligence-led policing inclination was more oriented towards national priorities and high-level crime and prosecution.

As with community policing, we can examine problem-oriented policing on the scale of the breadth of crime and disorder problems that the approach is targeted to resolve (the vertical axis in Figure 4.2). From a conceptual position, problem-oriented policing has a broad mandate though slightly less broad than community policing. In recent years, POP techniques have been applied to a growing variety of crime problems. For example, the Center for Problem Oriented Policing (www.popcenter.org) now has guides to address witness intimidation, bomb threats at schools, exploitation of trafficked women, meth labs, panhandling and prescription fraud. Furthermore, situational crime prevention techniques, closely aligned to problem-oriented policing, have featured in recent work on terrorism prevention (Clarke and Newman 2006; 2007). These topics reflect the broad applicability that Herman Goldstein intended. Problem-oriented policing places more emphasis on the crime events (collectively as a problem) than on arresting offenders (though a crackdown or arrest strategy is not out of the question, as Clarke and Eck 2005 point out). This realisation is reflected in the position of problem-oriented policing in Figure 4.2.

Problem-oriented policing therefore can be summarised as a conceptual framework that, while easy to define, is difficult to adopt. Adoption

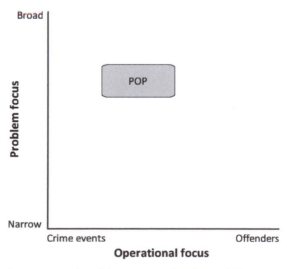

Figure 4.2 Two dimensions of problem-oriented policing (POP)

requires investment in analytical resources (both human and technical), a desire to move beyond responding to single incidents to addressing repeat calls for service as indicative of an underlying problem. It requires a police department to allow priorities to be grounded in analysis, and it demands a commitment to evidence as the basis for designing responses and evaluating outcomes. This all requires a considerable culture change within police departments, one where more autonomy is given to lower ranking officers, and where the reward structure rests less on arrests and more on alleviation of problems.

Compstat

Compstat is a police managerial accountability mechanism. In a Compstat-oriented police department, mid-level commanders are made accountable to the executive level of the police department for the management of crime in their basic command units. By encouraging accountability, it is believed that precinct captains and managers will make use of regular, detailed crime intelligence and from this intelligence flow determine an appropriate crime reduction strategy.

Compstat is easy to define. The crime reduction mechanism of Compstat involves four principles:

- timely and accurate intelligence;
- effective tactics;
- rapid deployment;
- relentless follow-up and assessment.

When Compstat meetings started in early 1994, maps of crime in New York City were projected onto a wall. This allowed the meeting participants to concentrate on crime hot spots, and pressure was placed on precinct commanders to address emerging crime hot spots. Within Compstat, the application of the term *intelligence* is slightly at odds with how the word is more commonly used. Within the Compstat framework, *intelligence* more usually refers to mapped data and is more akin to *information* than the integrated crime intelligence that this book describes.

While crime data and geographical information systems (GIS) play a role in Compstat, it is more than data crunching: it is a marriage of crime mapping, operational strategy and accountability among mid-level commanders. In essence, it is a combined technical and managerial system (Moore 2003). As Silverman (2006) argues, the key to the success of Compstat was the organisational changes that allowed precinct commanders to have the freedom to try new tactics and approaches to crime reduction.

While mapping local crime hot spots forms the focus for timely and accurate intelligence (McGuire 2000), commanders must then devise effective tactics to combat new and ongoing crime concerns. Unlike with community policing, which devolves responsibilities to line officers, the pressure is squarely placed on these middle managers (Weisburd *et al.* 2006). In New York, Police Commissioner William Bratton replaced over a third of his precinct commanders within a year and a half: 'To Bratton, Compstat was police Darwinism – the fittest operational commanders survived and thrived, and the weakest lost their commands' (Walsh and Vito 2004: 60). Rapid deployment of resources is central to Compstat as, without a rapid response, the value of the 'timely' intelligence diminishes. The last part of Compstat often takes place at subsequent Compstat meetings where a review of the crime situation since the last meeting indicates the success (or not) of the previously-adopted tactics.

Compstat was associated with a significant reduction in crime in New York City (McDonald 2002), and as a result the strategy rapidly spread throughout the world, fuelled by media, public and law enforcement enthusiasm (Firman 2003). However, the accuracy of the claim that Compstat caused the significant reduction in crime that occurred in New York is difficult to determine (Moore 2003). For example, Levitt questions whether Compstat and other innovations encouraged by Bratton were responsible for the crime reduction in New York City in the early to mid-1990s, citing other possible explanations such as increased recruitment of police in the city, a levelling of the crack-cocaine market, and the delayed impact of the legalisation of abortion from the 1970s (Levitt 2004). Homicide rates in New York had already been dropping for four years before the introduction of Compstat, and crime rates were declining in Newark, New Jersey; Minneapolis, Minnesota; and Lowell, Massachusetts, prior to their police departments starting Compstat meetings (Weisburd *et al.* 2006).

In support of the crime reduction benefits of Compstat is a thorough empirical study from Australia, where the largest police department in the country, the New South Wales Police, introduced Compstat under the name 'Operation and Crime Review' (OCR). The OCR panels started in January 1998 and were based on the New York model. This involved a three-screen set-up, with maps and temporal trends graphically displayed in a large meeting room in Sydney, the state capital. Police local area commanders were not encouraged to adopt zero-tolerance tactics, but instead were to focus on hot times and places, search for illegal weapons and target repeat offenders, especially those with three or more convictions, those with outstanding arrest warrants, or those whom local intelligence officers suspected were active in the local crime scene (Chilvers and Weatherburn 2001b). In this last activity, it clearly shares similarities with the offender focus of intelligence-led policing. The researchers focused on burglary, a significant problem in Australia, and built a complex time series model that controlled for a number of other possible causes of any crime reduction. These included controls for the level of economic activity in the country, the local unemployment market, and the size of the local heroin-using population. The results suggest that OCRs were responsible for a significant reduction in burglaries across the state, and provide substantial evidence that much of the reduction in burglary was the result of targeting recidivist offenders (as much a supporting argument for intelligence-led policing). Recent work, also from Australia, has found that from inception in August 2001 until the end of June 2004, the Queensland Police Service's Operational Performance Review process cost AU$1,611,500 in salaries, equipment and travel; however, it was associated with reduced crime estimated at saving society AU$2,773,675, for an impressive overall cost benefit of over AU$1,000,000 (Mazerolle *et al.* 2007a).

There is growing evidence that any organisational changes – for example, organisational flexibility, data-driven decision making, and innovative problem solving – that represent any sort of substantive change from past management ideals remain a challenge for police departments (Fleming and Lafferty 2000; Weisburd *et al.* 2003; Willis *et al.* 2003). It has therefore been argued that, while the aims of Compstat remain laudable, in practice it is implemented in a manner that 'has been focused more on reinforcing and legitimating the traditional bureaucratic military model of police organisation than on innovation in the practices of policing' (Weisburd *et al.* 2006: 298). Furthermore, the use of mapping challenges police commanders to interpret intelligence products that are spatial in nature, and devise crime reduction strategies that are geographical in scope, something that few police commanders are trained to do (Ratcliffe 2004a).

Some researchers have noted that Compstat has a theatrical component whereby style and delivery in the large auditoriums where Compstat is played out can become a more effective means of surviving the meeting than providing substantive crime reduction. As a result, the crime reduction aspects can play a secondary role in the meeting. As Maple points out, during the Bratton days in New York City, it was more important to know what was going on and to be on top of the crime picture than to be effective at reducing crime (Maple and Mitchell 1999). Of course, these matters may be more issues of implementation than problems with the management strategy of Compstat itself; if Compstat does reduce crime, fixing the implementation issues may be time well spent.

In summary, we can say that Compstat is relatively easy to define, and fairly easy to adopt, because it does not require a significant cultural change within policing at the street level, though at the managerial level the change in culture and attitude can be significant. Some commentators claim Compstat requires organisational adaptations, while others argue that, in practice, Compstat reinforces the traditional hierarchy of law enforcement. It is oriented to the reduction in recorded crime across police administrative areas, and is driven by a top-down approach that reinforces

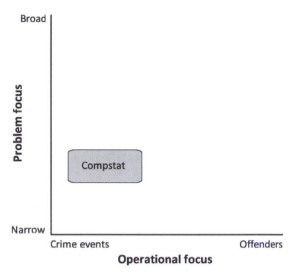

Figure 4.3 Two dimensions of Compstat

the police command and control system. The aim is to reduce crime in police administrative areas such as districts, precincts or basic command units, and if crime figures are reduced (even if only in the short term), then this is an indication of success in crime reduction.

On the two continuums of operational and problem range, Compstat sits more towards the crime side (Magers 2004) and focuses on reducing violent, property and public disorder crime through strategies that tend to target crime reduction and suppression (Moore 2003) rather than specific offenders (though the targeting of individual criminals is not theoretically outside the remit of Compstat). In practice, the general aim of most Compstat sessions is to address street crime, such as robberies and assaults, and property crime, such as vehicle theft and burglary. Compstat has not been widely applied to more esoteric crime activity, such as organised crime or transnational crime (though it has been proposed as a counter-terrorism tool; see Kelling and Bratton 2006), and it is not often applied to broader areas that community police units may address. This places Compstat on the problem/operational foci continuum as shown in Figure 4.3.

Conceptual confusion

The previous sections have identified key movements in modern policing, approaches to the business of law enforcement that are often confused or merged with intelligence-led policing. However, as yet, we have not approached a definition of intelligence-led policing. To get there, we must wade through some of the conceptual fog that swirls around the business of policing. Generally, one has to infer the meaning of intelligence-led policing from researchers and practitioners who write about the subject. Some have sought to articulate their vision of intelligence-led policing as a new direction for policing, while others have tied intelligence-led policing to existing policing paradigms. More generally, there has been a lack of clarity in regard to policing paradigms and the frameworks by which academics and practitioners articulate their vision of how policing should function.

For example, it has been suggested that Compstat is a tool of community policing (Carter 2004), or that intelligence-led policing grew out of problem-oriented policing (Borglund and Nuldén 2006). Some writers have noted that proactive policing has built on the paradigm of community-based policing, using community policing as a foundation for intelligence-led policing (Clarke 2006), or that intelligence-led policing is synonymous with Compstat and Compstat is an evolution of community policing (Dannels and Smith 2001). There does, however, appear to be disagreement with a linking of community policing and Compstat. In particular, this perceived relationship runs counter to the 'undisguised contempt for some of the ideas behind the community policing paradigm' (Walsh and Vito 2004: 63) expressed by the originators of Compstat, William Bratton (1998) and his colleague Jack Maple (1999). Walsh and Vito conclude from their review of the writings of the key players from New York City that

> it is apparent Bratton, Maple and Mayor Giuliani were unsympathetic to the organizational message of community policing. They rejected this paradigm. From its very origin, Compstat was not designed as a vehicle to implement community policing. It was put into action to resolve the inability of community policing and of the nation's largest police department to address crime and to provide community security. (Walsh and Vito 2004: 65)

When broken down into constituent components, there are substantial differences between Compstat and community policing, and these are summarised in the earlier sections of this chapter, and in Table 4.1. In many of the same ways that there is confusion about the unique components of Compstat and community policing, so intelligence-led policing is significantly different from community policing. Here again, there is considerable confusion among commentators and practitioners.

For example, even though the development of intelligence-led policing was a repudiation of the crime focus of the community policing movement, there are still claims that there is a connection between intelligence-led policing and community policing (for a recent example, see McGarrell *et al.* 2007), that 'in many ways, intelligence-led policing is a new dimension of community policing, building on tactics and methodologies developed during years of community policing experimentation' (Carter 2004: 41), or that 'intelligence-led policing is a recent evolution from the strategies of community oriented policing and problem oriented policing' (Dannels and Smith 2001: 111). There is clearly a need for clarity in this conceptual area. Community policing emphasises increased contact with the public and the community and decentralisation of resources, yet Chris Hale and colleagues, with their considerable experience of intelligence-led policing with the Kent Policing Model (Anderson 1997), argue that an intelligence-led policing approach centralises resource control and would 'probably reduce numbers of officers in daily contact with local communities' (Hale *et al.* 2004: 303). Given that a central tenet of a proactive approach is less reliance on crime reporting and more crime recording taking place over the telephone, *reduced* contact with the public is a more likely outcome (Amey *et al.* 1996). Community policing and intelligence-led policing are different policing models that require an organisational realignment to move from one to the other (Deukmedjian 2006). Furthermore, community policing's central aim is an increase in police legitimacy, while intelligence-led policing strives first and foremost to reduce crime. These are substantial conceptual differences.

The Global Intelligence Working Group has one of the few definitions of intelligence-led policing, calling it 'the collection and analysis of information to produce an intelligence end product designed to inform law enforcement decision making at both the tactical and strategic levels' (GIWG 2003: 3-4). In this, they are linking intelligence-led policing to the intelligence cycle – a series of analytical steps by which information is converted into intelligence and disseminated to users (the intelligence cycle is described in Chapter 5). However, while the explicit linking of intelligence-led policing to the intelligence cycle is a fairly common phenomenon (Gill 1998; Dannels and Smith 2001), it may not be entirely accurate. The difficulty with directly associating intelligence-led policing with criminal intelligence or to the intelligence cycle is that these are processes for analysts, rather than a business model for the police service. This approach emphasises the *intelligence* in 'intelligence-led policing' rather than the *policing*.

This linking of intelligence products to the overarching conceptual framework is quite common. For instance, EUROPOL, in announcing the public version of the European Union's first Organised Crime Threat Assessment, claimed the threat assessment document 'is a core product of the intelligence-led policing concept and its drafting is one of EUROPOL's top priorities in 2006' (EUROPOL 2006: 3). While it may be a product, it is not the embodiment of the intelligence-led policing concept as it stands per se – welcome addition though it may be. There is no requirement of the police service (or anyone else) to action the intelligence, nor for the intelligence to be used to influence resource allocation. As a result, the development of an end product could be seen as the successful resolution of the process, yet singularly fail to influence policing or effect any crime reduction or disruption.

Overall, there is definitely a threat to intelligence-led policing, one that Osborne (2006) referred to in the intelligence world as 'diluting intelligence by calling everything intelligence'. Without clarity, there is certainly the chance that intelligence-led policing could suffer in the same definitional manner as community policing. As the following viewpoint from Deborah Osborne points out, a lack of clarity regarding the conceptual models that police departments employ has significant consequences for the quality of products that analysts produce.

Viewpoint

Policing conceptual frameworks from the analyst's perspective

Deborah Osborne

Police managers have differing understandings of Compstat, community policing, problem-oriented policing (POP), and, now, intelligence-led policing. Whatever conceptual model employed, most law enforcement analysts, unlike their national security and military counterparts, receive little direction from law enforcement managers. They rely on outside training, their own particular expertise, and the influence of their peers in order to decide what types of analysis they will provide. Police managers and officers rarely go to analytical training and thus do not know what an analyst is supposed to do, could do, or what tools they need to do their job. The police management's adoption of one of the conceptual models may help analysts decide what to do in their agency, since analysts generally know what the concepts mean more than their commanders.

In agencies that focus on Compstat (or an adaptation of it) an analyst often becomes little more than a technician – someone who can produce statistics and pin maps on the computer. In this case, the analyst rarely analyzes – he or she is so busy creating descriptive data that there is no time for any in-depth analysis. Since Compstat focuses on timely, accurate intelligence, the analyst seldom, if ever, has time to do strategic assessments. Compstat management systems are more concerned with the here-and-now.

In community policing environments, the focus on the community's perception of problems makes it difficult for the analyst to objectively analyze all relevant data. Problems are determined by the community, not the data. Citizen surveys, citizens' complaints via 911 calls, and complaints to other political entities influence the direction of analysis. Community policing is supported by analysts through provision of community statistics and crime maps, which, as in Compstat models, is more description than analysis. Analysts may work with motivated community police officers to assess problems and recommend solutions, but more often on an individual case basis than system-wide.

Few analysts have the support, time and resources to conduct analysis for problem-oriented policing. In agencies that use POP as a model, generally officers choose projects and use analysts to help them obtain the data they need to work on their specific projects. While POP should integrate the analyst into every step of the process as an active member of the team, generally the analyst is not central to the process, but, rather, works on an as-needed basis.

True intelligence-led policing would expand and move the role of the analyst to centre stage. Adequate analytical staffing and tasking will be crucial to intelligence-led policing's success. Education and training focused on fully understanding analysis is mandatory for police officers and managers if we are to implement a concept that requires high-quality analysis. Officers need to know how to gather critical data and analysts need to know what officers need to affect change. Historically, analysts are blamed for producing irrelevant products, but this happens because – without the decision-makers' direction – the analyst is forced to be a mind-reader. Good results become based on lucky guesses. Analysts will be glad if intelligence-led policing can change that paradigm.

Deborah Osborne, a police analyst for ten years with the Buffalo Police Department (New York State), is 2007–08 President of the Society of Police Futurists International and author of the book Out of Bounds: Innovation and Change in Law Enforcement Intelligence Analysis.

Intelligence-led policing defined

Original tenets

Having just identified the need for a clear definition of intelligence-led policing, the next sections aim to approach an answer. The original articulation of intelligence-led policing by the Audit Commission (1993) and the Home Office (HMIC 1997), and as first operationalised by David Phillips, then Chief Constable of Kent Police, had the following central themes:

- *Target prolific and serious criminals.* 'The fundamental objective in recommending a clearer management framework ... is to generate a capacity for proactive work which targets prolific and serious offenders' (Audit Commission 1993: 54).

- *Triage out most crime from further investigation.* 'The [Audit Commission] report ... recommended the reduction of duplication in visits to crime scenes and the establishment of crime desks. These would handle all initial calls and screen out from further investigation, those where there would be no apparent benefit from doing so' (Heaton 2000: 345).

- *Make greater strategic use of surveillance and informants.* 'Even the smallest force needs access to a surveillance capacity ... [and] one aspect of the enhanced supervisory role of [detective sergeants] should be to encourage detectives first to cultivate informants and then task them to produce information on high-priority crimes and criminals' (Audit Commission 1993: 57).

- *Position intelligence central to decision-making.* 'The intelligence function must be at the hub of operational policing activities' (HMIC 1997: 1).

This placed intelligence-led policing, at least initially, at the same level as Compstat on the problem focus continuum (Figure 4.4). While the Audit Commission used burglary as an example crime, and Phillips concentrated on property crime in Kent, intelligence-led policing also became associated with serious organised crime. As such, it did not initially address the wider array of policing problems to which it is now being applied. The initial model orientation therefore located intelligence-led policing to the middle right (ILP #1) of Figure 4.4.

Revising the original model

These original components struck the initial tone; however, intelligence-led policing is definitionally an evolving concept. The last few years have seen a 'revisionist approach to intelligence-led policing' (Hale *et al.* 2004: 304), one that seeks to move intelligence-led policing more towards the crime-focus and problem-solving methodology of problem-oriented policing (Oakensen *et al.* 2002). This has been in line with government thinking in the last few years. The Home Office has articulated a more integrated model, with intelligence and problem-solving working hand-in-hand, such that 'whilst initial investigation into a crime is always undertaken, effective problem solving also requires the routine consideration of related intelligence' (HMIC 2000: 96). I reflected on this move towards integrating preventative problem-solving into intelligence-led policing when proposing a tentative early definition of intelligence-led policing as 'the application of criminal intelligence analysis as an objective decision-making tool in order to facilitate crime reduction and crime prevention through effective policing strategies and external partnership projects drawn from an evidential base' (Ratcliffe 2003: 3). The notion that intelligence-led policing was more an instrument than a philosophy found some support from Sheptycki, who, writing in 2005, defined intelligence-led policing as 'the technological effort to manage information about threats and risks in order to strategically manage the policing mission' (Sheptycki 2005).

But these definitions of intelligence-led policing as a tool or device do not do justice to the recent concerted efforts to position intelligence-led policing as a conceptual model that explains how the business of policing should be conducted, as exemplified by the National Intelligence Model. The recent revisions move intelligence-led policing away from being a tactic or tool to be employed as part of another conceptual model, and into the realm of a business model and conceptual philosophy for policing in its own right. These revisions also take a wider view of intelligence-led policing, such that it is increasingly being associated with the idea of identifying and analysing a problem (Hale *et al.* 2004). Given a greater acceptance of analysis at the core of decision-making, it was probably inevitable that the general processes would be applied to non-crime areas that are still within the domain of police, such as 'traffic, patrol and partnership activities' (Maguire and John 2006: 71). It was this thinking that inspired Merseyside Police to initiate a 'holistic strategy' that used an intelligence-led approach to all key areas of police business, not just crime (Barton and Evans 1999).

So, while still retaining the central notion that police should avoid getting bogged down in reactive, individual case investigations, intelligence-led policing is evolving into a managerial model of evidence-based, resource allocation decisions through prioritisation. It is also a philosophy that places greater emphasis on information sharing and collaborative, strategic solutions to crime problems, a concept that incorporates the 'reflexive notion of policing through partnerships' (Deukmedjian 2006: 531).

Intelligence-led policing components

With the caveat that intelligence-led policing has been an evolving concept, we can infer the tenets of intelligence-led policing from published work, given that it is relatively detailed and well defined in this way (Hale *et al.* 2004). For example, intelligence-led policing is closely aligned with the UK National Intelligence Model, which is designed to prioritise targets for increased intelligence gathering, prevention strategies and enforcement tactics into a control strategy (NCIS 2000). This control strategy is the basis from which local police commanders set priorities for:

- the targeting of offenders;

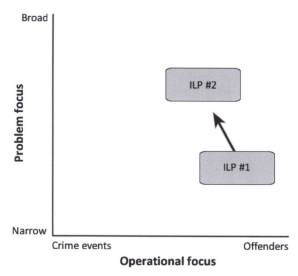

Figure 4.4 Two dimensions of intelligence-led policing (ILP) over time

- the management of crime and disorder hot spots;
- the investigation of linked series of crimes and incidents;
- the application of preventative measures.

(NCIS 2000: 14).

The decision-making process is effectively a top-down one, with managers controlling uniform, traffic and detective resources and how they are deployed (Amey *et al.* 1996). Once those resources are deployed, Tilley (2003b) notes that increased arrests and reduced crime are expected benefits and indications of success. These realisations help to complete the intelligence-led policing column in Table 4.1.

The move towards a greater integration with problem-solving moves the target focus away from the far right of Figure 4.4, and to a more central position (while still retaining the offender slant). Greater use of intelligence targeting to a wider range of criminal activities, such as terrorism (IACP 2002; Loyka *et al.* 2005) and organised crime (Sheptycki 2004a; Harfield 2006; NJSP 2006a), broadens the range of applicable crime areas to which intelligence-led policing can be applied, and therefore the revised location of intelligence-led policing on the two continuums of Figure 4.4 is reflected in the position of ILP #2.

A further piece of the puzzle is required before it is possible to attempt a definition of intelligence-led policing. The term *intelligence* has long been misunderstood within and outside law enforcement, and has often been associated with subterfuge and moral ambiguity. Moreover, it has also been misunderstood to mean the type of information gathered from informants or surveillance.

> A clear and general understanding of the meaning of the term 'intelligence', and an acceptance that it involves wider interpretations than perhaps traditional police-oriented explanations have allowed, is essential. This would include the interpretation of crime and incident data through analysis, and community information on a range of issues, as well as that more commonly used information gleaned from various sources on the activities of known or suspected active criminals. (Oakensen *et al.* 2002: 7)

Chapter 5 discusses the various definitions of intelligence, and how they can impact on the work of analysts; however, for now it is helpful to define *crime intelligence* as analysed information that blends data from crime analysis of crime patterns and criminal intelligence drawn from the behaviour of offenders. Here the term crime intelligence is used to reflect a realisation that good intelligence stems not only from knowledge about offenders (criminal intelligence) but also about crime events (crime analysis).

This all suggests that intelligence-led policing

- is a management philosophy/business model;
- aims to achieve crime reduction and prevention and to disrupt offender activity;
- employs a top-down management approach;
- combines crime analysis and criminal intelligence into crime intelligence;
- uses crime intelligence to objectively direct police resource decisions;
- focuses enforcement activities on prolific and serious offenders.

Furthermore, the model of intelligence-led policing practised in some places recognises the complementary nature of the long-term benefits of problem-oriented policing.

With these central tenets, intelligence-led policing is operationally the antithesis of community policing. Where community policing aims primarily for police legitimacy and is organisationally bottom-up and community centred, intelligence-led policing aims for crime reduction, is top-down and hierarchical, and uses crime intelligence to focus on offenders. Though there are stylistic similarities to Compstat (crime-fighting emphasis and organisationally hierarchical), the strategic approach to combating offender behaviour is substantively different. The offender focus differentiates intelligence-led policing from problem-oriented policing, even though this gap is shrinking as problem-solving becomes integrated into the crime disruption and prevention language of intelligence-led policing. Indeed, the 'revisionist' (Hale *et al.* 2004: 304) approach to intelligence-led policing has been increasingly to intertwine components of intelligence-led policing and problem-oriented policing. For example, Lancashire Constabulary explicitly sought to overlay intelligence-led policing (through the National Intelligence Model) over their existing problem-oriented policing approach (Maguire and John 2004).

Finally, it is sometimes said that police departments have been doing intelligence-led policing for a long time, but this is not the case. Intelligence has traditionally been used in police departments for case support, and not for strategic planning and resource allocation. The move from investigation-led intelligence to intelligence-led policing is the most significant and profound paradigm change in modern policing.

Summary

Defining policing frameworks can be like trying to nail jelly to a tree. Various practitioners and commentators have tried to tie intelligence-led policing theoretically to existing conceptual frameworks of policing. However, if intelligence-led policing is truly a new paradigm in policing, then it should be recognised as significantly different from previous ways of policing (the policing models from this chapter are summarised in Figure 4.5). As said earlier, the degree of generalisation necessary even to try to conceptualise these comparative models into a simple framework highlights differences that are not always as severe in practice. Academics devote whole books to elucidating particular styles of policing, and many police departments operate models that are hybrids of these different approaches. The simplifications described herein should be interpreted as such.

From this chapter it should, however, be clear that there is a great deal of daylight separating intelligence-led policing and community policing (though see the GMAC PBM framework described in Chapter 7 for an example of an attempt to integrate more closely the business model aspects of intelligence-led policing with the collaborative ideals of community policing). If there is one fundamental difference between community policing and all of the conceptual frameworks for policing discussed in this chapter, it is that reduced crime is a by-product of successful community policing, and not a primary aim. The primary aim of community policing is increased police legitimacy, whereas reduced crime is the primary aim of the other models.

While sharing some similarities, intelligence-led policing can have a broader problem range and more specific offender focus than Compstat. In

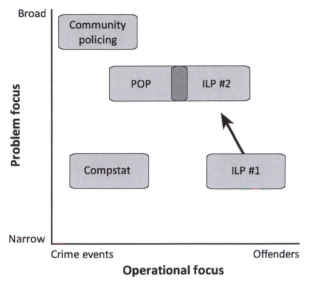

Figure 4.5 Various policing models represented on two focal continuums.
POP: problem-oriented policing; ILP: intelligence-led policing

many regards, intelligence-led policing tries to address many of the same problems as problem-oriented policing, though in a different organisational manner (more allied to traditional hierarchical command models) and with a greater emphasis on enforcement. In light of the philosophical revisions that have occurred in recent years and with a broader definition of intelligence, it is possible to propose a definition as follows:

> Intelligence-led policing is a business model and managerial philosophy where data analysis and crime intelligence are pivotal to an objective, decision-making framework that facilitates crime and problem reduction, disruption and prevention through both strategic management and effective enforcement strategies that target prolific and serious offenders.

Intelligence-led policing is thus a business model for policing that sees crime intelligence as a combination of what is more commonly known separately as crime analysis and criminal intelligence, and it works in an information management framework that allows analysts to influence decision-makers, and where a range of enforcement and longer-term, problem-solving prevention solutions are drawn from an evidence base that suggests their likely effectiveness. This definition also recognises the evolving nature of intelligence-led policing to be a more inclusive model able to incorporate areas of policing activity (such as accident reduction and missing person enquiries) that are not related to crime per se but are still significant problems for police agencies. With this evolution, intelligence-led policing is moving to become the 'all-crimes, all-hazards' business approach that is sought by many in policing.

There are a couple of points to note from this. Problem-oriented policing is usually defined according to its goal – reducing problems. Intelligence-led policing is too often defined according to the mechanism of how it is supposed to function. Therefore, the definition I propose here retains a similar goal-oriented approach; in other words, to use an objective, decision-making framework not as an end in itself, but as the means to achieve crime and problem reduction, disruption and prevention. Furthermore, Figure 4.5 shows a crossover of intelligence-led policing and problem-oriented policing. I share with a number of people the view that problem-oriented policing could benefit from greater use of crime intelligence and an offender focus, while intelligence-led policing could benefit from the strategic problem-solving capacities of problem-oriented policing.

The next chapters in this book will explore the role of analysts in making this vision a reality, and will introduce the 3-i model as a way to conceptualise how intelligence-led policing functions.

5

Analytical frameworks

While the preceding chapter defined intelligence-led policing, a formal description is of relatively little value if the user does not understand the underlying conceptual process of how it is supposed to work. One significant cause for confusion in the analytical world begins with the range of different definitions of key roles and functions, as the first part of this chapter will show. A further cause of problems (especially among police executives) is a misunderstanding of the differences between data, information, knowledge and intelligence. The chapter aims to clarify the distinction between these terms.

The core of this chapter explores the range of models that have been applied to the crime analysis and criminal intelligence fields. Models are 'a device for simplifying reality so that the relationship between variables may be more clearly studied' (Rogerson 2006: 2) and, as simplified representations of the real world, they must be approached with caution. However, models are also able to clarify relationships between key variables; in the case of intelligence-led policing, relationships between variables within the intelligence process or in the broader enforcement domain. The role of these models should not be underestimated; they send a signal to both analysts and intelligence clients as to the role each plays in intelligence-led policing.

Awash with terminology

The fields of crime analysis and criminal intelligence are filled with a variety of terms and definitions that are poorly policed, if at all, by the analytical community. What is operational analysis in one organisation is tactical intelligence at another, and network analysis in one police department is called association analysis or link-charting at the neighbouring jurisdiction. This can give the impression that police analysis is an impregnable field where understanding the mysteries, science and art of the business is available only to an initiated few who can comprehend the lingo. The conflicts in terminology were recently identified by a forum of crime analysts, intelligence practitioners and policymakers as a significant hindrance to better integration of crime and intelligence analysis (Ratcliffe 2007). The following sections give examples of these contradictions.

What is criminal intelligence?

Nowhere is this terminological conflict more obvious than with the myriad definitions of *criminal intelligence* that currently exist. For example, the Association of Chief Police Officers (ACPO) suggest that 'criminal intelligence can be said to be the end product of a process often complex, sometimes physical, and always intellectual, derived from information that has been collated, analysed and evaluated in order to prevent crime or secure the apprehension of offenders' (ACPO 1975: para. 32). The International Association of Law Enforcement Intelligence Analysts (IALEIA) refer to criminal intelligence as 'information compiled, analyzed, and/or disseminated in an effort to anticipate, prevent, or monitor criminal activity' (IALEIA 2004: 32), but they also refer to *intelligence* as 'analyzed raw data' (p. 3). The definition of *intelligence* is later expanded to 'the product of systematic gathering, evaluation, and synthesis of raw data on individuals or activities suspected of being, or known to be, criminal in nature. Intelligence is information that has been analyzed to determine its meaning and relevance. Information is compiled, analyzed, and/or disseminated in an effort to anticipate, prevent, or monitor criminal activity' (p. 33). Intelligence (or criminal intelligence) is therefore perceived to be a product that is generated from information. The National Centre for Policing Excellence (NCPE) defined *intelligence* as 'information that has been subject to a defined evaluation and risk assessment process in order to assist with police decision making', with an afterthought: 'In addition to being evaluated, information is analysed' (NCPE 2005a: 13). IALEIA's law enforcement intelligence analysis definitions include entries for *analysis*, *crime pattern analysis*, and a whole smorgasbord of other types of analysis, including *association analysis*, *network analysis*, *criminal analysis*, *demographic/social trend analysis*, *financial analysis*, *flow analysis*, *geographic analysis*, *indicator analysis*, *results analysis*, *spatial analysis*, *telephone record analysis*, and *communication analysis*. Quite a bewildering list!

While conceptualising intelligence is a challenge for policing, the one thread running through most definitions is that intelligence is more than mere information (Osborne 2006). The complexity of existing definitions is reflective of the scope of the crime intelligence business; it is often simultaneously a process, an outcome, and a product. The IALEIA move to establish common standards for defining the activities of their members is in part a response to the realisation at the International Association of Chiefs of Police (IACP) Criminal Intelligence Sharing Summit that there is a lack of common understanding of criminal intelligence terminology and processes, a situation that hampers information sharing between agencies (IACP 2002).

The cause of this range of definitions is unclear, but may be related to the role of the analyst. There can be a tendency to subvert the meaning of criminal intelligence to reflect a particular operational role or job description. For example, an intelligence analyst listening to wiretaps in a long-running investigation is not really conducting intelligence analysis: the activity is more accurately investigative support. The analyst might relate the covert information from the wire to the broader picture of the crime syndicate under investigation, but there is often little suggestion that a new course of action will follow or that this feeds into new knowledge about the broader criminal environment. However, if an officer is given the job title *criminal intelligence analyst*, there is a presumption that whatever that officer does must be criminal intelligence analysis. There is a tendency for definitions of criminal intelligence (and associated phrases) to reflect the job description of the individual performing the work, rather than an industry-wide definition. It is no wonder the IALEIA have attempted to promote a set of standard definitions, and their definition for criminal intelligence cited earlier is the most commonly used.

What is crime analysis?

Crime analysis is, as Rachel Boba (2005: 6) describes it, the 'systematic study of crime and disorder problems as well as other police-related issues – including socio-demographic, spatial, and temporal factors – to assist the police in criminal apprehension, crime and disorder reduction, crime prevention, and evaluation'. Alternatively, it is 'a set of systematic, analytical processes directed at providing timely and pertinent information relative to crime patterns and trend correlations to assist the operational and administrative personnel in planning the deployment of resources for the prevention and suppression of criminal activities, aiding the investigative process, and increasing apprehensions and the clearance of cases' (Gottlieb *et al.* 1998). Similar, but not the same. The website of the Massachusetts Association of Crime Analysts describes crime analysis as 'a discipline of public safety analysis, which provides information support for the missions of law enforcement or criminal justice agencies', shifting the focus to a broader definition. IALEIA defines *analysis* as 'the evaluation of information and its comparison to other information to determine the meaning of the data in reference to a criminal investigation or assessment', and *crime pattern analysis* as 'a process that looks for links between crimes and other incidents to reveal similarities and differences that can be used to help predict and prevent future criminal activity'. Given the range of activities performed by crime analysts, a definition is quite elusive, and

Boba (2005) dedicates a chapter of her book to the task. Osborne (2006: 7) notes:

> Virtually all of the skills used in crime analysis can be applied to intelligence analysis. The intelligence analyst may have to learn new ways of looking at crime in order to cross over to the crime analysis field, but the critical thinking skills used to analyse organized crime and support investigators are applicable as well to the analysis of street crimes.

Ron Clarke and John Eck do not promote a particular definition of crime analysis, but note that a crime analyst has to be an individual who not only performs analysis but is also a local crime expert, understands and applies problem-oriented policing, employs environmental criminology to understand crime patterns, performs in-depth analysis, identifies solutions, communicates effectively with police leaders and evaluates the outcome of attempts to solve the problem (Clarke and Eck 2005). Quite a tall order for someone often at the lower pay scales of the department.

I have been using the phrases *crime intelligence* as a way to integrate better these fields that examine crime and criminality (used in this book, and in Ratcliffe in press). There are numerous reasons for this. First, many police departments do not employ individuals in separate roles. These police analysts end up doing whatever is necessary to achieve the department's aims. Analysts may do link chart analysis of a gang one day (a role more traditionally associated with intelligence analysts) and create a map of local burglaries the next (a crime analyst role). Secondly, the distinction between intelligence and crime analysts is one that is largely absent outside the US, and analysts from outside the US cannot understand why two separate strands of law enforcement analysis have emerged in America (Osborne 2006). In other countries, analysts often have a broad range of skills and are expected to perform whatever functions that the operational need demands – a situation the US would do well to mimic. Lastly, I am trying to promote this terminology to replace *crime analysis* and *criminal intelligence*, terms largely redundant given the advances that analysis within the policing field has made in the last 20 years. Increasingly, the two disciplines are seen as interdependent, and it is to be hoped that they will completely merge in the coming years. Moving towards that future became one of the aims of the November 2005 forum organised by the Police Foundation, a forum that recommended a more integrated approach to analysis (Ratcliffe 2007).

Data, information and knowledge?

When I joined the ranks of the police, every police station had a *collator*, a police officer who had the job of collating information on known criminals.

The job title itself indicates one of information storage rather than information usage, and the term has thankfully fallen into redundancy. The analyst role has now grown beyond that of information storage. Crime intelligence analysts are pedlars of information, intelligence, *and* ideas.

To use a term popularised by Ericson and Haggerty (1997), there is a growing realisation that police have moved beyond the simple storage of information and have become *knowledge workers*, using information to generate greater insight into the criminal and policing environments (Brodeur and Dupont 2006). Brodeur and Dupont's work is valuable for clarifying the concept of knowledge within a policing situation. It is possible to consider that criminal intelligence, with its more extensive history within policing, represents an example of *old* knowledge in this regard, while crime analysis is *new* knowledge – taking advantage of the digitisation of the last 20 years (Ratcliffe 2008). The term *knowledge* has certainly become mainstream; the website of the Serious Organised Crime Agency (SOCA) describes 'knowledge management departments' within their intelligence wing. But stating that police are knowledge workers does not necessarily clarify the place of this knowledge within business models of law enforcement such as intelligence-led policing. What is needed is greater clarity of the scope and limitations of various information sources.

Many texts on criminal intelligence define intelligence as the product of information and analysis, and this relationship is often displayed formulaically as 'information + analysis = intelligence'. This definition fails to recognise the wide range of data and information sources that are of variable applicability and quality. Readers who have spent time observing the crime intelligence world would be right to point out that many people consider information and knowledge as synonymous, and throwing *data* into the mix can rapidly lead to confusion. At best, the formula 'information + analysis = intelligence' functions as an idealised conceptualisation of the intelligence cycle, in much the same way that the 3-i model (described later in this chapter and in Figure 5.6) serves to explain the conceptual framework of the role of analysis in policing. However, while 'information + analysis = intelligence' simplifies the intelligence cycle concept to the level where it can be easily taught, it does so at the expense of reflecting the reality of the situation on the ground.

From the chapter that defines intelligence-led policing, it is clear that I consider crime intelligence as pivotal to determining strategy in an objective, decision-making management framework. Crime intelligence therefore moves beyond knowledge into the realm of action. Davenport's information ecology approach (1997) conceptualises data, information and knowledge on a continuum, and in the next section I extend that by adding the vital action component of *intelligence*. The DIKI continuum (data–information–knowledge–intelligence) is a way to conceptualise the necessary information and data sources that create knowledge, and introduces intelligence into the mix as the mechanism to convert knowledge into intelligence.

DIKI continuum

Data are the observations and measurements we can make about crime. Examples include features of criminal activity that are easily quantified (such as uniform crime reports and other crime statistics), databases of offenders, and intelligence databases where information has been prescreened, categorised and entered onto the system. Data are simple observations, unencumbered with additional meaning, inference or opinion. Data can refer to crime scenes, modus operandi characteristics, weapons, stolen vehicles and suspects (Boba 2005).

Information is data with greater relevance and purpose (Davenport 1997). John Grieve, former Director of Intelligence for the Metropolitan Police, argues that intelligence is information designed for action where the emphasis is on action (Grieve 2004). Information is endowed with meaning and context and, in a policing environment, can often be unstructured in nature. For example, information from the transcript of a wiretap might represent a greater understanding of the relationship between a drug distributor and a street-level dealer. To be entered onto a database, the information needs to be given a context and assessment by an officer, and categorised according to systems designed by intelligence professionals (see Chapter 10). Information is therefore harder to transfer without some common unit of measurement that makes sense to both the transmitter and the receiver.

Knowledge has recently entered the language of operational policing. Whereas, previously, it was a more esoteric term used to discuss concepts of information management within policing by academics outside the blue ranks, it is now one of the latest buzzwords. For example, the National Intelligence Model (NIM) talks of 'knowledge assets' and 'knowledge products' (NCPE 2005c). Knowledge is 'valuable precisely because somebody has given the information context, meaning, a particular interpretation; somebody has reflected on the knowledge, added their own wisdom to it, and considered its larger implications' (Davenport 1997: 9). Knowledge is difficult to structure, store or communicate, yet it is also immensely valuable to an organisation.

Knowledge is also considerably more intangible than data. As such, it becomes vulnerable to organisational and cultural barriers to knowledge transfer; a problem not necessarily open to a technological solution. While naively thinking that resolving information technology (IT) problems can create knowledge, the 9/11 Commission at least recognised that within the pre-9/11 FBI there was little opportunity to develop knowledge products: 'The FBI's information systems were woefully inadequate. The FBI lacked the ability to know what it knew: there was no collective mechanism for capturing or sharing its institutional knowledge' (9/11 Commission 2004: 77). Throwing money at IT departments is not, however, necessarily the best way to initiate information sharing. In the study of one UK police force, Collier and colleagues found that 'without addressing the cultural barriers, an investment in technology may not yield the appropriate changes in behaviour. To achieve this, technology needs to be integrated with working practices in order to reduce organisational reliance on informal methods of communication' (Collier *et al.* 2004: 466).

One of the most illustrative of examples (from the most tragic of cases) can be found in the Bichard Inquiry Report. Following the murder of two 10-year-old girls (Holly Wells and Jessica Chapman) in Soham, Cambridgeshire, in August 2002, an inquiry into the handling of intelligence systems in Cambridgeshire Constabulary and Humberside Police found that, in Humberside, problems with the intelligence systems and practices were 'systemic and corporate', a situation caused by

- few effective management audits or inspections to check that the systems were operating properly;
- inadequate training of police officers;
- the guidance on record creation, review and deletion being either non-existent or, at best, confused;
- little evidence of sufficient strategic review of information management systems;
- no real awareness among senior managers of the scale and nature of the problems.

(Bichard 2004: 7)

The report went on to note that at no time did the record creation system work as it should, and the only intelligence report relating to the murderer, Ian Huntley, had been deleted from the system. Regretfully, many leaders in policing, no doubt spurred on by their IT managers, see investment in technology as the solution to problems that are often inherently human and not as easily quantified as a difficulty in transferring bytes of data.

The sort of special knowledge that comes from a real understanding of the criminal environment certainly has not only an allure (the same allure that sends hundreds of students to criminal justice and criminology classes in the often vain hope of becoming a crime scene investigator or a profiler), but also a power that can be informally traded. As Gill (2000: 36) notes, 'Reciprocity and trust are the name of the intelligence game; information is a "currency" which one might spend in order to get more. Power thus comes to be defined not in terms of hierarchical office but in one's reputation for having "knowledge".' If Brodeur (1983) is right that policing has moved to a situation of 'high policing' – where the capturing of knowledge and retention of intelligence is seen as a functional role of policing – then knowledge becomes an essential commodity. Knowledge management is certainly central to the design of the NIM, and is an intensive activity for police in an intelligence-led policing environment (Collier 2006). However, I have found analytical units in many places and countries that have possessed a wealth of knowledge, but who have little influence over decision-makers. Much police knowledge remains forever locked up inside the heads of detectives and analysts, retained for when that knowledge can become useful; that is, useful when it is to the advantage of the individual rather than necessarily to the organisation's crime reduction efforts.

From knowledge to intelligence

So why the extra step of adding *intelligence* to the continuum? It is due to the fact that intelligence products are inherently action products. In other words, knowledge products can generate understanding, but intelligence products are supposed to generate action (de Lint *et al.* 2007). Within the crime intelligence environment, knowledge has an extra hurdle to overcome before it can be used to good effect. The policing world does not automatically defer to the analysis arm of the service when making decisions; people prefer their instincts. This problem of 'gut-feeling' decision-making is not unique to policing: it is an issue that impacts from the corporate world (Davenport 1997) to the national security arena (9/11 Commission 2004). It is, however, particularly acute in law enforcement. The military, while having no shortage of intelligence failures over the years, does have a history of employing military intelligence to direct operational decisions, and there is both a culture and an organisational structure that places the intelligence arm within the decision-making ethos; in most policing situations, that structure and culture are rarely evident.

For many analysts, the gulf between knowledge production and intelligence production is substantial, requiring analysts to move beyond the descriptive and to know better their client's environment. The skills required are considerably different from the ones they were initially employed for. 'Relationship management' is not a term that many analysts are probably familiar with, but perhaps they should be. Managing the relationship between analysts and the consumer of their products – the client – is essential if the knowledge possessed by the analyst is to be converted into actionable intelligence. The need to manage this analyst–client relationship is the most vital skill that an analyst should possess, according to Nicholl (2004). It requires a less technical set of skills and a finer appreciation of the internal (sometimes infernal!) dynamics of the police department. The client–analyst relationship is so important that I dedicate a chapter to the topic of influencing decision-makers (Chapter 7). If intelligence is actionable knowledge and the defining criterion of actionable is client-specific, there should be no generic intelligence products. Instead, products should be able to convey intelligence that is situated within a solid understanding of the capacity limitations and organisational priorities of the client situation.

To place the DIKI continuum in context, consider this example. At a local police station, a computer database records and retains the location of residential burglary incidents. These computer records are *data*. When a crime analyst accesses the data and recognises an emerging pattern of new burglaries in an area not normally plagued with a break-and-enter problem, then this becomes *information*. In essence, raw data have been enhanced with sufficient meaning to recognise a pattern. If the analyst subsequently talks to a detective and shares this information, and the detective remembers that a new pawnshop has just opened in the area and that known burglars have been seen entering the pawnshop, this collective wisdom becomes *knowledge*. Various information strands have coalesced to enable the detective and the analyst to build a picture of the criminal environment in their minds, a picture that undoubtedly has gaps, but that also has enough substance to support hypotheses and contain implications. This is the structure of knowledge. Finally, when the crime analyst and the detective take their knowledge to a senior officer who agrees to investigate the pawnshop and mount a surveillance operation to target burglars and gather further information, then this knowledge becomes *intelligence*. In other words, somebody uses it explicitly to try to reduce crime.

Levels of crime intelligence

Given the great variation in police agency types, it is not surprising that crime intelligence analyst roles vary considerably. As there is a recognised need for different types of analysis, many policing organisations also recognise that analysts need to be employed at different structural levels in order to address different echelons of criminality or policing problem.

The traditional approach is to define intelligence as being utilised on two or three planes of operation. I have previously described these as *tactical* (support for front-line areas, investigations and other operational areas in taking case-specific action to achieve enforcement objectives), *operational* (supporting area commanders and regional operational commanders in planning crime reduction activity and deploying resources to achieve operational objectives), and *strategic* (aiming to provide insight and understanding, and make a contribution to broad strategies, policies and resources) (Ratcliffe 2004d: 4–5). Most organisations use some variation of these descriptions but sometimes in a rather haphazard way; some do not have an operational level while others describe their tactical level as their operational level, and so on.

A few organisations use the term *administrative crime analysis*, a term that seems counterintuitive to crime intelligence. Administrative analysis appears to be used to address analysis of organisational characteristics instead of crime, and is more concerned with the presentation of findings than with crime analysis per se (Boba 2005). Analysing organisational characteristics is thus more akin to policy analysis or management statistics. I do not include further reference to administrative analysis in this book because the crime and problem scope of administrative analysis is incorporated into the tactical-operational-strategic triumvirate of crime intelligence, and I feel that any analytical issues falling outside the domain of crime or problem analysis should not be conducted by police analysts. Where any work relates to presenting findings and influencing decision-makers, that is an integral part of the job of an analyst and does not require a separate title.

Tactical intelligence is the most widely employed application of analysis to crime control, though it is often misconstrued to be synonymous with investigative case support. Most crime analysts and intelligence officers do not stray far from the 'sharp end', and tactical intelligence that seeks to maximise the impact of enforcement (Cope 2003) is favoured by both analysts and managers. When O'Shea and Nicholls conducted a survey of crime analysis units in America, they found that executives demanded that analysts concentrate on tactical outcomes and investigative support rather than on analysis of underlying community problems, and this offender-based mentality permeates from decision-makers to the analysts themselves: 'Most analysts that we spoke with resented engaging in activities that cannot be linked directly to the identification and apprehension of offenders' (O'Shea and Nicholls 2003: 19).

The operational and strategic components of intelligence practice are largely absent from many police organisations. Many police departments and analysts do not recognise the operational intelligence arena, but this is one of the fastest growing areas of information management within policing. Sandwiched between the offender focus of the tactical area, and the strategic nature of intelligence to form 'strategy, policy and long term plans' (Quarmby 2004), the operational imperative that can drive crime reduction activity and resource planning is arguably the key component of both intelligence-led policing and Compstat. The strategic end of the spectrum has always suffered in terms of achieving legitimacy, with a distinction between tactical and strategic that is 'not just a matter of definition or semantics, [but] has real organisational consequences and permeates the analytical process' (Gill 2000: 217). Yet, it also has the potential to be the most significant aspect of crime intelligence due to the ability of strategic products to influence overall strategy and resource decisions (John and Maguire 2003).

While these distinctions have organisational consequences for the management of information and the application of intelligence, on the

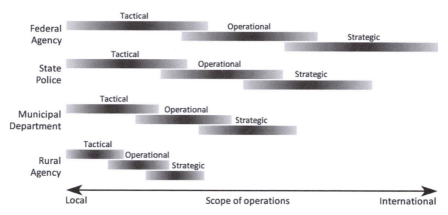

Figure 5.1 Scope of crime intelligence within different types of agency (adapted from Ratcliffe 2007)

ground the distinctions can be fairly abstract, can merge organisationally, and are largely dependent on the size and mission of the agency. Figure 5.1 is a simplified model of the crime intelligence scope of various agencies. Note that these definitions are often fluid, as reflected in the diagram with the overlap of tactical, operational and strategic, for every type of agency. What is a strategic issue for a municipal department is often an operational one for a federal agency with a national responsibility. Further down the continuum of departments, strategic issues for a rural agency are unlikely to have the scope of strategic importance for state or even large municipal departments. This is not to say that a rural agency does not have strategic crime concerns; quite the contrary. It simply reflects a different distinction of what constitutes *strategic*, an issue more of scale than conceptual difference. As Brian Flood notes, 'in NIM terminology, "strategic" is not a term related to exclusively national or whole law enforcement perspectives but is one that is applied to the process of business planning and resource allocation at each of the structural levels within UK policing' (Flood 2004: 42).

NIM levels

The NIM approach recognises a tactical and strategic level, but houses these within three 'business levels' (NCIS 2000), the structural levels referred to by Flood (2004: 42). Local issues are dealt with at Level 1, while factors that address a whole force or region are assessed both tactically and strategically at Level 2. Serious and organised crime that can impact on the UK and is usually national or international in scope, is addressed at Level 3.

Level 1 is a level that will feel the most familiar to analysts reading this book, and analysts who conduct strategic work for federal or national agencies will recognise some of the issues likely to occur at Level 3. It is at Level 2 that many operational challenges materialise. It has been argued that although local, geographically configured law enforcement has a role in addressing organised crime, the basic structure of geographic limits on operational boundaries is not suited to tackling transnational and global-scale criminality (Harfield 2000). If there is a flaw in the implementation of the structural levels of the NIM, it might be in the lack of accountability at this level. At Level 1, local commanders are answerable to the police chief, and police chiefs to their political masters. The accountability at Levels 2 or 3 is less clear.

The very nature of cross-jurisdictional operations and intelligence work in a collaborative environment without a clear hierarchy entails a potential weakness in the structure of law enforcement that criminals may seek to exploit. While a modest risk in the UK, this is a significant concern in the US, where the lack of any coherent structure to the country's 18,000-plus law enforcement agencies creates an accountability gulf that state police agencies are hard pressed to address. Level 2 NIM issues do occur in the US, as demonstrated in the Viewpoint in Chapter 2.

The NIM has at least brought strategic crime intelligence back into the centre stage of police operational planning, and there is modest evidence from the US that at least in one example strategic documents can feed relatively quickly into operational priorities (Ratcliffe and Guidetti 2008). It does, however, appear that strategic intelligence was thrust into the limelight a little prematurely for the crime intelligence industry. Nicholl (2004) is right to lament that 'many intelligence reports curiously suffer from a fundamental misunderstanding of what was originally asked', and that the risks are substantial when a client (decision-maker) is unhappy with an intelligence output: a 'product produced for an unreceptive audience is likely at best to receive minimal attention or at worse face a concerted effort to destroy it' (p. 53). Strategic products are expected at Level 3; however, there is undoubtedly a continuing need for the intelligence community to convince police executives of the need to incorporate a level of strategic thinking into their operational priorities at structural levels of policing (Ratcliffe 2004d).

Yet, for all of the problems with the NIM and its levels, as the following Viewpoint from R. Mark Evans shows, there are certain critical factors that enable the NIM to succeed as a holistic business model for policing.

Viewpoint

A practitioner's perspective on the National Intelligence Model

R. Mark Evans

Intelligence-led policing is manifest in the Police Service of Northern Ireland (PSNI) through the systems and processes described in the UK National Intelligence Model (NIM). In the early years NIM was largely ignored ('ridiculously over complicated. And anyway I'm already doing it all', as one 25-year veteran described it). As it struggled to gain early momentum, many picked holes in the jargon and detail; some challenged its validity and almost everyone initially questioned whether it had practical value at a local level. The tipping point was reached in 2004/05 – some five years after its introduction – when all local command units and key specialist areas had established a local crime intelligence and analytical capability – and positive results were starting to flow as a matter of routine.

From 'concept' NIM has now become the way PSNI does the bulk of its volume, serious and organised crime business and this is locally joined-up with wider national security work. It is starting to make inroads in other operational areas (like traffic policing) and in the foreseeable future is the possibility of a genuinely whole-of-force approach. In the PSNI, NIM is associated with the building of a more accountable, operationally effective and performance-driven culture. There are a number of critical success factors:

- NIM is a corporate business process and management philosophy which provides a common thread underpinning core policing activities. Good 'police analysts' – the choice of title is deliberate to avoid crime/intelligence analyst distinctions – working to properly understand problems are the lifeblood of an effective NIM process. Therefore analysts should be flexibly deployed, have a wide remit, need to avoid being labelled with specialist titles, and should be embedded around decision-makers at every level.

- The use of a common language and broadly consistent service-wide NIM processes is crucial. When the command team understands what a 'Tasking and Coordination meeting' looks like and how it should really work, participants can focus on taking action – instead of arguing about inputs and responsibilities.

- The use of standard NIM products provides a common way of exploring problems which allows aggregation and understanding across areas, regions and national boundaries. Some observers and academics believe NIM restricts the quality and range of analytical work. Maybe in the short term. But for years good analysts had no reliable outlet for their work. NIM ensures every product is focused on a problem that someone owns. This is good for the police, good for partner agencies and good for the community.

● Critical mass is vital. While the technical aspects of NIM don't need to be fully understood by everyone, a few staff promoting it in isolated areas is a recipe for failure. Over the longer term NIM is a way of thinking and working every day. It is not a concept that can be applied once and then forgotten about.

Many advocates of community oriented and other similar styles of policing have traditionally regarded NIM with a mixture of contempt and frustration. They are missing an opportunity. NIM provides the cultural and organisational framework that values more forward-looking, evidence-based approaches to decision-making and problem-solving at every level. NIM gives us the best chance of aligning actual resources against real problems. How we do this will always be a matter of local style and context.

R. Mark Evans is the Director of Analytical Services for the Police Service of Northern Ireland. He is currently on secondment with the New Zealand Police as National Manager: Intelligence.

Conceptualising analysis

Numerous models have tried to conceptualise the analysis process and how analysis fits into the wider conceptual framework of policing. Particular models in this section are

● the intelligence cycle;
● Gill's cybernetic model;
● the SARA model;
● the NIM business model;
● the 3-i model.

One thing we can usually guarantee is that neophyte analysts can recite the core analytical process of the business by heart: the intelligence cycle.

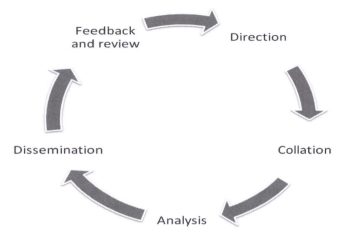

Figure 5.2 The intelligence cycle
Source: Ratcliffe 2004d: 6, reproduced with permission

The intelligence cycle has many minor variants but follows much the same format. The cycle starts with *direction* (some versions of the intelligence cycle have *planning* as a first stage). After identifying or receiving a task requiring analysis, analysts are required to *collate* all of the available information and data on the issue, conduct an *analysis* (referred to as interpretation by Cope 2003), and *disseminate* a product (a *knowledge product* if we are being current and trendy) to the client or customer who ordered the product. At some point in our intelligence utopia, analysts will receive *feedback* and a *review* of the value of their product, and possibly a new tasking, and the whole cycle starts again. Simple to understand, easy to convey, and summarised in Figure 5.2 (for a more expansive variation on the model shown here, see the Viewpoint by Lisa Palmieri in Chapter 7). This approach feels logical and nicely cyclical, and working within the cycle provides a structure and process that is ordered and repeatable. It also helps analysts work through the analytical process from start to finish.

The model emphasises the *intelligence* in intelligence-led policing, but not necessarily the *policing*. Therefore, from the broader perspective of a conceptual model of policing, there may be some limitations in thinking in this way. First, I have yet to meet experienced analysts who work within the strict regime of the cycle. In reality, analysts have to bounce from point to point in the intelligence cycle, simultaneously collating data, analysing information, speaking to clients, and revising taskings. Rarely, if ever, do they receive feedback and review. As Peter Gill points out, the intelligence cycle is an ideal of what is actually a 'highly complex and frequently messy process' (p. 23), a modus operandi that is always vulnerable to the time constraints of modern law enforcement (Gill 2000). In fact, after reading

Gill's comments, I was encouraged to recommend that analysts under a time constraint give consideration to reversing the intelligence cycle and think back from the type of product the client wanted, and from that the type of analysis that would produce the answer, and from that the type of data they would have to collate to complete the task. The value of thinking this way is that it limits the amount of data collation necessary (Ratcliffe 2004b). This approach might sound like intelligence heresy, but it is realistically what many analysts already do in our data-rich, knowledge-poor world.

A second problem I see is that the intelligence cycle, if viewed in isolation, divorces the analyst from the decision-making heart of the law enforcement process. The intelligence cycle might work as a way to visualise the job of an analyst if viewed from within a secluded, internal process of some abstract conceptualisation of *intelligence*, but it does not explain the role of an analyst in an *intelligence-led policing* environment, where equal emphasis rests with the word *policing*.

Gill's cybernetic model (2000), which, he argues, is still 'highly simplified', moves towards recognition of this wider environment by encompassing the intelligence cycle within a 'ring of secrecy' and placing constraints on the flow of information and knowledge along some of the 11 processes within his cycle (Figure 5.3). The filters (he uses the term 'power screens') represent interruptions to the flow of information around the model, sites where some information transfer is delayed, prevented or sometimes accelerated. Responsibility for these screens is laid at the doors of both 'agency' – the actions of people within the system, and 'structure' – institutional procedures and practices (p. 23). Given the exponential growth of digitalised data in policing, I would argue that we can add to this list 'technology', expressed here both as a manifestation of the capacity

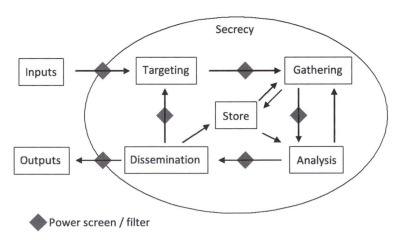

Figure 5.3 Gill's cybernetic model (*Source*: Gill 2000: 22, reproduced with permission)

of information technology to improve or degrade the ability of information to move in and around organisations, and as a measure of the common overenthusiasm to revert to technological solutions in an attempt to fix problems that are more often problems of agency and structure.

The addition of Gill's filters to the intelligence cycle is a welcome realisation of the systemic, internal issues that affect the intelligence function, and Gill's work is a solid addition to the literature on the role of analysis within policing (though the model at Figure 5.3 may not be a suitable one for an agency to try and emulate!).

The SARA model (see Chapter 4) takes a fundamentally different theoretical approach to the analytical process. Rather than being prescriptive regarding the analytical process and taking an isolationist view of the role of analysis within policing (as the intelligence cycle does), the SARA model has police and analysts scan for repeating crime problems and patterns, analyse the problems to identify the underlying causes, decide on a suitable response to alleviate the problems, and then assess the results of chosen response. Clarke and Eck (2005), in writing one of the most effective analysis guides specifically directed to problem-oriented policing, emphasise the place of analysis within the policing domain. In the first of 60 steps, analysts are exhorted to not only analyse data, but to also develop new sources, become more conversant with the effectiveness of police strategies, actively participate and make recommendations to the crime reduction team, learn about environmental criminology, communicate with practitioners and enhance the profession. This expansive approach to the role of the analyst steps far outside the comfort zone of many in the intelligence domain. As one New Jersey State Police analyst said to me, 'Nearly all the analysts want to do case support. ... Analysts are terrified of making recommendations. I can only think they are terrified of being slammed, or so insecure about their own abilities' (reported in part in Ratcliffe and Guidetti 2008).

NIM business model

In the UK, the NIM is entwined with intelligence-led policing: 'For the Police Service to become intelligence-led, the NIM business process must become embedded in local and national levels of policing' (NCPE 2005a: 13). John and Maguire (2003) posit that it is a misconception to conceptualise the NIM as only about intelligence-led policing. They argue that the developments in UK policing, developments that include greater interagency partnerships, increased use of non-police sources, and a wider interpretation of outputs and outcomes, mean that the NIM is conceptually broader than intelligence-led policing. They may be right, but recent versions of the NIM business model from the National Centre for Policing Excellence (NCPE) do not necessarily reflect this. Earlier graphic versions

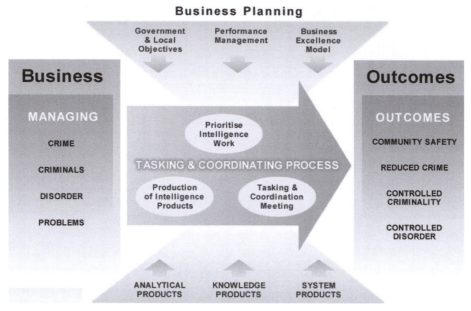

Figure 5.4 Original NIM CD homepage

of the NIM (Figure 5.4), while more complex diagrammatically, had clear equivalency with the SARA model.

Lancashire Constabulary (UK) saw the parallel and implemented the NIM alongside their existing commitment to problem-oriented policing: *Business* (NIM) was equivalent to *scanning* (SARA), the *tasking and coordinating process* (NIM) equivalent of *analysis* and *response* (SARA), and NIM *outcomes* equated to SARA *assessment* (John and Maguire 2003). More recently, the NCPE has refined the model to demonstrate better the process flows within the system (Figure 5.5), an 'ambitious' (Gill 2000: 252) attempt to create a model that can be applied to all law enforcement agencies in both the tactical and strategic spheres. In this refined model, the NIM is oriented around the Strategic and Tactical Tasking and Coordinating Groups (STCG and TTCG), from which flow a tactical resolution to a particular problem, followed by an operational review that influences subsequent tasking from the coordinating groups.

Parallels with SARA and the intelligence cycle still exist. There is a dedicated collation component (NIM's information/intelligence recording), SARA's *Analysis* stage can be found in the Research and Development component and response phase in the tactical resolution, and the operational review is reminiscent of both the SARA *Assess* component and the *feedback and review* part of the intelligence cycle. However, in the NIM, the assets used to drive the model are applied across the whole business structure.

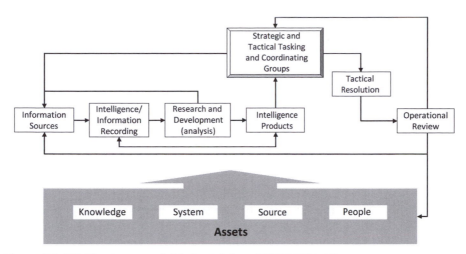

Figure 5.5 NIM business model (adapted from NCPE 2005: 14)

NIM System Assets address the need for security and correct management of classified information, while NIM Source Assets consider the benefits of information from forensics, CrimeStoppers, victims and the community, as well as from traditional covert information sources, such as *covert human intelligence sources* – to use the current UK term for confidential informants. NIM People Assets recognise the importance of people in the business process and clarify roles and standards within analysis, though saying little about the role of clients and users of intelligence.

Curiously, *knowledge* in the revised NIM mechanism does not relate to a deeper understanding of the criminal environment and the steps required to disrupt it. Here it has a more prosaic and bureaucratic meaning, relating to familiarity with current legislation and case law, codes of practice, manuals of standards and ACPO guidance, force policies, and briefing products (NCPE 2005a: 18). Within the NIM, knowledge assets therefore relate to processes rather than a product, a situation that analysts have found to be confusing and inaccurate (Gill 2000). These issues aside, at the broad level the considerable similarities between the SARA model and the NIM business process remain.

The 3-i model

All of the models to this point have been process models. For the remainder of the book, I will use a simpler, conceptual model. I have been using the 3-i (or 'three-i', or '3i') model for a number of years, to try to convey more explicitly to analysts and police executives the role that each plays within intelligence-led policing. It was adapted from a diagram used by the Australian Federal Police, and first published a few years ago (Ratcliffe

2003). Unlike the previous models in this chapter, it is a conceptual one rather than the more process-oriented models such as the intelligence cycle. The 3-i model is shown in Figure 5.6.

In the model, the crime intelligence analysis section actively *interprets* the criminal environment. The specific activities of the section depend on their tasking and operational environment. For example, a federal agency is likely to have a very different tasking than an analyst working in a small rural police department. In the model, the arrow runs from crime intelligence analysis to the criminal environment, an indication that the interpretation of the criminal environment must be an *active* activity. Readers with a systems approach to diagrams will find the direction of the arrow frustrating in this model, but the model is a better expression of the reality of the intelligence environment. While a *push model* works in a policing utopia where analysts send out information requests and patrol officers and fellow analysts rush to furnish a response,

> the push model does not work well in practice. The bureaucratic structure and culture of law enforcement agencies militates against the effective communication of intelligence requirements. The culture also thwarts the push model because large volumes of intelligence remain tacit, 'inside officers' heads', rather than recorded in intelligence records which can be shared at the push of a button. (Higgins 2004: 80)

Therefore, analysts have to succumb to a less-efficient *pull model* for information collection. As the direction of the arrow suggests, the analyst *actively* canvasses intelligence from contributors and *actively* hunts down the information required by interviewing investigating officers and debriefing handlers of confidential informants.

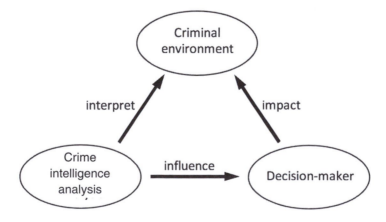

Figure 5.6 The 3-i model (interpret, influence, impact) (adapted from Ratcliffe 2003)

The second arrow runs from the analysis unit (however it is named) to the decision-maker. The 3-i model is not specific about the decision-maker, and this is often a real challenge for analysts to determine. Many decision-makers are not the people who initially commissioned the intelligence product, and many are also outside the immediate law enforcement environment. Furthermore, multiple clients for an intelligence product may exist, sometimes without the knowledge of the analyst when first tasked. The importance of clarity in the task definition stage of a project is therefore vital (Nicholl 2004).

The *influence* part of the 3-i model requires analysts to influence the thinking of decision-makers. In this, they have to be conscious of the need to identify the real decision-makers who can have an impact on the criminal environment while simultaneously being mindful that such decision-makers may not be their initial clients. Influencing decision-makers is a problem for many analysts, some of whom shy away from directly making recommendations to their clients.

When I was academic coordinator of Australia's National Strategic Intelligence Course, a residential course that brought strategic intelligence analysts together from leading law enforcement agencies in Australia and beyond, the appropriateness of analysts making recommendations was a hotly debated topic on every course. Analysts with an investigative intelligence background often felt that their role was simply one of investigative case support, providing output and descriptive analyses of wire-taps, suspect interviews, and information from confidential informants. Their job did not involve making recommendations. Likewise, analysts who had their formative training in the military came from an environment where military commanders receive extensive education in the interpretation of intelligence documents and where the military has a long tradition of using intelligence products to influence operational thinking. The military training generally instilled a purist approach to intelligence, with a doctrine that analysts do not make recommendations. This approach is based in the traditional view that it is important to maintain a distance between intelligence and decision-making, a belief that Marrin (2007) argues to be largely a myth. As Marrin points out, the gap does not protect the objectivity of intelligence analysis because, first, it is impossible to achieve truly unbiased analysis, and, secondly, faith in the existence of an idealised decision-making system is misplaced. The result is that a lack of proximity between analysts and decision-makers limits the ability of intelligence products to integrate into policy.

In the end, the managerial environment of law enforcement is significantly different from the military (Ratcliffe 2004c), and from the perspective of the 3-i model – where the analyst's role is significantly different from an investigative case support function – making recommendations is vital in an intelligence-led policing environment.

Traditional intelligence processes (such as the intelligence cycle) could be deemed successfully concluded when a product is disseminated to an intelligence client. This may be why there are a number of definitions of intelligence and criminal intelligence that have the creation and evaluation of a product as the end state (or place where the cycle restarts). Not so with intelligence-led policing. As I argue in this book, the end state of intelligence-led policing is an attempt to reduce the effects of criminality, either through prevention and disruption or by effectively deploying the criminal justice system. As such, intelligence-led policing does not occur if *interpret* and *influence* are the only components of the 3-i model that occur. For crime reduction to result, decision-makers must bring about an *impact* on the criminal environment.

Some might argue that this part of the conceptual model is beyond the remit of an analyst; the effectiveness of a crime reduction strategy is the domain of police leadership, which should carry the can for any failures. However, in an intelligence-led policing environment, strategies are chosen with an eye to the crime intelligence available about the target, and therefore there is a relationship between the intelligence product and crime reduction tactics. Many tactics that can reduce crime over the long term do not involve operational policing (Sherman *et al.* 1998; Scott 2000), and many traditional policing strategies are often expensive and futile. Even though there is a growing literature on police effectiveness in crime reduction, operational commanders too often rely on traditional enforcement tactics (such as investigations and saturation patrolling) as the sole response to crime problems, and there is a lack of accountability among police management to change this mindset.

All three *i* components of the 3-i model must exist if true intelligence-led policing is to take place. The crime intelligence analyst must *interpret* the criminal environment, the analyst must then use that intelligence to *influence* the thinking of decision-makers, and decision-makers must direct resources effectively in order to have a positive *impact* on the criminal environment.

When presenting the role of crime intelligence within policing, I prefer to use 3-i rather than other approaches, such as the intelligence cycle, because it deals with the big-picture environment of the law enforcement world. In the intelligence cycle and Gill's cybernetic model (2000), the decision-maker is largely absent, leaving analysts with the impression that their work is divorced from the action component of policing. It gives an impression that crime intelligence is independent of the consequences of that analysis, whereas the requirement in the 3-i model to influence the thinking of a decision-maker ties the intelligence process directly into the decision-making one, where it should be. It also gives both analysts and executives a clearer indication of their respective roles in intelligence-led policing.

Can models reflect reality?

A number of the models here attempt to provide a path to either the analytical process or the role of analysis within the larger domain of policing. Gill (2000) asserts that the reality of the intelligence cycle is that time and other constraints play a limiting role on the ability of this 'ideal-type' process to function as a cycle and that the process is in reality more messy and complex, and that each stage is autonomous. The problem with models such as those presented in this chapter is that they can lead to an assumption that the reality of analysis and crime reduction in the policing world actually follows these models.

For example, the process models generally include some form of feedback or evaluation; however, there is a widespread paucity of evaluation of police tactics and the intelligence process. The impact of policing is rarely examined because the police are constantly addressing new and emerging threats, or are limited in terms of time, resources and qualified staff (Cope 2003: 345). Without feedback, there is no evidence, and without evidence there is no learning and improvement for the future. Furthermore, evaluation can actually present an internal threat to an organisation. If a police operation is found to have been unsuccessful, this might reflect badly on officers, and senior officers in particular. It is often perceived to be better to label the operation in question a success (perhaps because many arrests were made) than to examine whether the operation actually had an impact on the criminal environment. Once labelled a success, the next course of action is usually to move swiftly on to the next operation without any potentially damaging assessment.

The NIM has come in for criticism from a number of authors, including Gill (2000), specifically for the use of terminology and the case study in the original version of the NIM (NCIS 2000). NIM terminology is a recurring theme, being described as unapproachable and overly technical (John and Maguire 2003; Sheptycki 2004b). One intelligence sergeant said,

> NIM is a simple concept made very difficult. It is academic. If you carve it up you can get the hang of it. ... But also police officers can be very basic in their approach. My own impression is that it was meant to be a management tool, that it was never meant for police officers. ... It contains a level of sophistication that turns people off. (quoted in John and Maguire 2003: 41)

In the end, few of the models presented in this chapter are capable of adequately describing the importance of key relationships between the analyst, the client and the business; however, useable models must address these key aspects of an intelligence-led environment. The intelligence cycle is a functional operational model for analysts but is inadequate at recognising the importance of analysis within the larger domain of policing, and is arguably a hold-over from a simpler time when intelligence was no more than an adjunct to investigations. More functional models that incorporate the policing role, such as SARA and the NIM, do address this bigger world and place the analysis role within a model that has an action component. The 3-i model places the emphasis on the relationships between the analyst and the client, and while being less prescriptive in terms of identifying products and processes, it identifies the key relationship in developing intelligence-led crime reduction.

Summary

The field of crime intelligence and the paradigm of intelligence-led policing are in a state of flux. Both are trying to integrate *new knowledge* from crime analysis with *old knowledge* from covert sources (Ratcliffe 2007; 2008), work with decision-makers who are from an occupational culture not versed in utilising crime intelligence (Christopher 2004), synchronise terminology, and convert a generation of police officers to the value of intelligence products that emanate from an office and are often created by civilian staff. It is not surprising that crime analysis has been described as 'the antithesis of action-oriented police work' (Cope 2003: 357).

Within this changing environment, models help the crime intelligence industry to articulate the processes and ideas that it wants to identify with, and the relationships that are essential to the delivery of crime reduction. The intelligence cycle, while a stalwart of criminal intelligence training and conceptualisation, is inadequate at representing the conceptualisation of analytical processes in a broader decision-making environment. What then is a suitable model for a replacement? Given the incredible variation in types of law enforcement agencies, that may be best left as a decision for the individual agency. Certainly, in the UK, the NIM business model is enshrined in legislation and will undoubtedly evolve. Importantly – and uniquely for the paradigm of intelligence-led policing – strategic intelligence is 'inextricably linked' to intelligence-led policing (Christopher 2004: 190) and has a place within the NIM, a situation that is both a challenge and an opportunity.

As the 3-i model addresses a simple but broad conceptual framework for intelligence-led policing that is likely to be applicable to most agencies, the next chapters of this book explore each *i* component of the model (*i*nterpret, *i*nfluence and *i*mpact).

6

Interpreting the criminal environment

A few years ago, Herman Goldstein (2003) identified a pressing need for better-trained crime analysts to implement problem-oriented policing and develop intelligence-led policing. The police analysis business is changing rapidly, and new analysts now often come into the crime intelligence field with backgrounds not in criminology but in other disciplines such as geography (Clarke 2004). This is partly an indictment of the quality of much criminological training – a problem based in the unwillingness of mainstream criminology to embrace a research agenda for both policy and practice that is evidence-based (Bradley *et al.* 2006: 173) – and is also reflective of the range of skills necessary to interpret the criminal environment of today. The 3-i model argues that this analytical stage is only one of three symbiotic conceptual parts of the business model of intelligence-led policing. However, the decisions made in the interpret phase dominate the rest of the model. Analysis and the accurate interpretation of the criminal environment are essential to intelligence-led policing and crime control.

The first part of this chapter addresses a key component of crime and intelligence analysis, that of initial target selection. With the growth of interest in offender profiling, the chapter examines in particular the potential for modus operandi details to influence targeting. The second part of the chapter examines the challenges facing analysts as the range of analytical techniques they are expected to master grows. Various government agencies and analyst associations have widened the scope of their training materials and courses to improve the range of skills education available to the analytical community. The purpose of this second part of the chapter is therefore not to provide a basic instruction guide in analytical techniques; there are numerous instructive manuals and undergraduate texts on the market that can fulfil this function. Instead, I aim to place these techniques within the broader conceptual framework of intelligence-led policing and explore the implications of widening the scope and influence of crime intelligence analysis. If analysts are to embrace their newfound status at the hub of intelligence-led policing, there are training, technical and cultural issues to be addressed before intelligence-led policing can become a routine business model.

Target selection

Prior to their move towards intelligence-led policing, I visited a number of divisions of the New Zealand Police and interviewed crime analysts and command officers. I found at the time that most analysts were self-directed and, even though a tasking (a formal request for intelligence on an issue) is often the first stage of the intelligence cycle (Andrews and Peterson 1990; SCOCCI 1997; McDowell 1998), few received any direction. As one analyst commented, 'I make my own decisions. I target the worst offenders.' Another intelligence manager said, 'I've been set a performance management plan. It is updated yearly.' Beyond that, she had not been given notice of any divisional objectives or specific crime targets (Ratcliffe 2005). At the time I thought this unusual, but Gundhus also noted that the organised crime unit at the Oslo police district tended not to discuss targeting priorities, as the unit was too concerned with rounding up drug traffickers (Gundhus 2005). There are of course many analysts who appreciate the chance to do their job without interference and would welcome the chance to be self-directed. However, while common, this arrangement runs contrary to the notion within intelligence-led policing that management sets a *control strategy* for local and regional crime priorities.

Irrespective of whether analysts are self-directed or receive a control strategy to work from, most targeting decisions are based on interpretation of the data and information available at the time.

Recording crime details

When analysts examine crime patterns and try to determine appropriate targets, they are generally not short of data. The digital explosion since the 1980s has resulted in a revolution in police data recording. Where data were originally just retained for statistical reporting purposes (Chainey and Ratcliffe 2005), there is now a tendency to record all sorts of information just for its own sake rather than with a specific aim in mind (Ericson and Haggerty 1997; Osborne 2006). Yet, as an analyst in New Zealand told me, while they recorded burglar modus operandi and details of property that had been stolen, 'nobody has time to analyse the stuff' (Ratcliffe 2005: 443). If crime analysis is dominated by a tendency simply to count the instances of crime (O'Shea and Nicholls 2002), what inputs might be required to achieve a more effective analytical foundation? Cope (2003: 343) identifies seven information requirements, key variables she feels are vital to the analytical process:

- nature of offence (the legal category of the crime);
- location (space and place of crime);
- time of offence;
- method of offence (modus operandi);
- target details;
- victim characteristics;
- physical and social circumstances of the offence.

Hidden within this seemingly straightforward list is a bewildering array of potential crime-recording and analytical challenges. For example, most crime recording systems are designed by IT professionals who rarely understand the subtleties of law enforcement and criminal behaviour. As such, there is a tendency to want a single value for each crime event. In many property crime cases, however, the time of offence is not known. While there are techniques that can derive meaningful analysis from high-volume crime where the exact offence time is not known (for example, aoristic analysis; Ratcliffe 2002a), this requires police officers to record start and end dates/ times that indicate when a crime victim last saw their stolen property and when they first discovered it missing. Many police departments do not record these vital details. Furthermore, information regarding the last of Cope's variables – the physical and social circumstances of crime offences – is rarely reported, and, beyond basic demographics such as age, gender and race, victim characteristics are usually sparse, if recorded at all.

Beyond Cope's list, other variables no doubt spring to mind, but even within just these seven variables there is considerable potential for variation in recording practices. Modus operandi is a particularly slippery notion, stretching across offender choice of target, method of entry (if to a premises), crime scene behaviour, property stolen or damaged, method of escape, and so on. Yokota and Watanabe (2002) found that increasing the number of modus operandi variables recorded by police increased the chance of matching a crime to an offender, as long as the offender was previously known. However, the same researchers noted that variation in the recording of crime event data, the choices available to offenders at the time of the crime, and inconsistency in offender behaviour all influenced the accuracy of the search algorithm. Bennell and Canter (2002) noted that even with a wide variety of modus operandi variables regarding crime scene behaviour to draw upon, the distance measured between burglaries was the most effective predictor that crimes were linked. They found that for every 1 km increase in the distance between burglaries, the chance that they were committed by the same offender reduced by 38 per cent (p. 159), and that this spatial similarity is a 'consistent and stable aspect' of burglary behaviour. Conversely, Ewart, Oatley and Burn, using 966 residential burglaries committed by 306 offenders in a large British city, found that geographic and temporal characteristics of offender behaviour were *least* useful for generating a suspect list compared with modus operandi variables (Ewart *et al.* 2005). Given the inconsistencies in the research findings, the value of modus operandi as a pattern recognition tool is still unclear.

One might think that if there was one situation where detectives reported modus operandi details accurately, it would be with homicide. It is on this concept that the Violent Criminal Apprehension Program (ViCAP) was founded. Accurate reporting of modus operandi characteristics, reported to the FBI, is supposed to allow violent crimes committed by the same offender to be linked anywhere in the US by similarity of crime scene characteristics. Unfortunately, after ten years, it was found that less than 10 per cent of homicides were reported to ViCAP; the information was perceived to enter a black hole and never emerge; and cities with the highest numbers of homicides were not reporting them to the ViCAP database (Witzig 2003). Given that the ViCAP form had 189 questions, the comparative value of the data that were reported from agency to agency – even from case to case – was questionable. While ViCAP has been redesigned (including squeezing the number of questions to just under 100!), the value of ViCAP is still in question.

The reality is that crime reporting is a highly subjective activity, and analysts hoping to use modus operandi as a method of crime linkage are relying on the optimistic notion that crime victims will recount details accurately and police officers will record the facts of a crime scene in a similar manner to other officers. Data entry and recording problems are common and well known (Ratcliffe 2005), and, unfortunately, detectives and police officers often ignore the modus operandi details of a file because they know that the data are unreliable. As a result, the modus operandi file is a 'grossly underused resource' (Forst and Planty 2000: 133). Even in the unlikely situation where modus operandi could become a standardised analytical variable, O'Shea and Nicholls (2002: 17, 41) found that less than half of US police departments record modus operandi details on a computerised system, and that hardly any possess either the statistical software or the advanced training necessary to even approximate the studies reported here. Police departments should start by ensuring they can get the basics right, and develop robust mechanisms to map the time and place of crime. These two parameters still provide the most reliable indicators of linked cases and problem areas.

Threat assessments

Target selection takes on greater significance when amplified in scope to the regional or even national level. National agencies such as SOCA, CISC and EUROPOL use unclassified annual threat assessments to raise public awareness and law-enforcement-sensitive versions to inform both 'law enforcement priorities for tackling serious organised crime and other relevant initiatives, such as changes in legislation, regulation or policy' (SOCA 2006: 5). This last distinction is illuminating in demonstrating the strategic aim of these assessments. They are the product of strategic intelligence work, and the target audience are policymakers, legislators and those with a macrolevel capacity to have an impact on crime. Many national, federal and state departments issue threat assessments at regular intervals. There is even an Association of Threat Assessment Professionals.

Anecdotally, discussions I have had with heads of agencies suggest that few organisations have the capacity to investigate more than about 5–10 per cent of the organised crime groups they are aware of, so prioritisation of the available resources is vital. Prioritisation of resource allocation should include not just a measure of threat but also a recognition of social harm, something that James Sheptycki and I called for a few years ago (Sheptycki and Ratcliffe 2004), and that now appears to be creeping into the products of agencies with strategic responsibilities.

Harm (to use the simple definition from CISC 2007, 'the adverse consequences of criminal activities') has become a central factor in further refining estimates of the impact of criminal groups for many agencies. For example, SOCA's responsibility is to reduce the harm caused by serious organised crime; however, they note that 'harm remains difficult to define clearly and to size accurately. … This takes various forms, from direct and indirect financial losses and costs, to damage to communities and individuals through, for example, drug addiction and increased fear of crime' (SOCA 2006: 6). CISC (2007: 10), building on the work of the Metropolitan Police in London, define four major types of harm:

- *social* – negative physical, psychological or emotional consequences that cannot readily be expressed in cash terms (as in homicide and assault);

- *economic* – with negative effects on an individual, community, business, institution, government or country (in as theft, counterfeiting and fraud);

- *political* – with negative effects on the political stability of a community or institution (such as in corruption, loss of confidence in government or law enforcement);

- *indirect* – secondary adverse consequences of criminal activities (such as environmental damage from clandestine drug labs).

As strategic assessments improve in methodology, the term *threat assessment* may need revision. Within the intelligence community, *threat* refers to the likelihood of an adverse outcome that can cause harm, and measuring the threat simply relates to the chance that an adverse criminal activity will take place. The harm that events cause may range from insignificant to catastrophic. *Risk* refers to the 'estimation of the likelihood of an adverse event balanced against the possible harm caused by the event' (Bond 2004: 120). CISC (2007) provide the example of crimes that can have a high volume but low harm factor, such as burglary, and crimes such as counterfeit pharmaceuticals that are low volume but have a high harm factor. The inclusion of a harm measure may be problematic for intelligence agencies in assessing the risk of various criminal enterprises, but it is essential if the public and other stakeholders are to appreciate law enforcement priorities and be engaged in the search for solutions to the crime problems we face today. Priority setting will gain greater public support if harm, specifically social harm, is used as a central criterion for police targeting decisions. With these definitions in place, we may in the future see the term *risk assessment* replace threat assessment.

Objective targeting and offender self-selection

For most police agencies, the chief concern is still the reactive management of recorded crime, that is, the crime events that the public report to them. Recorded crime is the benchmark against which success or failure in crime control is measured, and it relies on the public's willingness to approach police and tell them about criminality. For other agencies, such as state police investigation bureaux that have responsibilities for policing street gangs, narcotics, fraud, terrorism and organised crime, the volume of crime reporting from the public is minimal, and reported crime is an unrealistic benchmark or indication of workload (Ratcliffe and Guidetti 2008). These agencies are more likely to scan their operating environment and identify targets that fall within their purview. This is often the start of the criminal intelligence process, and the decisions made at this early stage will have a huge influence over the outcome of the operation (Gill 2000). For example, the initiation of an investigation by the New Jersey State Police into the Sex-Money-Murder gang was a snowballing target selection process resulting from knowledge and covert information gained during the investigation and arrest of many of the Nine Trey Gangsters in Operation Nine Connect (discussed in Chapter 1 and in Ratcliffe and Guidetti 2008). This approach to investigative targeting – based on intelligence priorities – is in line with the trend in the UK and other locations where police believe they can identify the main criminals (Gill 2000: 24). The challenge is to design a process that does not necessarily snowball from one organised crime group to another, but seeks a reappraisal of the criminal environment before every new significant targeting decision.

Of course, targeting known offenders, criminals who are leaders and innovators in the criminal world, is a cornerstone of proactive policing (Audit Commission 1993; Flood 2004), and for investigative agencies there is a comfort in targeting known offenders. The snowball approach to rolling investigations is often understandable given the need to establish a rationale on which to expend limited resources in an environment where the criminal fraternity outnumber the capacity of even the best resourced departments. That these decisions are not random is known, but the problem with basing targeting priorities on volume of information or the likelihood of getting a prosecution is the increasingly myopic nature of intelligence production, running the risk of continually rounding up Gill's 'usual suspects' (2000).

This positive feedback loop (Sheptycki and Ratcliffe 2004) is aptly demonstrated by Sheptycki, who describes the initial attempts by the Royal Canadian Mounted Police (RCMP) to produce a reliable consensus among intelligence analysts as to the relative hazard posed by different organised crime groups. When first introduced, the Sleipnir process (see the Viewpoint from Chapter 3) used a Delphi technique to survey experts in the area of organised crime; however, those experts were predominantly drawn from the criminal intelligence community. Sheptycki argues that the RCMP assessment that outlaw motorcycle gangs were a significant threat was 'more reflective of the amount of police resources dedicated to monitoring "outlaw" motorcyclists and less the result of an accurate measure of their objective threat to Canadian society' (Sheptycki 2003: 500). This self-fulfilling prophecy consistently drew attention to motorcycle gangs over a number of years. Recently, the Sleipnir methodology has been significantly refined by CISC (CISC 2007). They have enhanced Sleipnir by improving the matrices that constitute the central organising mechanism. These matrices rank and score organised crime groups by a variety of criteria, such as their degree of criminal experience, mobility, group cohesiveness and links to extremism. They are also in the process of incorporating a measure of harm.

It may be a challenge to move away from targeting particular criminals simply because the offenders draw attention to themselves at a time when police are looking for targets. The whack-a-mole policing strategy is hardly objective but surprisingly common (see, for example, Maple and Mitchell 1999). Opportunist target selection, if taken to an extreme, can result in a sting operation, where police create an opportunity for offenders to indulge in criminal activity and thus invite offenders to provide an opportunity for enforcement action. While there are often ethical questions raised regarding sting operations, police have used entrapment techniques for many years (Langworthy 1989).

A less extreme approach, and one that is probably seen as more ethical by the public, is to identify certain minor criminal acts that can be used to identify prolific offenders. Some of the best examples of this process of *offender self-selection* include (from the UK and US, respectively) the Yorkshire Ripper (caught with false licence plates on his car) and the Son of Sam killer, who was captured after parking by a fire hydrant (Roach 2007).

There are numerous advantages to identifying existing criminal 'triggers' that can spotlight offenders of more serious crime: there is less suggestion of harassment or entrapment if police are seen to be responding to existing crime events; the triggers are likely to be continually present; and, irrespective of whether the individual targeted is involved in more serious crime, the perception of police action is likely to be perceived as justifiable if offenders have already committed the trigger offence (Wellsmith and Guille 2005). Researchers working with traffic wardens in the Yorkshire town of Huddersfield discovered that, compared with cars parked legally nearby, vehicles that were illegally parked in disabled parking bays were nearly 10 times more likely to be of immediate police interest, at least 10 times more likely to be owned by someone with a criminal record, and more likely to be driven by someone with a history of traffic violations (Chenery *et al*. 1999). The difficulty with this approach is the probability of significant numbers of false-positive cases. In other words, while a greater percentage of cars illegally parked in disabled bays were of interest to police, a significant number of these cars were not of interest, raising the potential spectre of overenthusiastic police action. Offender self-selection has to be employed judiciously.

Offender selection for targeting is limited by the pool of candidates available. One of the rationales for a middle tier of the National Intelligence Model (NIM) is an acknowledgement of the significant gap that exists between the local level and the national arena (Flood 2004). Level 2 of the NIM is designed to address the increasing 'void' (Gill 2000: 56) that exists between local areas and larger structures of the policing environment, and increase the pool of cross-jurisdictional offender candidates. Good target selection at this level is challenging, given that this is a region where there is less incentive for police officers to share resources and information. There are many reasons for this reticence, as the next section discusses.

Playing well with others

One way for agencies to select appropriate targets for enforcement action is to get a better perspective on the relationship between their local crime problems and trends at the regional and national level. Information sharing became the buzzword of American law enforcement in the immediate aftermath of the terrorist attacks of 9/11. A direct result of those attacks was the creation of a National Criminal Intelligence Sharing Plan (IACP 2002), a plan that identified some key problems with information and intelligence sharing across the US. Specific problems included 'the absence of a nationally coordinated process for intelligence generation and sharing; the "hierarchy" within the law enforcement and intelligence communities; local, state, tribal, and federal laws and policies that unduly restrict law enforcement access to information; the inaccessibility and/or disaggregation of technologies to support intelligence sharing; and deficits in analysis' (GIWG 2005: 1). Quite a list. The unspoken assumption behind the plan was that addressing these deficiencies would help prevent future attacks. It is unclear whether improved information sharing would have prevented the 9/11 attacks; however, the attacks have provided an opportunity to address a long-standing problem within American policing.

In the US, the structure of the law enforcement world directly militates against information sharing. The vast number of small agencies that are fixated with their own jurisdiction excludes the possibility that collaboration or information sharing with outside agencies will ever be a priority unless a problem directly and explicitly affects an agency's taxpayers. Furthermore, many local law enforcement agencies are so small that they have neither the resources nor crime volume to warrant their own analytical capabilities (Osborne 2006).

Memorandums of understanding between law enforcement and national security agencies are often cumbersome and convoluted, placing layers of bureaucracy in the path of timely information sharing. Generally, no standard procedures exist to share information outside agencies (see, for example, Gundhus 2005). Even if the bureaucratic hurdles could be overcome, there are other, more intangible problems. While there would seem to be no significant reason that criminal intelligence is not shared, the underlying reality is one of a web of interagency competition, local and national laws, security clearance issues, turf protection and rivalry, all of which inhibit actual cooperation (White 2004). American police executives in particular strive hard to protect their independence such that cooperation between the different tiers of US law enforcement (federal, state, local) is often strained at best.

Many analysts prefer to use informal networks through contacts built up over time as a way to circumvent the 'formality and systematic nature' of strict agreements, contacts established through professional contacts, joint operations, and secondments, or by contacting former colleagues who now occupy positions at other agencies (Bigo 2000; Gill 2000). Little is known about informal networks because the majority of research has been on formal models of intelligence systems, models that have explored the hierarchical information flows and rules (Sheptycki 2004a). The problem with informal intelligence networks is the amount of time that an analyst must be in the business to establish the necessary connections and trust, and it relies on each analyst possessing certain tacit interpersonal skills as a basic requirement to circumvent a formal regulatory system. These informal information-sharing networks are used by analysts to gain information when formal systems prove too cumbersome, or where local agency rivalries preclude 'fraternising with the enemy'.

Law enforcement agencies have tried a variety of ways to address information-sharing problems. The lack of collaborative arrangements among federal agencies and state and local police organisations is a particular problem. The post-9/11 approach to tackling terrorism in the US was to expand the number of joint terrorism task forces (JTTFs) from 35 to 66 (Casey 2004), and in September 2003 the FBI created field intelligence groups in all 56 field offices to better work with state and local agencies (Spiller 2006). To aid the process of integration, the FBI set up written memorandums of understanding with local agencies as well as paying for all expenses incurred by local and state officers assigned to the JTTF (Casey 2004). However, in terms of broader counter-terrorism information-sharing partnerships, the quality of relationships is often determined by geography, culture and the history of previous collaborations between agencies. New information-sharing arrangements are never written on a blank sheet; there is always a watermark residue of prior successes or failures, a watermark that can shape future relationships. This may explain why the relationship between the FBI and the largest US police department, the NYPD, was, for a number of years after 9/11, a rancorous one (Miller 2007).

A one-directional way that large agencies communicate with smaller police departments is through the free distribution of intelligence products. When the Serious Organised Crime Agency (SOCA) absorbed the National Criminal Intelligence Service they took on responsibility for production of the annual *United Kingdom Threat Assessment of Serious Organised Crime*, producing both law-enforcement and public versions (SOCA 2006). The Australian Crime Commission continue the tradition of the (now defunct) Australian Bureau of Criminal Intelligence in producing an annual illicit drug report (ACC 2006), and the *Annual Report on Organized Crime in Canada* is one approach to fulfilling the mandate of Criminal Intelligence Service Canada to 'facilitate the timely and effective production and exchange of criminal intelligence' (CISC 2006a: 3). In the US, the federal government distributes a plethora of reports, summaries and raw data sets, so much so that it would be a full-time job just keeping up to date with the mass of information pushed out by the myriad agencies. In many cases, one is inclined to suspect that these documents are less intended to inform local police than to establish a presence for the particular agency and to show, in a public fashion, that they are 'doing something'. It remains unclear how much these national reports influence targeting decisions at the local police level.

At the regional level, in cities such as Los Angeles and New York, the city police departments have taken the lead in developing relationships, building links with colleagues within their regional geography. For example, Operation Sentry is the NYPD programme to forge collaborations with agencies within 200 miles of New York City (Miller 2007). But accessing information is not just an interagency problem; in some cases it is an intra-agency problem. The 9/11 Commission lamented that, prior to 9/11, FBI analysts had problems getting access to information that existed within their own organisation, such that 'the poor state of the FBI's information systems meant that such access depended in large part on an analyst's personal relationship with individuals in the operational units or squads where the information resided' (9/11 Commission 2004: 77).

A different approach is to embrace the informal nature of information sharing. I was always partial to the 'liaison event' run once a month on a Friday afternoon by the Australian Bureau of Criminal Intelligence (ABCI) as a great way to encourage informal contact between agents and analysts from a variety of public and private agencies that had an intelligence support function. The Australian National Strategic Intelligence Course is also specifically designed to bring analysts together and have them work on group projects for two weeks, with the aim of fostering better interagency contact and collaboration. To encourage informal networking, places on each course are offered to analysts from each state agency as well as to analysts from overseas through the Australian Federal Police (AFP) Law Enforcement Assistance Program (LEAP) (Walsh and Ratcliffe 2005). The New Jersey Regional Operations Intelligence Center (ROIC) (known as the 'Rock') – the state's fusion centre – has an analytical workplace specifically designed so that analysts from different federal, state and local agencies share communal eating and refreshment areas (Guidetti 2006). This area is also used for a morning 'huddle' that brings all of the analysts together for a few minutes at the beginning of the day to discuss briefly their individual projects.

Yet, however good the liaison with other agencies and the careful selection of targets for further information gathering or enforcement action, the reality is that decisions will always be made on the basis of incomplete evidence. Some offenders help by self-selecting themselves and bringing attention to their door; however, many choices are made on incomplete crime recording and a lack of information from outside the individual police department. Bureaucratic hurdles and mistrust between agencies (institutional friction) are among many unfortunate organisational pathologies afflicting analytical units (Sheptycki 2004a). Ways to improve information sharing, given that information sharing is a benefit not only to target selection but also to analysis, are considered later in this chapter.

Viewpoint

Information sharing at the national level

Peter Stelfox

The failure of police agencies to share information has been a recurring observation of researchers and a constant complaint of police managers and policymakers. In his 1796 *Treatise on the Police of the Metropolis*, Colquhoun identified the gathering and sharing of intelligence as an essential prerequisite of an efficient policing system. By 1839 the first Parliamentary Commissioners to enquire into the state of policing in England and Wales reported numerous examples of what we would now call intelligence-sharing failures, remonstrations that continue today (for example around the destruction of the World Trade Center). On this evidence, generations of police officers have failed to be persuaded of the benefits of sharing information, or, if they have been persuaded, have failed to respond. How accurate is this picture?

My time as head of Crime Operations in the Greater Manchester Police – with responsibility for investigating organised crime and homicide in Britain's second largest force – naturally involved working closely with many other forces and national agencies. Looking back, the sharing of information was extensive and certainly did not fit the picture often painted. At a routine level, a huge amount of information sharing takes place through systems such as the Police National Computer, the National DNA Database, and the Serious Crime Analysis System. It is difficult to measure the quantity of information that is shared in this way at a national level, but it is clearly extensive. At the operations level, there are large numbers of investigations and other operations where forces and national policing agencies work together and freely share information.

Whilst policing may not be the most exclusive club in the world, it is one of the biggest and its members can usually be relied on when help is needed. This includes sharing information, which happens day-in, day-out, in many hundreds of operations ranging from the unusual to the routine. If there are failures by policing agencies to either join such operations or to share information once they have joined, then this is more likely to be a symptom of a failure to agree common objectives and manage their achievement properly.

It could be argued that the routine harvesting of intelligence or sharing it in joint operations is not the issue; rather, it is the unwillingness of investigators to share information on those occasions when they are not forced to do so systematically or through self interest. This could be expressed in terms of 'if everyone pooled their information about x a better outcome could be achieved'. The problem with this approach is that it is particularly easy to ask for information about x, once you know it to be a problem. It is significantly harder to do so beforehand.

A second line of reasoning argues that it is precisely because the world is full of potential problems that we should pool information to better identify them and hopefully avoid their consequences. But it seems to me that based on that conclusion, the only rational response is to put effort into designing intelligence systems that routinely harvest information of interest and motivate investigators to share it by setting objectives into which they can buy. Criticising detectives for failing to make up for shortfalls in poorly designed systems, processes or procedures, or for not spotting a problem that no one else spotted, is hardly a sophisticated approach.

I hope that Patrick Colquhoun would be impressed by the level of information sharing that has been achieved since his time. It would be naïve to suppose that investigators and agencies share information well on every occasion; but it is equally naïve to assume that a lack of information sharing is the root cause of all intelligence failures. In my experience, problems are as likely to result from failure to design and implement good intelligence systems or to develop common goals amongst investigators as they are to result from choices made by individuals not to share information.

Dr Peter Stelfox is Head of Investigative Practice for the UK's National Policing Improvement Agency

Information collation

Once a targeting decision has been made and an analyst has been directed to undertake a particular project (or, as is often the case, the analyst is self-directed), then, according to the rubric of the intelligence cycle, a collation phase is undertaken. In reality, information collation is often conducted as part of the process of deciding what targets law enforcement has the capacity to tackle. Effective information collection and collation requires communication with the client that originated the tasking and interpretation of their intelligence requirements (Higgins 2004). Therefore, some understanding of the client's requirements and the look and feel of the likely final product is required before information collation can take place. Understanding the aims of the client's intelligence requirement is an aspect of crime intelligence analysis that is often overlooked. There is a tendency for many analysts to divorce themselves from the business reality of the environment occupied by the managers they support. If the experiences of police commissioners in Australia is anything to go by, police executives have 'no chance of being effective without a healthy dose of "political acumen and awareness"' (Dupont 2003: 3). The analyst should be prepared to invest time in understanding the client's business better, manage client expectations, and, if necessary, in refining the tasking to better suit the client's needs (Nicholl 2004).

There are particular areas of information collation that are a challenge for modern policing. These include (as are discussed below) improving information sharing, the question of whether liaison officers can resolve information-sharing problems, and the role of information from confidential informants in strategic decision-making.

An *intelligence requirement* can be used to address issues of what data and information are currently available, and what the analyst will need to collect before proceeding further. Intelligence requirements are structured approaches to gathering and collating information about a particular issue or person. They are often differentiated into Strategic Intelligence Requirements (SIRs) and Tactical Intelligence Requirements (TIRs) (Sheptycki 2004b). Documentation of the intelligence requirement is often helpful in projects involving multiple analysts. Operational or strategic projects will probably include a range of data and information requirements. Analysts with a technical or quantitative leaning often address data issues, while analysts trained as intelligence analysts favour information sources. The problem at this early stage in the intelligence process is that analysts have a tendency to rely on sources that they are better at accessing, be they electronic data warehouses or qualitative information gleaned from interviews with detectives. As explained in the previous chapter, a pull model of information collection requires the analyst to actively draw information from colleagues and outside agencies and hunt down the information required by interviewing investigating officers and debriefing handlers of confidential informants. As one analyst from the New Jersey State Police said about this more proactive model of information collation, 'We go to central bureaux and [a covert location] where the detectives are actively working on the wires and we sit down with them and talk with them there, and that is very helpful' (quoted in Ratcliffe and Guidetti 2008).

A limitation of many existing police collation strategies is the dominance of law enforcement as the only source of data and information. As James Sheptycki and I have argued, 'over-reliance on law enforcement data places considerable limitations on strategic intelligence analysis. It follows that liaison and information exchange with other agencies holds the promise of improving the quality of strategic assessments by incorporating complementary (or alternative) views and data' (Sheptycki and Ratcliffe 2004: 193). For this to take place, crime intelligence analysts have to enhance their collation mechanisms with information from outside, and this brings us back to the same information-sharing problems that affect the choice of appropriate targets.

In interviews and focus groups across numerous British agencies, as well as with research conducted with Dutch, Swedish and Canadian officials, Sheptycki identified a number of 'organisational pathologies' that were problematic to the flow of information and intelligence around organisations, both internally and externally. In particular, he found the following:

- *digital divide* (caused by incompatible information systems between agencies);
- *linkage blindness* (where crime series cross agency boundaries);
- *noise* (a problem of low-quality information volume exacerbated by increased sharing);
- *intelligence overload* (caused by a lack of analytical capacity in the crime intelligence system);
- *intelligence gaps* (caused by criminals operating in the spaces between police agencies either hierarchically or geographically);
- *duplication* (caused by separate agencies keeping the same information on isolated systems);
- *institutional friction* (between agencies with different missions, structures and methodologies);
- *intelligence hoarding and information silos* (caused by retention of information until it is most beneficial to the information-holder);
- *defensive data concentration* (whereby a concentration of resources in one area to address a short-term problem creates other organisational pathologies, i.e. duplication);
- *occupational subcultures* (both intra-agency as well as interagency)

(Sheptycki 2004a, 2004b).

These are all problems for analysts, but they are problems that require managerial intervention to fix. As such, these issues have to be addressed at the interface between the crime intelligence practitioners and the executive level clients they serve, an area commonly fraught with misunderstanding

(Nicholl 2004). In the end, sharing information and information management is time-consuming, incessant and an additional strain on the working lives of analysts already hard-pressed to meet current expectations.

Improving information sharing

Information sharing is not intelligence-led policing, and police departments that do share information are not necessarily practising intelligence-led policing; there is much more to intelligence-led policing, as this book aims to demonstrate. It can, however, enhance interpretation of the criminal environment even with the limitation of a fundamental contradiction in the police information setting: Better communication and information sharing would improve targeting and result in more objective resource allocation decisions, but the existing culture is one where information is power. And in policing, power is to be retained and used by individuals to demonstrate their worth in the workplace and for personal advancement through promotion, merit and prestige. Thus, the move to greater collective application of individual knowledge can run into 'firewalls of resistance' (Gundhus 2005: 141) where personal ambitions can trump organisational needs (Ratcliffe and Guidetti 2008). As Kelling and Bratton note, 'The problem for American policing is not so much getting the intelligence but making sense of it and sharing it with those who can use it' (2006: 5).

A 2005 gathering of intelligence analysts, crime analysts, practitioners and policymakers identified that even intelligence officers and crime analysts in the same agency may not communicate with each other (Ratcliffe 2007).[1] Organisational changes were identified as one solution, given that, as Mary Garrand (a crime analyst from Alexandria, Virginia) said at the forum,

> Intelligence and crime analysts are not in the same arena as far as chain of command. … By linking these two equally important analytical functions, serial crimes and organized crime groups can be detected more quickly and more cases can be solved. The days of 'this is my information and you can't see it' have to end. Separating crime and intelligence analysts within law enforcement agencies is a no-win situation.

Forum participants promoted numerous solutions, ideas that are designed to remove excuses, encourage compliance, explain the need, and decrease the effort required to share information:

- *Become intelligence-led.* Instil attitudes within the organisation that value objective intelligence and analysis.

- *Police chiefs should work closely with analysts.* Police chiefs have to spend time with analysts. This will engender a culture within the department that recognises the work of analysts because where the chief spends time sends a signal to the department.

- *Co-locate analysis and intelligence functions close to decision-makers.* The physical location is as important as the organisational location – analysts must have regular access to each other and to decision-makers or the aim of a more intelligence-led organisation cannot be met.

- *Articulate the analytical vision within the police department.* By describing an aim to combine crime analysis and criminal intelligence, the department makes a formal statement of its analytical aim.

- *Make the case for integrated analysis.* Many police executives may not have been trained to appreciate the bigger decision-making options that become available with a more complete picture of crime and criminality.

- *Create integrated reporting mechanisms.* Formalise the connection between all analysis that takes place and the decision-makers in the police department, so that contextual information from both sides is always available.

- *Develop informal information exchange mechanisms.* Although it is nice to think that formal organisational structures can create effective crime intelligence analysis, decision-makers should recognise that informal information exchanges still dominate both the crime analysis and criminal intelligence worlds.

- *Consciously collect feedback and respond to criticisms.* Analysts should document what they give to their commanders in terms of products and analysis and explore the outcomes from their work.

- *Create an analysis users group.* Bridging the gap between crime analysis and intelligence is likely to create some initial teething problems in terms of analysis products, and these can be resolved by focusing on the primary activity.

- *Get over the whole security issue.* The vast majority of information that is gathered by police departments is not so secret that it cannot be revealed to other analysts and people responsible for deciding crime reduction strategy.

- *Develop technology solutions but do not fixate on them.* There is a tendency in policing to believe that technology will overcome organisational and cultural barriers. Technological solutions to data management will certainly help but will not be able to address all of the concerns.

● *Be realistic about what can be achieved in your department.* In small police departments, it is realistic to expect that both the intelligence and crime analysis functions will often be combined in the job description of one or two individuals; however, midsize and large departments should strive for greater incorporation of crime analysis and criminal intelligence.

The forum participants noted that integration of intelligence and crime analysis units would have a number of benefits, including; allowing decision-makers to see a bigger picture of criminal behaviour, providing a greater range of enforcement options, creating an analysis model that better reflects the criminal environment, and creating a single point of contact for interagency communication. For more details, see Ratcliffe (2007). Yet the challenges are significant. Analysts and police leaders reading this should be cognisant of the sustained power of information in a policing environment. Overcoming traditional barriers to sharing, barriers that are reflected in reward structures and 'pay-to-play' systems of information trading, will be a long-term project.

A role for liaison officers?

Beyond the boundaries of individual police departments, the increasing globalisation of policing has resulted in new approaches to overcoming hurdles in interagency communication. It has long been recognised that international systems for sharing and cooperating on intelligence are hampered by different laws and local regulations, blockages that slow and prevent opportunities for collaboration (Johnstone 2004). Bigo (2000: 67) argues that the liaison officer is a 'new specialist' within the policing field, a role that has become crucial to the flow of information between agencies in the new porous Europe (and beyond). As Bigo argues, their numbers may not be huge, but liaison officers occupy a strategic position in a network of information sharing.

Liaison officers can be used as a general conduit between disparate agencies, or can be used to address specific needs. For example; the organised crime unit of the Oslo police district studied by Gundhus (2005) gave office space to a customs officer specifically to aid drug investigations; the Strategic Intelligence Directorate of NCIS and the ABCI both started a process of sending analysts out to other agencies as well as receiving analysts on secondment (Sheptycki and Ratcliffe 2004); and to improve liaison with other countries, the FBI maintains officers in over 40 Legal Attaché offices (or Legats) around the world to support operational activities (FBI 2004).

The growth of the liaison officer specialisation has become a necessity in the face of significant changes in the geography of policing. While traditional descriptions of policing suggested an organisation with hegemonic control over a specific, bounded territory, national and transnational mandates exist for police agencies with overlapping and shifting territorial boundaries (Manning 2000). The traditional autonomy of the local police chief is being eroded by the growth of competing pressures and demands that emanate from regional and national arenas. The growth of JTTFs is an example of a response to a problem that spans multiple agencies and simultaneously has policing implications from the transnational to the local level.

Liaison officers perform important information functions that are both technical and cultural. They stand at the interface of distinct organisations and provide the host agency with access to technical databases that are normally unavailable. Of possibly greater importance, liaison officers bring understanding of the knowledge processes, doctrine and organisational culture of the remote agency they represent. There is, however, a sense of failure associated with the need for liaison officers, as if agencies are resigned to the notion that their systems and structures are so Byzantine that a liaison officer is necessary to act as the bridge between disparate organisations. It is possible that, more than integrated databases and data-mining techniques, liaison officers with their understanding of the information culture of their respective organisations represent the future of collaborative and cooperative policing.

Confidential informants

Intelligence-led policing is not synonymous with covert policing – it is a business model for resource allocation; however, if there is one street-level tactic that is often used to epitomise an intelligence-led focus, it is the use of informants to aid interpretation of the criminal environment. Informant handling is on the rise, though informant use remains a sensitive and largely tactical activity.

As explained in Chapter 2, although the mistakes by some American police intelligence units in the 1970s hampered the development of criminal intelligence systems, US officers and detectives have always maintained formal and informal networks of informants, and a gradual shift in emphasis back to use of this covert information source is under way. This process has been accelerated by a greater enthusiasm for clandestine sources since the terrorist attacks of 9/11. The 9/11 Commission recommended that FBI agents and analysts receive sustained support and improved resources to become more effective intelligence handlers, and in particular they recommended rewarding FBI agents for recruiting informants (9/11 Commission 2004: 424–425). Outside the US, one of the more expansive law enforcement programmes has been Program Axiom, a $21.4 million, multiyear undercover policing programme conducted by the Australian Federal Police. Axiom has employed teams of covert personnel to collect evidence and covert information in the areas of high-tech crime, economic crime, money laundering, illicit drugs, counter-terrorism, people smuggling and corruption (Keelty 2004: 8).

When pushing for a proactive, intelligence-driven model of policing, the influential UK Audit Commission report described informants as the 'lifeblood' of the criminal investigation department, and that 'there is no doubt that they offer a very cost-effective source of detections' (1993: 39). The report claimed a phenomenal return rate for investing in informants; for every (British) pound spent on informants 12 times that amount in stolen property was recovered.

Confidential police informants are primarily used to identify offenders or suspects, collect background information on offenders and criminal organisations, provide information used to determine the target of future surveillance operations, trace stolen property, and locate evidence (Innes 2000). Informants have a range of motivations to provide information to the police, and not all of those motivations are benign. While crime victims generally want to have their crime solved and many witnesses are motivated by civic responsibility, insiders involved in the criminal world are less inclined to provide information to the police. As a result, police often need to gain leverage to elicit what they need. The reality is that few law-abiding citizens have detailed knowledge of criminal activity, and 'those individuals who do possess such information are the same individuals who often have the least incentive to provide it to the police' (Innes 2000: 363). For covert information, police often have to generate informants from within the very criminal environment they seek to disrupt.

Chapter 10 examines the ethical considerations of informant handling in greater detail, but for now it should be noted that the use of confidential human sources can often bring police officers close to ethical and legal boundaries, and raise questions of police legitimacy in the minds of some of the public. This might be a price worth paying if informants provided information that was of significant or strategic value to a police department; however, the evidence often suggests otherwise. Until recently, confidential criminal informants were used in a decidedly tactical manner, mainly to assist an investigation and affect an arrest for a single case investigation. This case-specific use of informants was, and largely still is, driven by a policing organisation and culture that rewards officers for good investigative work with a structure better suited to a close relationship between the informant and the police officer. As Flood notes, this results in a decidedly non-strategic application of informant power: 'By and large, most collection capability consisted of the use of informants whose exploitation was usually immediate and sometimes dependent upon the personal insights, priorities and determination of the informant handlers' (Flood 2004: 40). Thus, the informant role is predominantly a case-specific one.

One defining characteristic of intelligence-led policing is that informants should be used in a more strategic manner, and if confidential sources are employed in a more proactive, strategic and targeted way, the benefits may outweigh the risks.

Analytical techniques

Analysis is central to the work, status and role of crime intelligence analysts. The National Intelligence Model promotes nine analytical techniques (NCIS 2000) as a prelude to informed decision-making:

- *crime pattern analysis* – a rather broad term to indicate a range of skills, including trend identification and hot spot analysis;
- *network analysis* – used to understand the direction, frequency and strength of links between collaborators in a criminal network;
- *market profiles* – an assessment of the criminal market for a particular commodity, such as drugs or prostitution;
- *demographic/social trend analysis* – an assessment of the impact of socio-economic and demographic changes on criminality;
- *criminal business profiles* – used to determine and understand the business model and techniques employed by offenders or organised crime groups;
- *target profile analysis* – another broad term used to indicate a range of skills used to understand the lifestyle, networks, criminal activities, and potential interdiction points in the life of a targeted offender;
- *operational intelligence assessment* – evaluation of information collection to inform decision-making about an existing operation;
- *risk analysis* – assesses the scale of risks or threat posed by offenders or organisations to individual potential victims, police, and the public;
- *results analysis* – a process used to evaluate the effectiveness of law enforcement activities.

NCIS described results analysis as 'a *new discipline* which evaluates the effectiveness of law enforcement activities, for example the effectiveness of patrol strategies, crime reduction initiatives or a particular method of investigation' (NCIS 2000: 29; emphasis added). Many social scientists would be somewhat surprised to find what is essentially evaluation research described as a new discipline, given that evaluation research has a long history within the social sciences. In fact, it has been argued that intelligence work is simply applied social science research (Prunckun 1996). However, this minor criticism aside, to articulate the techniques that are deemed fundamental to effective analysis is a valiant enterprise, one subsequently continued by NCPE (2005a).

What skills and data resources are required to complete these analyses? As Boba (2005) points out, analysts should be able to draw on the police department's computer-aided dispatch system, records management system, vehicle database, known offender database, registered sex offender database, field information database, and geographic data system; the last of which should include such features as police stations, schools, hospitals, businesses, retail stores and restaurants, offices, places of worship, government buildings, transport stops and stations, streets, highways, rivers, rail systems, mass transit routes, buildings, census areas and data, car parks, airports, administrative boundaries, police beats, drug markets, and gang territories. Beyond what could be loosely termed a standard skill set of crime-analysis activities, more complex intelligence-gathering investigations require specialised skills, skills increasingly found only in the private sector. For example, the 'emergent anti-money laundering industry' (Schneider 2006: 285), one that incorporates aspects of forensic accounting and corporate investigation (Williams 2005), requires an ability to track financial transactions across multiple accounts in different jurisdictions and cope with money-laundering devices such as 'walking trust accounts' that automatically move funds to other locations when law enforcement enquiries are made (Levi 2002: 184).

To address even a proportion of this toolbox of analytical techniques and data needs places a huge demand on information resources; has training, support and time management implications; and draws on a far wider array of information requirements than the seven Cope identified for basic crime analysis (at the beginning of the chapter). There is a tendency for less experienced analysts to respond to the wealth of data and analytical options available by fixating on the intricacies of analysis to the point where analytical techniques – rather than the wider crime control issues – come to dominate their thinking. This can sometimes be seen in the plethora of technical questions on list servers dedicated to crime and intelligence analysis (for example, the LEANALYST list server administered by the IALEIA). Higgins is right to point out that 'intelligence professionals need to balance the requirement to understand the basic elements of what is happening now with the need to anticipate and the requirement (but more frequently the temptation) to understand a problem in all its possible permutations. "Paralysis through analysis" is as much a concern for the intelligence professional as the business person' (2004: 75).

A common response to paralysis through analysis is to invest in digital solutions that are perceived to reduce the burden on analysts. While there has been considerable investment in information-processing technology for police work, this does not necessarily mean that the standard of data analysis has improved (O'Shea and Nicholls 2003). Police departments have long suffered from a lack of internal analytical capability, and attracting the best candidates to do this work has often been difficult given that the role has, in the past, been low status yet challenging enough to pose considerable difficulties (Weatheritt 1986). As yet, it seems that pay grades and training opportunities are failing to keep pace with the increasing demands on analysts. The end result? Departments that should be developing skilled individuals are suffering from rapid turnover of staff disgruntled by low salaries and lack of career progression (O'Shea and Nicholls 2003).

Increasing the number of entrants into policing that are comfortable with computers along with improvements in information-communication technology will undoubtedly reduce the necessity for basic training, in the same way that greater intuitiveness in document-handling software reduced the demand for word-processing training. This does not, however, necessarily translate to better analysis; it may simply mean that training curricula will adjust to accommodate more complex tasks. But if police executives are to take advantage of the range of techniques advocated through the NIM, then issues of staff retention, career progression, salary, access to advanced technology, and training will have to be addressed before the analytical techniques identified in this section will begin to help interpret the criminal environment and influence decision-maker thinking in a meaningful way.

Strategic thinking

Strategic is a rather fluid term within analysis, given that (for example) the strategic demands of a small rural police department are different from those of a federal agency (see Chapter 5). Strategic thinking requires a skill set different from the usual toolbox that most analysts exploit in their tactical or operational work life. For instance, in looking at organised crime, EUROPOL's Organised Crime Threat Assessment 'puts an emphasis on the qualitative assessment of this complex and multi-faceted phenomenon' (EUROPOL 2006: 4). Strategic intelligence work requires a knowledge of more qualitative techniques such as futures wheels, competing hypothesis, force-field analysis, morphological analysis, Ishikawa diagrams, PESTEL, SWOT and Delphi analysis, and scenario generation (for descriptions and examples of these techniques, see Heldon 2004 and Quarmby 2004).

A more holistic understanding of long-term problems and their potential correlates would undoubtedly enhance strategic planning within policing. As Deborah Osborne, author of a number of crime analysis books, points out,

> Analysis of investigative data in aggregates rather than case-by-case could help in discovering new patterns that might enhance both investigation and prevention of crime. What are the characteristics of burglary victims in a neighbourhood? When are all the robberies occurring in a retail district? What are other factors that contribute to

crime in a specific region? Weather? Events? How might the police be better deployed to address some of these issues? How might the community become involved by enhancing capable guardianship? Who are our vulnerable population and how might they be better protected? (quoted in Ratcliffe 2007: 10)

Yet, for all this potential, analysis to support strategic planning is rarely undertaken. When it is, these activities are reduced to 'annual reporting and staffing allocation' (O'Shea and Nicholls 2003: 23) – activities that are unlikely to influence thinking about the criminal environment and have an impact on crime that reaches the threshold for functional intelligence-led policing I proposed earlier in this book. Strategic thinking should be forward-looking in orientation, attempting to articulate a range of possible futures that help law enforcement position itself advantageously to address emerging crime threats. Neil Quarmby (2004: 128-129) points out that for future work within a strategic intelligence environment to succeed, there must be:

- an identifiable decision-making system to support;
- a will to think ahead in both the intelligence system and the decision system to be supported;
- a will to apply the results in both the intelligence system and the decision system to be supported.

Given the risk-focus of modern policing and the desire to mitigate risk (Flood 2004), one would think that a future-oriented strategic approach would appeal to policing executives, but in general this appears not to be the case. It may be that the inductive approach common in strategic analysis is incompatible with 'a policing culture that is bred on deductive reasoning processes and the evidentiary dictates of the judicial system' (Quarmby 2004: 128). It may also be that an 'intelligence lacuna' (Christopher 2004: 177) still persists, or there is a perceived threat due to the exploratory nature of techniques that try to understand potential future scenarios (Heldon 2004). Whatever the cause, before strategic analysis becomes a mainstream analytical technique across policing, many of the organisational barriers identified in this chapter will have to be addressed.

Summary

This chapter has paid special attention to the issue of target selection. When intelligence-led policing emphasises the use of covert information gathering as an information resource, subsequent target selection can be dominated by intelligence gleaned from sources that have an isolated and myopic view of the criminal environment. This becomes an important consideration when analysts often have a free rein to determine priorities. The concept of offender self-selection is certainly worthy of further investigation, being a relatively ethical and productive way to target offenders (Roach 2007).

For a more holistic view of the criminal environment, analysts have to draw on a far wider array of data and information sources. This requires an increase in skill level, as well as a need to work collaboratively with other agencies. In regard to collaborative intelligence practice, addressing security classifications and procedures will certainly attain greater significance in the future. For instance, in the US all analysts and investigators assigned to JTTFs require top secret clearance, a process that can take up to a year, and is often perceived as a significant barrier to collaboration by local police agencies (Casey 2004). Integrated analysis models may be the way of the future, but there are considerable barriers to be overcome before crime intelligence analysis achieves the expected gains from a more holistic understanding of the criminal environment (Ratcliffe 2007).

Once targets are selected, and information is collated from various sources, the skill level for the analytical techniques that analysts are expected to employ is impressive (as Boba (2005) points out, some analysts even engage in computer programming in order to create software that fits their purpose) but far outstrips the pay grades and career opportunities that one would normally associate with this skill set. The result is rapid staff turnover.

It seems unfathomable to me that police departments are quite happy to pay good salaries to young police officers at the lowest ranks where most day-to-day duties have a social service component and an often limited impact on criminality, but resent paying an equivalent wage to staff that are expected to have mastery of statistics, analytical processes, GIS, intelligence writing, data management, publishing software, research skills, and presentation and briefing proficiency with an aptitude for strategic influence at the highest managerial levels of the police service. This is not to say I resent the salaries paid to sworn officers. Nothing could be further from the truth; however, recognition that analysts have the capacity to have a major impact on criminality if their products and skills are properly utilised might help to reassess their value in the workplace to a level more commensurate with their contribution to the crime reduction effort. Analysts generally strongly support the concept of intelligence-led policing (when it is clearly understood), but the loss of highly trained and experienced staff remains a significant policy area that law enforcement is going to have to address if intelligence-led policing is to succeed as a philosophy and business model.

Note

1   The section that follows draws on the findings and outcome from this forum, results of which have been published elsewhere by the Police Foundation. See Ratcliffe (2007).

7

Influencing decision-makers

When Gundhus studied the operations at one police station in Oslo, she found that the strategic planning unit gave up presenting crime statistics to the daily briefings because it was taking too much time. Instead, the information was presented to management meetings, a situation that the unit perceived negatively (Gundhus 2005). But was this move from a tactical briefing role to a strategic one more concerned with broader crime prevention policy and resource planning really a 'defeat' (p. 133)? There is considerable ambiguity among many analysts as to who the real decision-makers are that they support, and surprisingly little attention is paid to the relationship between analysts and decision-makers. From the research perspective, there is a paucity of literature to clarify this vital connection.

Until the formation of Crime and Disorder Partnerships in the UK, it was generally assumed that decision-makers were only found within the police service. The clients for most intelligence products were detectives and investigators working on specific cases, and there was a strong tactical focus with most of the output from analytical units. Now we have the UK National Intelligence Model (NIM) – predisposed as it is to strategic products geared towards higher-ranking police officers – and a growing recognition, through mechanisms such as problem-oriented policing and greater collaboration with industry and other crime preventers, that working outside the police is a viable alternative to achieving crime reduction goals. Given that the hegemony of lower-ranked officers as the predominant clients for crime intelligence products is slowly being eroded, this chapter begins by examining the vital question of who are the new decision-makers in the criminal justice and crime reduction universe.

It should be mentioned at this point that the chapter discusses decision-makers and clients. Decision-makers are people and institutions that can have an impact on the criminal environment. Clients are the people who commission or receive crime intelligence products. While they are often one and the same (and the terms are often used interchangeably), this should never be assumed. For example, analysts may find that in a hierarchical workplace, they are tasked by intelligence managers who could be considered the client for a project. However, the intelligence manager is unlikely to be the person who makes changes to deployment strategies, instigates a policy change, or sponsors new legislation. The intelligence manager is therefore not the decision-maker. Understanding the implications of this important distinction will help analysts achieve greater traction with crime intelligence products, and the central section of the chapter addresses some of the skills necessary to understand the institutional environment of clients and decision-makers.

Finally, it should not be forgotten that achieving traction with disseminated materials is the key to having an impact on crime. Maximising the influence of analysts is discussed in the last section of this chapter, and is arguably as important as identifying the decision-makers. Regretfully, many analysts are fixated on the *interpret* arm of the 3-i model; however, this chapter aims to redress the balance and explain the importance of *influence* in the workplace of analysts. The purpose of this chapter is succinctly summarised by Jonathan Nicholl:

> Knowing and understanding the client's current focus is an essential element of ensuring the work produced is welcomed by a receptive client as a relevant and timely contribution. Most critically, client understanding maximises the chance that the intelligence will be utilised and have a positive impact on the criminal environment. (Nicholl 2004: 66)

Who are decision-makers?

The 3-i model requires that while it is important to *interpret* the criminal environment, it is equally important to *influence* decision-makers. In the last decade or two, there has been, within the policing world, a gradual change in the perception of who are the decision-makers that can have an impact on the criminal environment. Problem-oriented policing has been pivotal in pushing the perception that a law enforcement solution is not the only way to resolve a crime problem and, indeed, in many situations is not a viable remedy of long-term crime issues at all (Goldstein 1990; 2003). In the UK, the development of Crime and Disorder Partnerships has accelerated this view. Once the mindset moves away from seeing a standard arrest strategy as a feasible option, the search then begins for alternative strategies, strategies that can be implemented by a range of different actors and decision-makers. As this section contends, there are a range of potential decision-makers from both within and outside the police service, including front-line police officers, senior law enforcement managers, actors from the private sector and industry, stakeholders from outside law enforcement, and (in ever increasing numbers and influence) security networks of collaborative agency partnerships.

Front-line officers

Patrol officers and detectives investigating individual cases have traditionally been the main clients for crime intelligence products. This situation is likely to continue, as it is often reinforced by the analysts themselves. O'Shea and Nicholls' extensive survey of crime analysis in America produced results that 'overwhelmingly suggest that crime analysts value tactical analysis (that supports short-range planning, primarily in crime control activities) over strategic analysis (that supports long-range planning, primarily interested in more complex organisational issues that involve departmental strengths, weaknesses, opportunities, and threats)' (O'Shea and Nicholls 2003: 13). They also noted that analysts resented being asked to conduct work that did not have this immediate case-support type role, a result that I found initially surprising but corroborated in interviews with some analysts in the New Jersey State Police (NJSP). While I, as well as some NJSP analysts, thought that having greater influence over the thinking of senior officers was an improvement in status and capacity to do good – 'I do like being at the captain's level because I like having that access and influence' (analyst quoted in Ratcliffe and Guidetti 2008) – many more analysts were threatened by the increased responsibility and pressure of potentially directing activities for sworn officers. As another NJSP analyst observed, 'analysts are terrified of making recommendations'.

The gulf between the analyst and the decision-maker in the 3-i model is bridged by the *influence* arrow, and not an arrow that says *inform*. This distinction is important because it is easy for analysts to inform patrol officers, but those same officers are relatively immune to being influenced by the analyst. Officers on patrol are at the beck and call of the public through the emergency telephone system (999, 911 or 000 depending on the country) and are slaves to the radio and dispatch system; thus, analysts often perceive that patrol officers do not have enough free time to engage in problem-solving or proactive work (Taylor *et al.* 2007). While there are times when officers are uncommitted to response policing, these times are sporadic and unstructured. Furthermore, these times are not monitored by supervisors, leaving officers with a great deal of flexibility in deciding whether or not to address any concerns raised by a problem or target profile. As an analyst from the New Zealand Police told me, 'Service from the troops is slowly improving but still poor. [There is a] lack of responsibility. It is better to go through the supervisor to get accountability' (quoted in Ratcliffe 2005: 444). The issue of achieving accountability for actions recommended in crime intelligence products is one that many analysts have yet to recognise as a significant barrier to the adoption of intelligence-led policing. As one middle-level commander in the New Zealand Police commented, 'My intelligence officer often gets frustrated with shift commanders. He is powerless without my support' (quoted in Ratcliffe 2005: 445).

Officers who work the streets every day generally see incidents in terms of their immediate impact on crime victims and the quality of life in an area, and thus work in a tactically focused environment. These are the group that most analysts turn to for information on the street. This relationship is thus a reciprocal one; analysts get a feel for the criminal environment through a close liaison with patrol officers and detectives, and in return this 'front-line' client group receives tactical products that assist their operational needs. In this complex and paradoxical arrangement, analysts need to be close to those in contact with the street and the criminals that operate there, so they can access the raw data and information necessary for more insightful products, yet there is greater opportunity to influence the targeting and resource decisions of the whole police department by disseminating products to a client base closer to the top of the hierarchical order.

The most common argument for providing tactical products is rooted in the desire to support case-specific investigations, and in the case of serial offending or crimes of particular brutality or barbarity, this is difficult to argue against. There is clearly a group of offenders where significant effort should be expended to prioritise their capture and incarceration. However, as I showed in a previous chapter (and I will elucidate this in the next chapter), a review of the crime funnel suggests a significant limitation in the ability of police to control and reduce crime through a general arrest and prosecution policy. And as stated earlier in this book, case-specific investigative support is not necessarily intelligence-led policing.

Police leadership

Both Compstat and intelligence-led policing have placed greater expectations on the leadership of the police, and especially middle and senior management. Experience with employing or understanding the basic tenets of intelligence-led policing is rarely a prerequisite of leadership positions, as the following quotation from the 9/11 Commission Report suggests:

> Performance in the [FBI] was generally measured against statistics such as numbers of arrests, indictments, prosecutions, and convictions. Counterterrorism and counterintelligence work, often involving lengthy intelligence investigations that might never have positive or quantifiable results, was not career-enhancing. Most agents who reached management ranks had little counterterrorism experience. (9/11 Commission 2004: 74)

The 9/11 Commission draw attention to the FBI, but in reality they identify the driving force for performance measurement across the whole policing domain. Arrests and prosecutions have been the benchmark for most of the history of policing, and are likely to remain so for many police departments. In the absence of robust mechanisms to measure the absence of crime, crime prevention activities are harder to validate than crime-busting operations. They are certainly less photogenic and do not result in impressive show trials. A requisite improvement in police statistical training for better appreciation of crime prevention has not happened yet, so police management in many places continues to view the value of crime intelligence products myopically in purely enforcement terms. As O'Shea and Nicholls' US survey discovered, 'crime control, narrowly defined as the identification and apprehension of offenders, dominated the demand for crime analysis' (2003: 11).

I have previously questioned the standard of police leadership training in the use and comprehension of crime intelligence products (Ratcliffe 2004a). The fault has been grounded in an assumption that senior police officers who have been in the job for many years have garnered sufficient experience to direct crime reduction and prevention activities, though where this belief originates from is unclear. When I give training and education sessions for senior police officers and unveil the latest research evidence of what does, and does not, work in long-term crime prevention, most of the audience are surprised to discover that projects and policies in which they have invested heavily are ineffective. When one asks senior officers what training courses they have taken since they left the police academy, they usually respond with a list that includes diversity education, budget management, community liaison and managerial training, but rarely have they attended instruction in crime prevention – supposedly the core activity of the police. This speaks to both a lack of insightful education for the middle and higher ranks and a lack of appreciation of evaluation as a steering mechanism for future policy. It also shows that political skills and administrative familiarity are considered suitable managerial experience for positions that really should require greater experience in crime reduction, disruption or prevention. At the highest levels of law enforcement, as the quotation from the 9/11 Commission at the beginning of this section illustrates, leaders of criminal intelligence agencies often do not have backgrounds in intelligence. John Abbott, former director general of the National Criminal Intelligence Service, admitted that his background in intelligence was 'not significant' and that he faced a 'steep learning curve' when he took the job (Johnstone 2004: 409).

My earlier research with the New Zealand police (prior to their recent positive engagement with intelligence-led policing) illustrated the disconnect some police executives felt with products produced by their analytical units. In my study none of the intelligence staff or police officers interviewed identified the district commander (the highest ranking officer at the local level) as a significant decision-maker and target for crime intelligence products. When discussing the intelligence system that was in place at the time, most officers never mentioned the district commander at any time, as if the local area commander was considered irrelevant to local crime reduction efforts. And the district commanders often felt the same way about intelligence and analysis. The disconnect was most apparent with a strategic analyst who said, 'I want to attend management meetings, be consulted more, be trusted more, be more involved' (quoted in Ratcliffe 2005: 444).

In response to this clear lack of training, some agencies have stepped into the breach. For example, the Jill Dando Institute for Crime Science runs a master class, 'Crime Reduction for Policy Makers'; the National Policing Improvement Agency (NPIA) has short courses for national intelligence managers and command unit commanders; the Manhattan Institute has developed leadership programmes for the New Jersey State Police and other US agencies; and the Australian Federal Police have developed a 'leadership in criminal intelligence' programme for senior intelligence staff that articulates into a graduate certificate and diploma. However, the majority of police department training funds, where they exist, are expended without considering the value of better informed decision-makers as leaders who should be influenced by analysts to use their knowledge and intelligence to drive a positive impact on the criminal environment. This is a shame, given that analysts seem to feel that managers are more supportive of their work than patrol officers (Taylor *et al.* 2007).

Non-law enforcement

Many non-law enforcement agencies maintain a crime prevention function less through the use of prosecution than through the deployment of regulatory or compliance-based processes. This does not mean that they do not prosecute; however, they have the advantage of being able to police criminality within their sphere of influence in a multidimensional manner, using a variety of sticks and carrots. This situation is dissimilar to traditional law enforcement, coupled as it is to a criminal justice system where prosecution is pretty much the only stick available to effect compliance. Law enforcement and community security appear to be moving to what Wood and Shearing (2007) refer to as *nodal governance*; networks of actors both within law enforcement and from outside agencies such as government and the private sector, all of whom have responsibilities to provide security. A good example of a private sector body with a security mandate is Center City District, a successful business initiative that has created a safe, clean and well-managed haven in the 80-block heart of Philadelphia (Greene *et al.* 1995). In a nodal governance environment, it is likely that analysts will have less control over the audience for their product, so the Center City District hybrid public/private model may have an impact on the way that intelligence products are produced and disseminated. In an original position contrary to much existing research (Gill 2000: 13), Ericson and Haggerty argue that the provision of crime data to non-police and compliance-based groups has greatly increased the visibility of police organisations and information systems: 'The primary locus of police activity is the risk communication systems shaped by external institutions. Through these communication systems, external institutions are able to routinely access police for knowledge useful in their own risk management' (Ericson and Haggerty 1997: 5).

Examples of non-traditional policing agencies include public organisations for housing, financial regulation, social security and the environment, organisations that often have to rely on police data to inform their decision-making. For example, mayors in many cities now use crime data to influence the provision of resources in an attempt to address crime in a multiagency fashion. In addition, private industry, either through encouragement or enforcement, has been instrumental in reducing theft. An example of this is the primary role of car manufacturers in increasing the difficulty to steal motor vehicles (Clarke and Harris 1992). Weatherburn (2004) notes that a significant car theft problem in Western Australia was brought under control, not by harsh penalties for offenders, but because of legislation that required new cars to be fitted with engine immobilisers.

A further example of private industry as crime preventers comes from the American experience with mobile phone fraud. In the early 1990s, offenders in the US identified and rapidly exploited weaknesses in the emerging mobile phone market (Clarke et al. 2001). The result was a

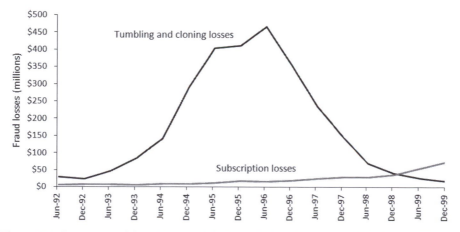

Figure 7.1 Semi-annual fraud losses, US, June 1992 to December 1999. *Source*: Clarke *et al.* (2001)

rapid growth in fraud cases caused by *cloning* (capturing mobile phone data with scanners and reprogramming the information into other phones) and *tumbling* (phones being altered to transmit illegally obtained numbers randomly to get free phone service). The costs of tumbling and cloning frauds to the mobile phone industry dramatic increased in the early 1990s (Figure 7.1) and spurred the industry to initiate significant technological counter-measures (Clarke *et al*. 2001: 7). As can be seen from Figure 7.1, the responses instigated in the mid-1990s not only were successful in reducing the instances of fraud but were also able to limit displacement to other offence methods such as subscription fraud (obtaining mobile phone service with details of another party).

Private industry is now a significant stakeholder in the provision of security across the world. From private security guards at housing estates, airports and businesses, to the growth of banks and other financial institutions that combat financial irregularity, it has become evident that modern crime intelligence analysts should recognise the wealth of possibilities for crime reduction and prevention by lifting their gaze beyond the law enforcement domain.

The general public

The community policing movement was anchored to the notion that greater community engagement would improve police legitimacy in the eyes of the public, and from this would flow greater information back to the police as well as greater incorporation of the public's wishes in the strategies that the police adopted (Fielding 2005). At least from a community policing perspective, the engagement of the general public is almost a prerequisite of any crime prevention activity, though how far American policing has truly moved to achieve this has been questioned (Kelling and Wycoff 2002; Mastrofski 2006). Intelligence-led policing takes a more pragmatic view of the role of the public in crime prevention, akin to the approach adopted by practitioners of problem-oriented policing: engagement of the public in the solution to crime problems is appropriate when they can help, but not an essential ingredient necessary to solve every problem.

Examples can be drawn from the various organised crime threat assessments produced and disseminated by national agencies such as SOCA (2006), CISC (2006a), and EUROPOL (2006). These documents have a public version and a law-enforcement-only version, indicative that the (at least stated) aim of the public versions is 'to educate and inform the public about the negative impact criminal organisations have on ... society' (CISC 2006a: iv). In any democracy, public support is clearly vital in achieving the basic mission of police; however, the specific role of the community in addressing and dismantling particular crime concerns is less clear. Many criminal intelligence units currently withhold information from their fellow officers and co-workers and thus fail to recruit other officers to the fight against drugs and organised crime, even though some police departments are beginning to recognise that a 'bottom-up' approach to gathering covert information on organised crime threats 'offers the best way of assessing the market and tackling the social harms associated with it' (HMIC 2005: 9). If intelligence units are reluctant to work with colleagues, then there is scant possibility of these units engaging with the public to prevent crime. It is nice to argue that 'a balance must be struck between making information as widely available as necessary to maximise potential benefits, and restricting availability to protect the security of sources, techniques and information' (NCPE 2005a: 22), but in a risk-averse policing world (Flood 2004), it is not surprising that the tendency is towards less dissemination than more. The flow of information to the public is always the first sacrificed.

Although the idea that community policing is effective for long-term crime prevention has been fairly well scotched (Sherman *et al.* 1998), the one area where a specific policy of greater engagement with the community may help is in counter-terrorism. Indeed, there appears in the US to be a growing recognition of the need to redefine community policing (where it is still practised) within an intelligence-led policing framework for counter-terrorism purposes (Loyka *et al.* 2005), even though most local law enforcement officers have never had intelligence training and thus would be hard-pressed to recognise, or know to share, information pertaining to terrorism that they may receive from the public (Docobo 2005).

The question of whether or not the public are decision-makers as a target for influence within the framework of the 3-i model will in the end come down to an assessment of the crime intelligence at hand. The thinking behind sex-offender registration and notification schemes, such as Megan's Law, is predicated on the notion that the public are able to make more informed decisions about where they wish to live and what routes they might tell their children to take to school. Whether this type of dissemination actually has an impact on the criminal environment and prevents crime is harder to determine. Similarly, considerable effort goes into the public dissemination of crime information through police websites and pages where maps of crime information can be viewed (Wartell and McEwen 2001), though, again, the long-term impact of these sites for crime prevention is not known (Ratcliffe 2002c). For the purposes of intelligence-led policing, it may be that disseminating to the general public has as much value in terms of maintaining and promoting public support as it does in engaging any crime prevention capacity.

Security networks

It is increasingly clear that if crime is to be managed, police have to recruit other agencies and actors to the fight, or even join other networks or groups involved in governance. The security field has grown beyond traditional police agencies to include customs and border control, immigration authorities, defence agencies, and organisations with national security responsibilities (Bigo 2000). Enthusiasm for partnership working between police and other agencies is improving, though in some places it could be accurately described as 'a coming together of organisations that in reality have a barely concealed contempt for each other; apparently united in pursuit of a superficially considered and ill defined purpose, but with the real aim of securing resources for themselves' (Brumwell 2007). The police reform movement has, however, embraced partnership working, especially in the UK where the 1998 Crime and Disorder Act made a statutory requirement of multiagency crime prevention initiatives. A recent review of the partnership provisions of the Act may change some of the structural arrangements; however, the general objective of partnership working remains, and it appears that the government's intention is to strengthen the visibility of partnerships (Home Office 2006b).

A range of legislation in the UK appears to have smoothed some of the data-protection issues that had previously inhibited data sharing between agencies. As a good example of what then becomes possible, it is worth considering the Greater Manchester Against Crime Partnership Business Model (a bit of a mouthful, so, hereafter, GMAC PBM). As Tim John and his colleagues explain,

> GMAC is fundamentally a business process model for partnership (multi-agency) working in the fields of Crime and Disorder Management and Community Safety. Developed by a multi-agency team, on behalf of the Crime and Disorder partners in [Greater Manchester], from an interpretation of the police National Intelligence Model (NIM), GMAC represents a significant development in partnership working. With the NIM as its foundation, the GMAC Partnership Business Model (GMAC PBM) has sought to build a structure whereby a multiagency approach across ten local authorities can contribute to a pooled resource for the conurbation, which constitutes the county of Greater Manchester. (John *et al.* 2006: 1)

The GMAC PBM is therefore an attempt to integrate a multiagency approach to crime problems while retaining a formal structure for action similar to the NIM.

This more collaborative approach to crime reduction has enabled some in policing to see benefits (and potential threats) in other agencies that orbit law enforcement agencies. The police are still central to policing, but 'they now are seen, and see themselves, as one node among others. Within this nodal context they have sought, with considerable ingenuity, to establish a role for themselves that recognizes and builds on the fact that they have been, and will continue to be, a fundamentally Hobbesian institution of governance' (Wood and Shearing 2007: 57). In other words, drawing on the ideas of Thomas Hobbes, the police are conceptualised as the pivotal representative of strong central government but within a network of partners in the provision of governance and security. Within this network, the central node status of the police is enhanced by playing a role as information and knowledge broker. The police can lever significant social capital to maintain their position as crucial to the network in a number of ways; deploying economic, political, cultural and social capital, and controlling the flow of information and intelligence can be central to this (Dupont 2003). As information and communication resources have expanded into every facet of modern life, this 'exponential development of information and communication technologies around the globe has, without any doubt, been instrumental in the collapse of all sorts of barriers that previously corseted institutions, organisations, communities and individuals inside limited roles and responsibilities' (Dupont 2004: 77).

New opportunities have enabled agencies that were previously inconsequential (in comparison with the social capital of the police) to engage with law enforcement on an increasingly equitable footing in the provision of security. Disseminating intelligence is thus not just a way for the police to maintain their hegemonic role and legitimacy at the centre of an expanding governance and security network; it is also a way for police agencies to enrol others in the fight against crime.

Security networks are growing not just within countries, but also between countries. As global concerns of illegal immigration, drugs, organised crime and terrorism (the new Four Horsemen of the Apocalypse, according to Bigo (2000)) expand to absorb more of the security agenda, transnational policing is redefining the concept of policing away from the notion of support for the sovereign status of the nation state to one where greater governance and collaboration are required to counter threats that span national borders. Certainly, if transnational policing becomes an issue of 'crucial concern in the coming years as social life is increasingly lived beyond the parochial confines of traditional ways of living' (Sheptycki 2000: 1), then decision-makers who reside beyond immediate boundaries, either organisationally or nationally, will become key determinants of public safety.

In Chapter 5, I extended Davenport's continuum of data, information, and knowledge to include intelligence as an adjunct that is a requirement beyond knowledge. Knowledge has to be converted into something that is used to influence decision-making, and this requires analysts and commanders to move beyond roles as processors of information. Peter Manning has suggested that 'the view of Ericson and Haggerty (1997) that police are "information workers", based on formal ties and networks, is somewhat problematic, in part because the argument refers to potential and form, rather than content and actual use' (Manning 2000: 194). In support of this position, the key to progressing from knowledge to intelligence is in the actual use of the product to influence decisions. One of the most valuable ways of increasing the use of crime intelligence is to influence decision-makers beyond an analyst's immediate establishment and to drive the crime reduction activities of other organisations. This requires analysts to understand the reality of the environment of their potential decision-makers, the subject of the next section.

Viewpoint

The responsibilities of intelligence-led police leadership

Lisa Palmieri

To adapt a popular philosophical riddle; 'if an analyst provides intelligence that never reaches a decision-maker, was it ever really intelligence?'

Much like the original question about a tree falling in the woods making a sound, the question of analysts having an influence on decision-makers is central to intelligence-led policing. This chapter's focus on decision-makers shines a glaring light on the missing link to successful implementation of intelligence-led policing. Analysts who have been properly trained and mentored are quite aware of their responsibility to present conclusions and recommendations to decision-makers. Yet barriers to accomplishing this are inherent in the culture of law enforcement. Intelligence-led policing cannot be successfully implemented in the current environment without a strong, educated executive and management cadre that values strategic approaches over the more audience-pleasing count of arrests and prosecutions.

The relationship of analysts to decision-makers has not been researched to any extent. In the absence of a clear relationship, communication suffers. What are the priorities of the department? Are analysts expected to be all things to all people without the proper resources? Is there a clear understanding by decision-makers regarding the capabilities and limitations of analysis? Do they appreciate the rigours of the intelligence cycle? I have heard more than one instance of commanders asking for 'intelligence' on a certain topic and expecting it 'by the end of the day'. Understanding that intelligence cannot flow without prior planning and investment, particularly in collection and analysis, seems to be lacking in many police agencies.

This chapter's distinction between clients and decision-makers is well made. In my conversations with IALEIA members from many different countries I have found that their experiences are eerily similar. Managers who task out products are generally not intelligence professionals, and don't understand the intelligence cycle; planning, collection, collation, analysis, dissemination, feedback. Their primary concern is *product*. Managers in police agencies are evaluated in the same manner as their peers in patrol and investigations – quantitatively. This lack of comprehension for the *value* of good intelligence accounts for all the crime reports ('that happened last week, this happened today') that masquerade as intelligence. What can a decision-maker really do with information on which no analysis had been performed?

The value of intelligence must be measured qualitatively by educated management. Managers can serve as quality control, but rarely do they ask the hard questions; what does this mean, and what can we do about it? Analysts should make recommendations to address these important questions. Some in law enforcement believe that police executives don't want recommendations, that they would prefer to simply react to crime than develop a new strategy or work with a non-traditional partner to implement a more strategic response to a problem. I hope this renewed interest in intelligence-led policing will change this mindset and have an impact at the highest levels of law enforcement.

There has been real progress in the executive ranks as far as trying to understand intelligence. Solving some of the issues identified in this book will move us further towards a real implementation of intelligence-led policing.

Lisa Palmieri is President of the International Association of Law Enforcement Intelligence Analysts (IALEIA) and is currently working for the Department of Homeland Security, assigned to the Commonwealth Fusion Center in Massachusetts.

Understanding the client's environment

Before talking about the importance of analysts understanding the environment of the client, it is worth pointing out that understanding, and the benefits it can produce, is a two-way street. As Jonathan Nicholl astutely observed, 'If the client's experience in dealing with intelligence as a decision-making tool is rudimentary and unsophisticated, the pressure on the analyst is accentuated. They will generally be unsympathetic to even reasonable requests for more information, more time or a response

153

indicating the question posed cannot be directly answered' (Nicholl 2004: 55). Analysts should always understand that educating decision-makers is, regretfully, a task that they will probably have to engage with for their entire careers, or at least until the use of crime intelligence and the intelligence-led policing model reach a stage of maturity and general acceptance. In the interim, understanding the decision-maker's environment can go a long way to smoothing the passage of crime intelligence products to acceptance and influence. There are three central points that analysts should recognise:

1. The decision-maker's institutional environment exerts considerable pressure.
2. Decision-makers demand actionable intelligence products over descriptive reports.
3. The evolution from knowledge to intelligence product is dependent on the nature of the decision-maker.

When I talk here about the decision-maker's institutional environment, I am referring to institutional and cultural domains in which clients move in their professional life. For example, consider the position of a police chief in a small town. While the 3-i model identifies the crime intelligence analyst as an influence in the decision-making of the chief, a more realistic picture would probably portray further bubbles of influence stemming from other institutional pressures, as shown in Figure 7.2.

While their contribution to the policing agenda is often criticised (see, for example, Neville (2000)), it is an unfortunate reality that the media

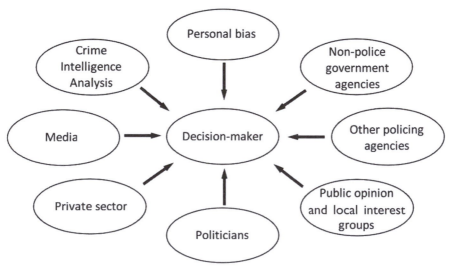

Figure 7 2. Institutional, community and personal influences on decision-makers

is hugely influential in driving decision-making, either directly through editorials, selection of stories and their placement in newspapers, radio and television, or indirectly through the media's influence on local politicians and public opinion. Other police agencies (such as at the federal and state levels) can try to drive the priorities of local police for their own benefit. Likewise, non-police government agencies, such as health departments, can enhance their own missions if local police behave in certain ways. External to clients and their organisations, there are myriad organisations that have a vested interest in the priorities and resource decisions of the police.

In addition, clients are likely to have their own personal biases regarding any issue that the analyst addresses. As the Commissioner of the Australian Federal Police commented, 'It is important to remember that intelligence is just one aspect of the decision making and policy development process – and I think this has been lost in the current debate – but the final decision takes into account many other factors' (Keelty 2004: 5). What must always be pointed out to decision-makers is that of all the influences shown in Figure 7.2, while crime intelligence may not always be the most persuasive, it is usually the most objective, and is often the *only* objective voice in the room.

Unfortunately, many analysts live in professional isolation, content with spending considerable effort on the *interpret* aspect of the 3-i model and paying scant attention to the outcome of their labours. If they did, they might find that their influence would increase with a finer appreciation of the pressures and constraints on their decision-makers. It was a recognition of the lack of action resulting from tactical intelligence products that drove the Organised Vehicle Crime Section in NCIS to change their operational approach to support better live operations (Brown *et al.* 2004). This change in the thinking of analysts is yet to materialise among many of the crime analysts that O'Shea and Nicholls interviewed:

> Analysts have no clear sense about which products are considered useful to the target. They produce, deliver, and through anecdotal evidence draw conclusions about the value of their work. Neither the analysts, nor the analysts' managers are clear about how and how well targets use their product. (2003: 16)

The second consideration is in regard to the importance to clients of actionable intelligence products rather than descriptive reports. One of the most noticeable limitations among the mass of output created by analysts that I have seen is the lack of analysis that goes beyond the descriptive and into the realm of actionable and useful. For example, one of the most common crime intelligence outputs that operational officers ask analysts to produce is a map of crime (Innes *et al.* 2005), either as a representation of crime events as a 'pin' map, or as a map of crime counts within administrative boundaries. Much of this 'analysis', while well-meaning, does not satisfy the demands of the decision-maker and is not 'fit-for-purpose' (Chainey and Ratcliffe 2005). Good decisions are not based on counts of crime, but arise where crime frequencies and rates are related to other criminogenic factors that can explain why the crime patterns occur as they do (Eck 1997). One analytical organisation has an annual crime bulletin competition that is judged by experienced analysts within the organisation, but I somehow feel it would be better judged by the bulletin's recipients, who could attest to how it changed their thinking and had a positive impact in reducing crime. Many bulletins are not targeted to the audience and can often be 'turgid' (Audit Commission 1993: 38) or mundane and repetitive at best.

The architects of the NIM decided that uniformity of formal intelligence products was important because the 'intelligence process in law enforcement cannot be merely a voyage of discovery but demands predictability in the delivery and content of intelligence products for managers' decision-making' (Flood 2004: 44). Thus, NIM analysts produce only strategic assessments, tactical assessments, problem profiles and target profiles. While practice on the ground may differ, from the NIM there is no encouragement of bulletins, flyers or other periphery that are rarely used for decision-making.

The final consideration is for analysts to recognise that the evolution from knowledge to intelligence product is dependent on the nature of the client. This requires the careful tailoring of every product to likely decision-makers. This is a recurring theme in this chapter, but is worth reiterating. Lack of this consideration may explain why so many criminal intelligence products do not get the airing they should. Broad dissemination of crime intelligence products is often seen as an end in itself in an age where information sharing is perceived as paramount; however, if a product is not tailored to at least one particular client, it may be that the product is unsatisfactory for *any* client.

In summary, it is important for analysts to track and take an active interest in the way their products are used and applied to decision-making. Given the pressures on decision-makers (see Figure 7.2), analysts will find greater traction when they recognise that their crime intelligence outputs may have to blend with or trump other institutional pressures to achieve acceptance. Crime intelligence products that run counter to prevailing currents are immensely valuable in refining how clients think, but also have to be introduced with a diplomacy that recognises that existing attitudes have cultural capital. As Weatheritt (1986: 16) noted, 'The incorporation of research findings into a new body of accepted wisdom is a slow and uneven process in which the intellectual persuasiveness of the research is a great deal less relevant than its political appeal'. This is not to say that analysts should mangle their products or change their findings; such an approach would definitely conflict with analytical integrity (Nicholl 2004). There are, however, many ways to tell the same story, and greater political savvy on the part of the analyst will help a crime intelligence product achieve greater acceptance.

Working with the audience

One of the best ways for analysts to tailor products to their target audiences is to understand how clients define success. For example, at a local station with patrol responsibilities and a reactive disposition, the types of knowledge and intelligence that are valued may be 'short-term based, useful, effective, freshly produced and practical' (Gundhus 2005: 136). The type of output that might support a joint terrorism task force might be substantially different, given that 'JTTFs do not have numerous arrests, search warrants, or seizures. Rather, the bulk of the work often relates to long-term surveillance, electronic court-ordered monitoring, source development, or interviews, none of which may garner significant statistics in the traditional law enforcement sense' (Casey 2004: 5).

In understanding the potential application of the final product, it is vital that analysts be allowed to interact with the client directly (McDowell 1998; Nicholl 2004). This may mean that an intelligence manager has to relinquish some control and, instead of acting as a conduit, permit a free flow of information between analyst and decision-maker for the sake of a more refined task definition. In the process, the decision-maker will better appreciate the subtleties and difficulties of the initial tasking, and the analyst can understand the constraints of the client. It will also help the analyst and the client appreciate the time constraints, the format of the final product, and the overarching aims of potential decision-makers.

Finally, a greater understanding of the possibility of multiple clients can help analysts tailor their product for maximum acceptance. The analyst should always be conscious of the possibility of multiple clients even when not specifically articulated by the person that initially requested the product (Nicholl 2004). For example, a three-page summary of an evaluation of a crime suppression operation that a graduate student and I wrote for a deputy commissioner in the Philadelphia Police Department made its way to the city managing director's office within hours of being finalised and was mentioned by the mayor in a public forum shortly after that. It probably need hardly be mentioned that it was a positive evaluation!

One advantage to drawing on data from outside the police domain when communicating with non-law enforcement audiences is an inherent suspicion attached to police data: 'Distorted, unschooled use of data by police administrators in the past has led to a widespread tendency to dismiss facts presented by the police as potentially biased and intended to support some deeply embedded police "value"' (Goldstein 1990: 89). Non-police data can also help clients understand the wider implications of crime prevention activity, and move towards a more strategic harm reduction framework grounded in the impact of crime in terms of social harm rather than just being focused on crime figures devoid of a broader context (Sheptycki and Ratcliffe 2004). Understanding the institutional environment and culture should be a central part of an analyst's role.

Maximising influence

> A misconception persists on the part of the public, lawmakers, and even some in the law enforcement and intelligence communities that information sharing alone will be the miracle counterterrorism solution. Information sharing is critical for homeland security. It makes prevention possible by enabling a better national and local understanding of threats. Indeed, information sharing moves usable information gathered by federal, state, and local agencies to the national level and back down again. But the key to successful information sharing is that the information is usable. (Loyka *et al.* 2005: 5)

Usability of information (or crime intelligence) is central to maximising influence, but it is not the only requirement of a successfully disseminated product that has an impact on the criminal environment. Some years ago I wrote, 'It is probably impossible to count the number of intelligence failures that have occurred due to an inability of the intelligence organisation to "sell" its product, or the failing of the decision-maker (the intelligence client) to recognise the value of the product' (Ratcliffe 2003: 4). This statement (while a little dramatic!) still holds true.

Achieving the widest distribution possible may help to reach decision-makers of whom both the client and the analyst are unaware. This runs contrary to the 'need to know' principle, which states that 'the dissemination of classified information should be no wider than is required for the efficient conduct of business, and should be restricted to those who have authorised access' (NCPE 2005a: 22). Analysts should resist this urge and request, as much as possible, to seek the widest and most proactive dissemination strategy. There are many advantages to this approach, given that 'dissemination is the final stage of the intelligence process and is crucial to the reputation of often-small and sometimes marginalised criminal intelligence units. Their ability to maintain credibility and thus enhance their organisational project is determined to a large extent by the perception of those to whom they disseminate their "product", whether members of the same or a different agency' (Gill 2000: 211).

One of the ways to maximise influence is to determine who the main decision-makers are, and then locate the analysis unit close to these main clients. This idea of geographic and organisational location for an analytical office has become the topic of some debate. According to the Audit Commission (1993: 38), locating the office away from the parade or briefing room for patrol officers is contributory to the lack of intelligence awareness among uniform officers. The corollary is the presumption that decentralised units are closer to the information sources they require and are better able to respond to their needs. However, the benefits of situating analysis units closer to operational and street units has been countered by the argument that they become inundated with trivial requests (for example, making banners for retirement parties) to the degree that it interferes with the central mission of the analytical function (O'Shea and Nicholls 2002: 15). There is also the problem of 'out of sight, out of mind'. At one New Zealand Police district, the intelligence office was located in a different building some miles from the office of the district commander, and the analysts there rarely had any contact with the command structure (Ratcliffe 2005).

The experiences of analysts in the reorganised NJSP is telling. Analysts generally report increased influence with senior officers through improved contact brought on by closer geographic proximity of offices: 'We do have that access now. Prior to the reorganization, I didn't feel we had access to the decision-makers. Now it has put me right in there. The Captain is down the hall' (analyst quoted in Ratcliffe and Guidetti 2008). At the time of our interviews, the impact of the organisational restructuring was still being felt, yet the trend was generally positive, as indicated by another quotation from an analyst from the same article:

> I didn't get much [information] prior to the reorganisation, but now I'm definitely in the know. Prior to the reorganisation, I didn't know command staff and I felt a disconnect in terms of what was going on. It is definitely much better. We need to fine tune our role in terms of products and what we produce and what balance of [strategic] assessments and tactical products.

It is not surprising that a forum of practitioners, analysts, and policymakers recommended that police chiefs work closely with analysts, and that an integrated office of crime analysts and intelligence officers should be located close to the decision-makers (Ratcliffe 2007).

Embracing networks

Even when it is not possible to place all the analytical and decision-making functions in close proximity, the impact of a loss of spatial immediacy can be minimised (to some degree) by a virtual or institutional proximity. Analysts can benefit from understanding and embracing the power of security networks to achieve long-terms aims of crime reduction, and this is true for analysts of all agencies from the local to the federal and national. Dupont (2004) usefully distinguishes four types of network, all of which can be leveraged to increase the influence power of crime intelligence:

- *local security networks* – initiatives that work with public and private resources available at the local community level to overcome the more intractable crime problems with origins in deteriorating social conditions;
- *institutional networks* – networks that smooth the progress of information flow between government agencies or enable disparate agencies to collaborate and pool resources;
- *networks without borders* – networks that, while similar to institutional networks, facilitate cooperation at an international level between agencies with national responsibilities;
- *informational networks* – the web of electronic and informational technologies that enable police officers to access vital information remotely.

Security networks are becoming central to the provision of long-term, multi-agency crime prevention activities, the sort of activities that individual agencies do not have the resources or cultural capital to implement. These collaborative networks increase the number of decision-makers, requiring analysts to consider not only the security implications of dissemination strategies but also the possibilities of utilising resources beyond their immediate agency in the fight against crime. Admittedly, some collaborative networks resemble at best a loose affiliation of feuding barons with little interest in cooperative action, each striving to gain the most resources for their agency in return for the least effort or investment. Others are, however, emerging as more collegial groups that put the larger picture in context.

Recommending action

In previous work, David Mackay and I argued that it is increasingly accepted that intelligence analysts should make recommendations for future courses of action or activity based on the findings of the assessment undertaken (Mackay and Ratcliffe 2004). Even when the client does not request suggestions, it is perfectly acceptable to canvass potential solutions from what has been found to be successful in social and policing situations similar to the client's environment (Nicholl 2004). This is an area with which analysts with a military background often struggle. Their formative intelligence experiences are with intelligence users trained and versed in the use of military intelligence. When analysts transition to the criminal analysis environment, they have two initial disadvantages; they are not used to making recommendations, and they do not have a thorough grounding in understanding fields such as situational crime prevention and environmental criminology from which to make suggestions.

Given the current trend towards civilian analysts (Osborne 2006), making recommendations for action can be equally difficult for civilians in a sworn-officer environment, given that 'analysts, in addition to being generally younger, better educated and more female than most police, find themselves between the rock of operational personnel and the hard place of ill-informed managers' (Gill 2000: 239). Yet the lack of training for police managers in effective techniques for crime prevention is one of the reasons that Clarke and Eck recommend that analysts become more conversant with recommending suitable tactics (Clarke and Eck 2005). The Center for Problem Oriented Policing maintains a wealth of updated information on potential crime solutions to a range of problem areas (www.popcenter. org).

Whether analysts make recommendations that are acceptable to decision-makers or not acceptable, there is often confusion as to the appropriate response from the decision-makers. As Nina Cope astutely observes, 'Emphasizing the distinction between the capacity to *make recommendations based on research and analysis* with the *capacity to make decisions about adopting recommendations and directing action* is necessary' (Cope 2004: 191; emphasis in original). In other words, while some police managers may feel that it is not the place of non-sworn staff to make recommendations, senior police officers still retain the capacity to decide whether to adopt those recommendations or to choose a different path. It is perhaps a fear of the reaction from senior police officers that spurred one NJSP analyst to comment on fellow analysts who do not suggest a course of action: 'I can only think they are terrified of being slammed, or so insecure about their own inabilities' (analyst quoted in Ratcliffe and Guidetti 2008).

In the current intelligence-led policing environment, targeted dissemination strategies are vital. Too often, analysts rely on long-winded reports that few practitioners have the time or inclination to read, oral briefings are poorly prepared, and bulletins are distributed with no appreciation of their readability. One former military analyst told me that near the end of one particularly long report, he inserted the comment 'in accordance with the prophecy' just to see whether anyone would read that far! At least he was rewarded by a few concerned telephone calls. Analysts are often hamstrung by the desire to demonstrate how hard they have worked and so expound their research to great length. An analyst I interviewed in New Zealand had written a strategic report of the future of crime in the local area that ran to at least a couple of hundred pages. While an undoubtedly intellectual and thorough piece of work, I could not find a single person at the station who had read it.

Alternatives abound. Written materials can be summarised in a single page of basic facts and action points, and then, if necessary supported by longer reports. The Australian Institute of Criminology has a popular series of reports that are never longer than six pages, and are written and paginated in an informative but readable style. All of their *Trends and Issues in Crime and Criminal Justice* reports, including an early piece I wrote on intelligence-led policing (Ratcliffe 2003), are downloadable from their website and have become admired among senior government decision-makers. The power of brevity was recognised by one analyst for a US national security agency, who said, 'If I write a 12-page self-directed piece that goes out as a community product, and somebody else writes one paragraph with two bullet points that goes into a daily brief, the guy who got in the daily brief is going to get the recognition. Why waste my time with the big products?' (Johnston 2005: 38).

Away from written documents, many analysts are comfortable briefing patrol officers, but need to extend this practice to briefing senior executives and managers. Good briefings and presentations with decision-makers in a face-to-face environment are far more effective than most paperbound communications. Unfortunately, few analysts are employed for their presentational dexterity, though, fortunately, this is a skill that can be improved with practice. The research of Mehrabian and Ferris (1967), while having been overgeneralised into the 7 per cent–38 per cent–55 per cent rule (i.e. that people perceive the meaning of a message by placing 7 per cent of their faith in the words, 38 per cent in the vocal tone, and 55 per cent in the non-verbal communication), does recognise that consistency of the whole communication is necessary to convey a message. When done correctly, the ability to influence decision-makers with a quick, insightful presentation far surpasses the passivity of written forms of communication. A myriad other options is possible. Cathy Lanier, chief of the Washington, DC Metropolitan Police Department, told me she uses short, informative videos to reach out to officers across the city. In another example, police in the centre of Oslo decided that young people in the city centre were decision-makers in the fight against pickpockets and violence, and so they arranged to send an SMS message one Saturday afternoon to 15,000 youths advising them to take precautions against crime (Gundhus 2005).

Summary

For intelligence to flourish it must prove to be useful and be seen to support the decision-maker. It cannot do this if it is not serving the decision-maker's needs. (Nicholl 2004: 67)

NCPE (2005a) have stated that all intelligence products should be actionable, but sometimes there is value in a policy of benign neglect if it allows law enforcement resources to be better employed elsewhere. This is where the strategic perspective comes to the fore. The ability to suggest strategic priorities to a decision-maker may be one of the most valuable services that an analyst can perform, in terms of both achieving value for money from policing and enlightening decision-makers to potential solutions they may not have considered. A strategic viewpoint is also vital in making tough decisions about which areas of criminality will receive less attention in favour of concentrating resources elsewhere. However, a strategic perspective will continue to be a rare activity while analysts and clients maintain a tactical myopia.

The first task for any analyst is to determine who the decision-makers are, especially if they are not the person who requested the original tasking. For too many police analysts, patrol officers and detectives are the only decision-makers in their line of sight; however, the crime funnel suggests that there are fewer opportunities to make a significant dent in crime as one gets further down the funnel. I expand on this position in the next chapter.

It is going to be hard to move beyond a fixation on tactical products that have a purely street-officer focus given the findings, at least from the US, that 'police managers insisted that crime analysis should concentrate on tactical operations (i.e., support efforts that can be directly linked to "catching the bad guy") and not on the analysis of underlying community problems' (O'Shea and Nicholls 2003: 11). I suspect the situation is not so different in other countries. However, moving beyond the tactical is going to be essential if intelligence-led policing is to make the significant inroads into crime that the originators claimed it would (see, for example, Audit Commission 1993).

When the gaze is lifted, and analysts see crime reduction opportunities in other decision-makers and clients, the challenge becomes understanding the institutional environment in which those distal clients operate. At the same time, it is important not to contort analytical findings to suit those environments to the level where they become a tool of a preconceived schema. What if an analyst only produces the intelligence product requested, even though the analyst knows there are other important considerations? The balance is to understand the client's environment and business, while maintaining analytical integrity (Nicholl 2004). As Australian Federal Police Commissioner Mick Keelty wrote:

> While intelligence needs to be aware of policy context and direction, these must not become drivers of intelligence outcomes. ... At the same time, I believe that relevant, actionable intelligence needs to be informed by the policy context. The trick is to ensure that analysts are

sufficiently independent so that they do not write into an actual or perceived agenda of the intelligence consumer. (Keelty 2004: 5)

Influencing decision-makers requires resolute accuracy in detail and fact, but also a flair for the imaginative in terms of getting clients' attention. The Internet has created the opportunity for a proliferation of reports to be researched, disseminated, and ignored. Influencing decision-makers is a vital component of the job of the analyst, equal to that of interpreting the criminal environment and worthy of as much attention being paid to it in the professional training and research world. The end result, of course, is to have a positive impact on crime, and this is the subject of the next chapter.

8

Having an impact on crime

Being a policeman in the 21st Century is like being the man who was standing on the bank of a very fast flowing river. In that river he could see hundreds of people being swept along struggling to stop from drowning. As each moment passes their numbers swell until there are thousands of people all gasping and shouting to the man on the bank to help them.

What do we do as police officers? Go in and help as many as we can? Or do we take a walk upstream and find out who is throwing them all in? I have a feeling that most of the time police have been wading in to the rescue!

And so begins a reactive cycle of uncontrolled demand and equally uncoordinated response. The police become like lifeguards frantically swimming against the tide from one incident to another, employing different tactics in a disjointed and unfocussed manner with little or nothing to show for it at the end of the day. (Stevens 2001: 2)

Sir John Stevens, former Commissioner of the Metropolitan Police, strikes a great analogy in the statement above, one that can be quantified through the crime funnel, as I do at the beginning of this chapter. The crime funnel can be used to estimate the implications of changes to one part of the crime funnel and how these changes will likely affect the rest of the criminal justice system.

To have an impact on crime, it is necessary to *reduce*, *prevent* or *disrupt* criminal activity. Regretfully, these terms are often used interchangeably; however, they have different meanings and thus have implications for the outcomes they generate, as explained in this chapter. Decision-makers are often unaware of these differences, and tend to ignore prevention or dismiss it as a viable option. In the criminal justice system, many managers lack training in the area of crime prevention and reduction and are often unaware of the research that exists. Within policing, there is often a perception that a commander who has made it to the highest stratum of policing, must instinctively know how to 'do' crime prevention, simply by virtue of having been in the business for many years. This mindset is reflected in the general lack of training courses that address this vital area of operational strategy. One year, a leading international police organisation offered only one course in crime prevention from 68 courses offered (Ratcliffe 2004a). Building on the previous chapter, this section of the book explores the changing role of leaders through intelligence-led policing, and develops further the argument for analysts making recommendations, especially in the area of crime prevention. The second half of the chapter is dedicated to outlining different ways that crime reduction and prevention can be achieved, predominantly from a law enforcement perspective, and points the reader in the direction of sources for further information.

Revisiting the crime funnel

Chapter 3 of this book introduced the crime funnel, the generalisation that for every 1,000 crimes that occur, about 410 are reported to police, 287 make it into the official record of crime, 75 are detected and cleared up by police, offenders are charged by the police in 37 cases, in 21 instances offenders actually have a court appearance, 15 of those cases result in a finding of guilt, and in only 4 of the original 1,000 does an offender receive a custodial sentence (reproduced in the first column of Table 8.1 but now with the decimal value for custodial sentences shown). We can continue the generalisation and explore a few scenarios to understand better the impacts on criminal justice policy.

The central tenet of the following approach is to understand that any impact generally flows down the funnel rather than up. Therefore, we know that 75 offences are detected, but that number is constrained by the 287 incidents recorded by police. If the number of offences recorded by police increases, perhaps as a result of a change in crime recording policy, it is possible that the detected number may increase, as could the number of cases resulting in a charge and appearance at court, and so on down the funnel.

However, increasing the number of offences recorded *by* police does not mean that the number reported *to* police necessarily increases, nor does it mean that the total number of offences increases. The original source for the increase would still be the 410 offences that the public decide are important enough to merit contacting the local police. Over the years, significant changes in the volume of crime in many countries have been attributed to changes in recording practices, while national crime victimisation surveys have not detected significant changes in the volume of crime experienced by the public. For example, increases in reported violent crime in parts of Australia were not reflected in crime victimisation surveys, a finding probably caused by changes in the way police approached the recording of assaults and changes in society's willingness to report violent behaviour (Indermaur 1996). So, impacts flow down the funnel, but not necessarily upwards.

With this *top-down effect* flow in mind, let us explore what would happen if prosecutors and police officers decided to take court action at an increasing rate and charged more offenders. With a 10 per cent increase in charges, the second column of Table 8.1 shows that this would mean that charges would increase to about 41, the already-stretched courts would have a 10 per cent increased workload, guilty findings would increase, and there would be a need for some extra jail space (the custodial sentence figure increases from 3.7 to 4.1 for every 1,000 offences). However, because the impact on the criminal justice system flows downward and not necessarily up, there is little evidence that this would have a meaningful impact on the 1,000 offences that affect the public.

Flood argues that a central precept of intelligence-led policing is the necessity to tackle and incapacitate the 'criminal leaders' and 'criminal specialists' (2004). One of the claimed benefits of a more proactive approach to police work, one that is more intelligence-led and offender focused, is that it would allow the police to focus on the prolific and persistent offenders committing much of the crime (Audit Commission 1993). This means that to have a meaningful impact on the 1,000 crimes that affect the community, police enforcement practices are going to have to concentrate on arresting and incarcerating the right (four or five) people at the bottom of the crime funnel, people who are the criminal elite rather than the low-hanging fruit. Chapter 3 explored what research exists on the ability of police to perform this activity, but for now we can see what would happen with a 25 per cent increase in the clearance rate for reported crime. Given the resources available to police, this is probably quite unrealistic; however, Table 8.1 shows that even with this optimistic view, the result would be increased arrests and paperwork, and greater pressures on the court and jail system.

The hope with intelligence-led policing therefore rides on the possibility that any increase in the custodial sentence rate manages to target the 6 per cent that cause about 60 per cent of the crime (see Chapter 3). Only then is it realistic to suggest that a policy of improved detections would have a chance of reducing the 1,000 actual offences at the top of the funnel. Unfortunately, little research has been conducted to quantify the impact of targeted arrest strategies or more intelligence-driven tactics, and of course this assumes that (1) the increased detections will target the right offenders, and (2) the cost-benefits of this approach – one that places increased stress on the whole criminal justice system – outweigh other crime prevention or reduction tactics. Some research that does examine the impact of a general policy of increased arrests on the crime rate is discussed later in this chapter.

The challenge in targeting the criminal elite is that they tend to be

Table 8.1 Revised crime funnels exploring hypothetical changes. Note: decimal values shown for custodial sentence rates only

	Original crime funnel (decimal values shown)	10% increase prosecutions	25% increase in detections
Actual offences	1000	1000	1000
Reported to police	410	410	410
Recorded by police	287	287	287
Detected offences	75	75	93
Charged or summoned	37	41	47
Proceeded against at court	21	23	26
Found guilty	15	17	19
Custodial sentence	3.7	4.1	4.7

very elusive. With my colleagues George Rengert and Sanjoy Chakravorty (Rengert *et al.* 2005: 15; see also Reuter 1990), I have previously argued that one of the side effects of greater US law enforcement on the lower levels of the drug importation community has been inadvertently to develop a 'corps of experienced and expert smugglers who have been able to remove the inexperienced competition'. Even though many police officers profess to wanting to catch the criminal elite, they are constrained by an organisational system that rewards them for the volume of arrests rather than the quality of their captures, a system that returns police again and again to nicking whichever crook was unlucky enough to stick his head above the parapet just when police were looking for their next target. As a result, the smarter criminals have developed elaborate mechanisms to avoid capture (Jacobs 1993). For example, drug sellers and distributors employ a range of tactics to minimise the impact of police interdiction, including paying lookouts, cooperating between sellers and buyers to identify undercover police officers, using a constantly shifting 'linguistics code' to 'screen' potential customers, and employing business practices that minimise the potential for surveillance (Johnson and Natarajan 1995: 54). As a result of their observations of over 300 crack dealers, as well as interviews with over 120 of them, Johnson and Natarajan estimate that experienced and higher-level dealers can use a variety of strategies to minimise the risk of arrest to one for every thousand drug transactions or more.

Even when the tools for targeting the top of the criminal food chain are provided, they are sometimes ignored. Levi (2002) laments that anti-money laundering legislation is used, at best, modestly, and that conviction rates in the UK from suspicious transaction reports during the early 1990s were as low as one for every thousand suspicious reports. There is little evidence to suggest that the situation has improved today. Arrest and prosecution, while often seen as the only tool that the police and criminal justice system have, is regrettably an inefficient one when unfocused.

Estimating prevention benefits

An alternative to arrest and prosecution is to consider the benefits of a crime prevention policy. As opposed to addressing crime problems at the lower levels of the crime funnel, crime prevention is designed to work at the top of the funnel. While the number of crimes reported to police is only a small proportion of the actual offences, their geographic dispersion is an indication of the likely concentration of the larger 'dark figure' of crime (Chainey and Ratcliffe 2005). Therefore, the true value of offences reported to police may be as indicators to the bigger problem. From this, police can at least glimpse some of the 1,000 crimes that the community experience.

If it were possible to initiate a policy that had a 10 per cent reduction in actual offences that affect the public, the crime funnel could be used to estimate the impact on the criminal justice system. As shown in Table 8.2, the impact of a reduction in crime flows down the crime funnel. Therefore, reducing the number of offences has the corollary of reducing the crimes reported to police, the number recorded and detected by them, the number of people going through the courts, and the size of the jail population. A cost-effective outcome all round!

Crime prevention is therefore the key to long-term crime control, but greater crime prevention can also improve our ability to bring serious and prolific offenders to justice. The scenario above paints a picture of an approach to the crime problem that suggests smaller jail populations and fewer court delays. Swifter justice and greater availability of prison space increases capacity to remove prolific and serious offenders from the general population, and with fewer arrests police could concentrate on these serious, recidivist offenders.

Of course, there are potential threats to this model. For example, one current measure of success in policing is the number of arrests. A

Table 8.2 Revised crime funnel with 10 per cent crime prevention.
Note: decimal values shown for custodial sentence rates only

	Original crime funnel	10% decrease in actual crime
Actual offences	1000	900
Reported to police	410	369
Recorded by police	287	258
Detected offences	75	67
Charged or summoned	37	34
Proceeded against at court	21	19
Found guilty	15	14
Custodial sentence	3.7	3.4

preventative focus would reduce the number of offenders from which an officer can demonstrate worthiness for promotion. A change in police managerial practice may be required to resolve this issue; however, a greater threat comes from an absence of political will.

Lab (2004) points out in four succinct premises why there is a general lack of enthusiasm for prevention from policymakers. Politicians like programmes with:

- immediate results;
- focus on outcomes that can be counted;
- a sensationalist streak;
- an eye to the immediate problems of the day.

First, politicians look for immediate results that will get them re-elected; therefore, any solution must work within the timeframe of an election cycle. Unfortunately, crime prevention activities, 'particularly those that require major changes at the community and societal levels, often require a much longer time period to have an impact than that provided by the election cycle' (pp. 684-658). Secondly, politicians prefer programmes that focus on things that can easily be counted, and this often leads them to discount prevention to focus instead on arrest, prosecution and punishment. A further reason for a lack of interest in crime prevention is that politicians, encouraged by the media, prefer policies that are sensationalist and are easily conveyed in the sound bites that seem to constitute in-depth news reporting these days. The result? 'Policies to address serious and heinous offences will grab the attention of the media, while community prevention programs or projects to invigorate the job prospects in struggling communities will receive less attention. Crime prevention simply does not play well in a 15-second sound bite' (p. 685). Lab's final premise is that politicians and the public continually fixate on the issue of the moment rather than seeking to address the long-term and more meaningful problems that affect society. So in the interests of appearing new and invigorating, every new political administration 'needs (or wants) to look good or active. Thus, changes are made. Often those changes may simply be for the sake of change, not because existing policies or practices are bad or ineffective' (pp. 685–686).

While crime prevention is a stated aim of intelligence-led policing, the focus on prolific offenders reduce crime if the right four or five offenders that find themselves incarcerated are the same ones that are responsible for a significant proportion of the 1,000 crimes committed against the public. Further prevention benefits may flow from disrupting the activities of prolific offenders. However, this more intelligence-led approach to tackling the criminal leaders and specialists demands more of police analysts and executives, a challenge to which only some are now rising.

Reduction, disruption and prevention

If the aims of intelligence-led policing are the reduction, disruption and prevention of crime, how are these approaches to crime differentiated? Crime reduction is cognisant of the available resources and is considered as an action that brings 'net benefits after considering the impact of displacement and diffusion of benefits, fear of crime and the impact from other programmes that may have contributed to any specific crime reduction activity' (Chainey and Ratcliffe 2005: 19). Crime reduction is one of the most pragmatic approaches to fighting crime because it specifically looks for cost-effectiveness. As Don Weatherburn and his colleagues in Australia have estimated, burglary in New South Wales could be reduced by 10 per cent at the cost of increasing the number of burglars sentenced to incarceration by at least 34 per cent (Weatherburn *et al.* 2006). However, as the authors point out, the financial cost alone is estimated at millions of dollars, and comes with the attendant dampening effects that the number of guilty pleas may decline (increasing court costs), the number of people with prison records would increase (reducing long-term employability and resulting in longer criminal careers), and there are ethical considerations (the public may not accept more draconian sentences for cases of burglary). The research team concluded that, 'The evidence that prison stops a lot of crime is very strong. The cost-effectiveness of further investment in prison relative to other options for bringing down crime, however, is very unclear, not only for burglary but for all other offences as well' (p. 9).

Given a widespread disenchantment within policing as to the effectiveness of the legal system, it was not surprising that the term *disruption* has become increasingly common in the lexicon of police services. Using the example of organised crime groups or criminal businesses, EUROPOL explains that disruption 'occurs when the business is hampered for a period of time, normally as a result of law enforcement action, but is not permanently disabled' (EUROPOL 2006: 17). While it is a temporary measure to stall crime rather than eradicate it, disruption is a primary aim of a number of police agencies, especially those tasked with combating organised and serious crime. It has even become enshrined in formal government policy to combat organised crime, part of a triumvirate of new tactics: reducing profit opportunities, disrupting the businesses and their markets, and increasing the risk of interdiction (Home Office 2004).

Some questions immediately arise. For example, while a strategic aim of the Australian Crime Commission may be the 'disruption and deterrence of serious and organised crime through operations into federally relevant criminal activity in collaboration with law enforcement partners' (ACC 2004: 8), how is the success of this goal to be measured? Disruption (and/ or dismantling) of criminal syndicates is a performance measure for the agency; however, the criteria by which significant disruption is assessed is unclear. When HIDTA (high-intensity drug trafficking areas) personnel were asked exactly when a drug trafficking organisation was disrupted or dismantled, their answers were 'vague and inconsistent' (BOTEC 2001: 5). EUROPOL (2006) points out that disruption activities that do not dismantle a crime group have only a short-term benefit, if any at all, though they provide no evidence to corroborate this assertion and they do not suggest what sort of disruption might have a long-term impact. Does an organised crime group have to curtail all of its activities, or only certain ones? Does it have to shut down for a year, six months, or a few weeks? These questions elude many policymakers wishing to assess the merit of disruption in an intelligence-led policing framework (Harfield 2006).

Of greater concern is the reality that disruption is a tactic that effectively negates the legal system. I have argued in this book that while there is a role for the criminal justice system in locking up prolific offenders, over-reliance on the system to resolve general crime issues is a recipe for failure (see the crime funnel). Beyond prolific criminals and criminal gangs, disruption is often a realistic tactic when trying to frustrate criminal behaviour that is unlikely to be contained by legal means; however, it does remove police activity from judicial oversight. As such, there is always the potential for abuse, and so organisations that actively engage in disruption as a strategic tool should be especially careful to implement supervision and monitoring structures that enable crime disruption to take place while simultaneously being responsive to legal constraints.

Crime prevention involves any activity by an individual or group, public or private, which attempts to eliminate crime either before it occurs or before any additional activity results (Lab 1988). Some criminologists have also included activities designed to reduce fear of crime in their definitions of crime prevention. Primary prevention identifies conditions of the physical and social environment that create, precipitate or provide opportunities for criminal behaviour (Brantingham and Faust 1976). Secondary prevention aims to reduce risks associated with those people vulnerable to involvement in crime, and to ameliorate the chance of high-risk offenders developing more serious criminal activities. Tertiary prevention deals with actual offenders and involves 'intervening with the lives of these offenders in a manner that prevents them from committing other crimes and includes arrest and prosecution, reform and rehabilitation, and institutional education programmes' (Chainey and Ratcliffe 2005: 17). From an intelligence-led policing perspective, all three levels of prevention are accessible. The primary prevention level allows decision-makers to identify the systemic weaknesses that offenders exploit so that more strategic problem-solving can gain a foothold. The secondary level provides opportunities to identify priorities for resource allocation and targeting, and the third level deals with prevention benefits from the arrest and prosecution of high-risk, prolific and persistent offenders.

In the end, these distinctions are simply different methods to achieve the same end: relief from the ravages of crime in our communities. Where the distinctions assist is in helping decision-makers conceptualise different ways to achieve their goals. Regretfully, all of these activities take place within a wider institutional environment where, as identified in the previous section, crime prevention is often relegated to a lesser role. To maximise the benefits of crime prevention and disruption activities, analysts (and decision-makers themselves) have to view the institutional situation through the lens of a decision-maker and adjust accordingly. Therefore, the next section explores the decision-makers' perspective in greater detail.

The changing leadership role

The 3-i model stresses the need for the analyst to understand the position of leaders and decision-makers. The recent paradigms of policing, such as problem-oriented policing and intelligence-led policing, now require a different skill level of senior decision-makers from that previously demanded. For example, many police commanders have in the past been identified as promotion candidates through their detective abilities and their competence in a world dominated by case-specific challenges. Other observers have also noted the importance within policing of 'doing time'; being seen to put the hours in and to have spent many years in the service as a key requirement of police leadership (Silvestri 2006). Doing time is often perceived as more important than actual ability; some police departments have promotion structures so union-controlled and ineffective that promotion is reduced to a time-served function. In this environment, embracing change and being more in tune with new ideas, such as the principles of crime reduction or the mechanisms of intelligence-led policing, requires more effort than some senior police officers feel they need to invest. There is no causal mechanism to suggest that just being around a lot makes a commander a good decision-maker or helps them to be versed in what would work to reduce crime. For intelligence-led policing to succeed, this may be a change that has to be addressed soon.

Other changes within law enforcement may help the development of intelligence-led policing. Police executives are now used to less autocratic and more democratic workplaces. Such new approaches to the work environment provide opportunities for officers with initiative, although the traditional approaches are heavily entrenched within policing, where an autocratic model predominates (Dupont 2003). While articulate academic debate demands that police leadership embrace an evidence-based and intelligence-led policing framework, there are other forces at play: 'The striking advances of an economic "rationality" and a new managerialism in policing have tended to obscure the fact that police leaders and managers manifest and sustain other rationalities in their leadership practices' (Adlam 2002). As Dupont's research and recorded interviews with Australian police commissioners show, time is required for senior officers and their staff to adapt to a new regime. As one commissioner said,

> We moved right away from a paramilitary structure to a much more flexible evolved team structure. ... Even those people who like the idea of [reform] were threatened by it, because they only have experienced, and are used to, total command and control and people who would always complain about not being given enough autonomy were nervous about the responsibilities that went with it. And in fairness to them, it took me a while to really appreciate the fact that they had not been trained or prepared for the acceptance of them. (quoted in Dupont 2003: 4)

Just as it takes time to adjust to new ways of doing business, new conceptual frameworks such as intelligence-led policing require an adjustment period. In terms of having an impact on crime, this is certainly the case. As a district commander I interviewed in New Zealand observed, 'We have people in leadership and management positions who were never expected to do the job I'm asking them to do' (quoted in Ratcliffe 2005: 449). Most police commanders have been groomed for leadership positions by subjecting them to training and experiences that are not related to crime reduction. Requiring decision-makers to understand the subtleties of what works and what does not work in crime prevention and crime reduction is akin to teaching them mathematics and then subjecting them to a geography test. I feel that we simply have not prepared the command levels of policing for the role they are being asked to perform.

As a result, law enforcement leadership has rarely demonstrated much enthusiasm for prevention. All levels of crime policy stress a bias for enforcement action as a first step, and not only at the local level. Much of the discourse regarding organised crime, and especially transnational organised crime, has been restricted to an enforcement approach, and little attention has been paid to mechanisms that would promote crime prevention or reduction (Sheptycki 2005).

Fortunately, a few leaders are starting to see beyond a preoccupation with arrests and see the benefits of a more strategic and intelligence-centric view. After moving to an intelligence-led policing philosophy and organisational framework, a senior commander in the NJSP said, 'It's not about numbers and arrests, it is about having an impact on the criminal entity. … In the past a lot of guys, myself being one of them, were rewarded by the number of scalps brought in. Now, I never ask for quantity of drugs or number of arrests. But I look at the number of intelligence entries going on to [the intelligence database]' (quoted in Ratcliffe and Guidetti 2008).

Viewpoint

The leadership role in intelligence-led policing

Rick Fuentes

For the New Jersey State Police (NJSP), the aftermath of 9/11 added a critical mission of homeland security to the day-to-day demands of a hometown public safety mission. Initially the new mission incurred considerable and costly overtime, as well as distractions from significant criminal investigations and highway traffic safety initiatives that could not be resolved by troopers thinned out and stretched along multiple fronts of responsibility. It became obvious that the old way of doing business was a poor fit with the post 9/11 operating environment.

For our Investigations Branch, the old way of doing business prioritized investigations and allocated personnel towards targets of opportunity. Advantage went to the leaders of criminal groups, the Mafioso, drug traffickers and the heads of criminal street gangs, who were well-insulated by layer upon layer of functionaries too visible and too tempting for the police to ignore. To maximize results and impact, architectural changes were made to the Investigations Branch and we began to focus upon gathering and analyzing information on those criminals and groups that had the greatest impact upon crime and quality of life in New Jersey. Breaking hard with decades of traditional techniques and investigative strategies, the NJSP adopted intelligence-led policing as its new operating system and multitasking process. Not simply confined to the realm of criminal investigations, intelligence-led policing has a much broader application to public safety. It offers a robust approach to traffic safety, absorbing information from accident reports and narratives on time of day, weather, location, road condition, severity of crash, contributing factors such as drugs or alcohol impairment and extent of injuries or fatalities.

Now, every commander is responsible for harvesting the information generated by subordinates and routing that information for analysis. The output is the development of current, early warning or long-range strategic intelligence through analysis. The intelligence product created by this process drives the priorities of the commanders through increased situational awareness of the operating environment.

For instance, gang surveys, informant information, and intelligence received from outside sources, are used to rank order the most violent gangs in the state. With this report in hand, commanders can most effectively allocate resources, reduce crime and create better, safer communities by investigation, enforcement and prosecution of gangs in that order. Intelligence-led policing creates a Darwinian paradigm for criminal groups, wherein the most violent groups are rank-ordered and thereby select themselves out of the herd for aggressive police attention. Ironically, the most violent gangs unwittingly compete for scarce police resources that would otherwise have focused upon the 'low hanging fruit'. Culling the criminal herd of its most aggressive members is one of the most powerful utilities of using investigative priorities grounded in intelligence-led policing.

Not only have we integrated our analysts into the heart of decision-making, but in addition, the intelligence products from the New Jersey Regional Operations Intelligence Center are used to guide policy decisions on the topical issues of the day. This continues to challenge not only leaders to be more intelligence-focused, but also analysts to step up with a more strategic product. This one change has had training implications for analysts, but especially for management. We are now heavily committed to managerial training and education to help our cadre of commanders become the intelligence-led, evidence-based leaders of the future.

As the first police organisation in the United States to provide an on-line guide to intelligence-led policing, we look forward to sharing our experiences with colleagues around the country. It is important to note, however, that the New Jersey State Police is still engaged in the process of learning and expanding intelligence-led policing within our organisation. Our recent expansion of the model throughout the whole organisation requires continual monitoring and encouragement to succeed. It is often easy for managers doing a difficult job under stressful circumstances to slip back into the comfortable and the familiar. But with encouragement and reinforcement of the core principles of intelligence-led policing they can and will develop the flexibility and versatility that intelligence-led policing demands of them, and for which they were selected and promoted. And the winners will be the people of the State of New Jersey.

Colonel Rick Fuentes was named the 14th Superintendent of the New Jersey State Police in 2003. A career police officer since 1978, he is currently the General Chair of the State and Provincial Division of the International Association of Chiefs of Police.

Steering the rowers in the right direction

Various analogies have been applied to the security governance field, the most common of which is the distinction between those that do the steering and those that do the rowing (Wood and Shearing 2007). Analysts and decision-makers wanting to have an impact on crime should seek to identify those doing the steering. Sometimes the middle-ranking officers with local leadership roles are steering in the wrong direction; an intelligence analyst in New Zealand lamented that in her attempt to drive more operational use of crime intelligence, 'We have a real blockage with some leaders, such as the Sergeants in the teams and sections' (quoted in Ratcliffe 2005: 445). One challenge is therefore to bring all levels of the police service to support the concepts of intelligence-led policing.

Some leaders are particularly resistant to prevention simply through their formal training. This is especially the case where chief law enforcement officers have a legal background rather than a criminological or crime preventative one. In the US, for example, the chief law enforcement officer for a county is often the prosecutor or district attorney, and their lawyer training blinkers them to any possibilities beyond application of the law. There is therefore a tendency to view arrest and prosecution, or changes to the law, as not only the best but the only solution to crime problems. They simply have not been exposed to crime prevention as a viable option. The move from prosecuting individual cases to one of managerial oversight of the whole crime issue on promotion to a leadership role exposes prosecutors to the broader and more complex nature of endemic problems; these problems often have their roots in structural and ecological stresses within neighbourhoods and communities, or are caused by failing to address rampant criminal opportunities. As cops know, many criminal opportunities will continue to be exploited by offenders until the opportunities are closed down, irrespective of the number of prosecutions pushed through the courts.

It may be necessary for analysts and decision-makers to formulate a long-term plan to instil a culture that is more evidence-based if crime intelligence products are to have the impact anticipated. Although the crime funnel would suggest a more preventative approach, and 'Although the gradual acceptance of prevention as the primary purpose of intelligence may precipitate improvement, law enforcement has a long history of strategies that respond to a current problem but rarely prevent or control an emerging or anticipated threat' (Higgins 2004: 72). Achieving a more strategic viewpoint is difficult in an environment where feuding barons spend much of their time seeking their own advantage rather than working collectively to reduce crime. Writing about early Tasking and Coordinating Groups used by the NIM, Tim John and Mike Maguire noted that unless the meetings were chaired effectively, they deteriorated into a scramble for the available resources, and 'personality rather than evidence from products was most likely to prevail' (John and Maguire 2003: 51). If intelligence products are to garner the attention it is hoped they deserve, greater store must be placed on the power of evidence and evaluation to drive objective, strategically focused decision-making. It may be that the steerers need to be steered correctly.

The police impact on crime

Whether crime intelligence analysts are working to support police commanders or community activists, whenever the conversation turns to crime solutions, the first question is often, 'What can be done?' The second question is usually, 'What can the police do?' It is therefore beholden on analysts to have at least a basic understanding of the impact of commonly discussed strategies. It is clearly beyond the scope of this book to summarise all of the research that has been conducted on crime prevention and reduction strategies. I will therefore restrict this section to the research most relevant to police decision-makers and analysts and, rather than bombard the reader with a daunting list of references, confine the literature reviewed to a number of key studies. We start with increasing police numbers and offender targeting strategies.

Does police targeting prevent crime?

When placed under pressure at Compstat meetings, police commanders will often respond by increasing patrols in a high-crime area, especially if the case can be put for more resources to staff the patrols (Willis *et al.* 2003). While the Kansas City Preventative Patrol Experiment (Kelling *et al.* (1974), though criticised on methodological grounds by, for example, Sherman (1986)) quashed the notion that random patrols are effective at preventing crime, more recent studies have examined the impact of police on crime from different angles.

Marvell and Moody (1996) examined US crime data and police numbers for 49 states and 56 cities. The researchers wished to determine whether there is a relationship between crime rates and the number of officers in a city or state. They found that while increasing crime did increase government hiring of officers, the magnitude of the impact of crime on police hiring was small. For every 10 per cent increase in reported crime, the average increase in police numbers was only 1.5 per cent – quantitative evidence of the demand gap from Chapter 2. They also determined that a 10 per cent increase in police numbers would, on average, result in a 3 per cent reduction in the major crime types for a city. The city figures were more impressive than the state-wide figures, and the impact of police was different across crime types, but the general point does well to dismiss the common notion that police do not prevent crime (see, for example, Bayley 1994b). Readers should be cautious of extrapolating this research too far; Eck and Maguire's meta-analysis of the research on police strength and violent crime found that 'hiring more police officers did not play an independent or consistent role in reducing violent crime in the United States' (Eck and Maguire 2000: 217). These research studies throw some light on the value of untargeted variation in police numbers, but the aim of intelligence-led policing is to target better *available* resources. It may be that the value of police officers is not in how many we have, but *how* they are employed.

There are some interesting studies that have looked at the benefits of concentrating law enforcement resources. Focusing on police patrols at 100 crime hot spots in Minneapolis, and building on a data set of over 6,000 observations by nearly 30 trained observers over a 1-year period, researchers found that the presence of police officers alone – irrespective of their activity – had a dampening effect on criminality (Koper 1995). Moreover, the presence of an officer had a residual deterrence effect (Sherman 1990) after the officer left. Koper found that officers must stop for a minimum of 10 minutes at a crime hot spot for there to be any lasting effect, but, interestingly, the benefits of waiting at the hot spot beyond 14–15 minutes diminished as time spent at the hot spot increased. The study shows that police can 'maximize crime and disorder reduction at hot spots by making proactive, medium-length stops at these locations on a random, intermittent basis' (p. 668). In another study in Kansas City, overtime was used to provide for two, two-officer patrol cars to concentrate on a high-gun-crime beat for 29 weeks. The officers performed a number of high-visibility activities, including vehicle and pedestrian checks, conducted with the aim of finding firearms and preventing gun violence. According to Sherman and colleagues (1995), in the first six months 45 per cent of firearms were recovered when offenders were searched on arrest, 21 per cent of guns were observed in plain view by officers, and 34 per cent were found when the outside of offenders' clothes was patted down as an officer safety precaution (in the US this is commonly termed a *Terry stop and frisk* or, more commonly, a *Terry stop*, and is based on the US Supreme Court case of a *Terry v. Ohio*, 392 U.S. 1, 1968). As a result, gun seizures increased more than 65 per cent while gun crime was cut in half. One gun was found for every 28 traffic stops, and for every gun seized more than two gun crimes were prevented.

However, the news is not always good. First, the experiments conducted in the previous paragraph have not been replicated in substantial numbers such that we can place complete confidence in these methods. It may be that the gun reductions seen in Kansas City would not occur in Philadelphia or Nottingham. Secondly, a substantive review of the literature on policing for crime prevention found that while there appear to be substantial benefits from 'focusing scarce arrest resources on high risk people, places, offences and times', this does not hold so well for drug markets and drug corners (Sherman *et al.* 1998). The review concluded that while increased directed patrols at street-corner hot spots of crime and proactive arrests of serious repeat offenders were effective ways to prevent crime, arrests of some juveniles for minor offences, drug market arrests and community policing with no clear crime-risk factor focus were not effective.

These studies suggest that while generally increasing numbers of police can help, it is more useful to consider *how* officers are deployed. Random patrol is not an effective tactic to reduce crime, but more focused tactics that are drawn from an evidence base (a fundamental component of intelligence-led policing) can have crime prevention benefits beyond the amount of time officers spend at a crime hot spot. These residual benefits extending beyond the time that the officers are actively employed are essential in getting value for money from preventative policing. Longer-term effects have been attained when police mix increased enforcement strategies with preventative work to coerce or encourage local businesses to assist with enforcement aims. While drug market arrests do not seem to work on their own, drug markets appear vulnerable when civil code violations and nuisance legislation are applied to the properties where dealers gather, at least in reducing disorder-related calls for service (Green 1995; Weisburd and Green 1995). A recent review of the existing research found that 'proactive interventions involving partnerships between the police and third parties and/or community entities appear to be more effective at reducing both drug and nondrug problems in drug problem places than are reactive/directed approaches' (Mazerolle *et al.* 2007b: 115; see also Mazerolle *et al.* 2007c).

Does increasing arrests reduce crime?

As we found in an earlier chapter, crime is highly concentrated in certain locations, and a small percentage of the population are responsible for a significant percentage of the crime – often against the same victim (Everson 2003). Can this knowledge be turned into an operational strategy? As we shall see, there are numerous encouraging examples.

In Australia, New South Wales Police Commissioner Peter Ryan started a Compstat-like process (called Operation and Crime Review, or OCR) that encouraged local police commanders to focus on crime hot spots and hot times, spend more time searching people for illegal weapons, and target recidivist offenders. Within six months, the prison population began to rise and 18 months after the start of OCR had risen by 13 per cent, swelled to a degree by police activity that targeted people with both outstanding warrants and criminal records (Chilvers and Weatherburn 2001b). Chilvers and Weatherburn were able to determine not only that the introduction of the OCR process reduced crime, but also that the reduction in crime was attributable to the increased arrest rate rather than other extraneous factors. Further analysis allowed the research team to estimate that a burglary was prevented for every two arrests, a vehicle theft was prevented for every five arrests, and a robbery was prevented for every 30 arrests (Chilvers and Weatherburn 2001a: 11).

In another example from one part of the Killingbeck area of Leeds (UK), police identified the key burglars that were targeting the neighbourhood and commenced a focused detection and incapacitation strategy. Offenders were chosen who were known to be prolific burglars, not currently in custody, and who were suspected of committing numerous offences. This intelligence-led strategy was supported by a consolidation phase that emphasised crime prevention activities, such as target hardening, educating elderly people about the potential risks of burglary by deception, and youth outreach programmes (Farrell et al. 1998). As a result, residential burglary fell by 60 per cent, with no evidence of displacement and some evidence for a diffusion of benefits to surrounding areas.

However, it should not be assumed that offender targeting is always a successful strategy. In one UK police force, local intelligence officers nominated 46 offenders that they deemed were criminally active in the local area. When the historical crime patterns and the incarceration rates going back 19 months were examined, it was found that the incarceration rate of these 46 did not, in general, appear to affect significantly the crime rates in the police area (though one police sub-area did see a significant reduction when higher numbers of car thieves were in jail) (Townsley and Pease 2002). The difficulty with this research is that it is difficult to establish whether the lack of crime reduction was due to a poor choice of targets from the intelligence officers, whether 46 was too small an offender pool to have a significant impact, or whether targeting offenders does not work. At least, the findings regarding vehicle crime were encouraging; the more car thieves incarcerated, the lower the car crime rate. In Canberra, officers of the Australian Federal Police conducting Operation Anchorage were able to target recidivist burglars and incarcerate them to an extent that, although the police operation lasted for 18 weeks, the crime reduction benefits lasted a further 45 weeks before burglary reached the pre-operation rate (Makkai et al. 2004). Operation Anchorage is a particularly illuminating example, and I will discuss this research further as a case study in the next chapter.

By targeting over 20 chronic drug dealers with long criminal histories, the police in Brightwood, Indianapolis (Indiana) were able to make a number of arrests and gain long-term jail sentences for many. This operation is credited with a two-year reduction in calls for service in the neighbourhood (Nunn *et al.* 2006). It may be that in a smaller neighbourhood setting, the incarceration of about 1 per cent of the males aged 14–29 provided the required tipping point to effect long-term change in the neighbourhood.

In summary, I suggested earlier that the crime funnel is structured such that there is no guarantee that increasing efficiency in a lower component of the model would improve matters at the top of the funnel. The evidence appears to support the position that increasing random arrests may do little to prevent or reduce crime; however, targeted arrests might have a significant crime reduction potential.

Intelligence-led crime reduction

As with the drug market and the Leeds studies mentioned above, police strategies appear to be most effective when combined with other problem-solving and preventative tactics. Given the broad assortment of criminogenic factors (for a concise summary, see Weatherburn 2001) – most of which are beyond the power of the police to influence directly – it would appear prudent for police to pool resources with agencies that have a more direct capacity. This may be the thinking behind the British government's enthusiasm for more partnership work and collaborative problem-solving. A greater focus on problem-solving is emanating not only from the street level, where problem-oriented policing was originally intended to function, but also from the high policing domain. An example comes from the Serious Organised Crime Agency in the UK, where 'the vision the Government has set for the new Agency is far closer to problem-solving "policing" in the sense of sustaining safer communities than the "law enforcement" paradigm of criminal investigation inherent in the modern police service with its performance emphasis on detections and prosecutions' (Harfield 2006: 747).

Earlier in the book, I defined intelligence-led policing as a business model and managerial philosophy where data analysis and crime intelligence are pivotal to an objective, decision-making framework that facilitates crime and problem reduction, disruption and prevention through both *strategic management* and effective enforcement strategies that target prolific and serious offenders (emphasis added). A lengthy meta-analysis conducted by a team organised through the University of Maryland (Sherman *et al.* 1998) concluded that incapacitating offenders who continue to commit crimes at high rates is a successful strategic management tactic for long-term crime reduction. Beneficial non-enforcement options include family therapy by clinical staff for delinquent and pre-delinquent youth, short-term vocational training programmes for older male ex-offenders no longer involved in the criminal justice system, and prison-based therapeutic community treatment of drug-involved offenders. Promising tactics (but that have to be evaluated further) include gang violence prevention focused on reducing gang cohesion; battered women's shelters for women who take other steps to change their lives; housing dispersion programmes; Enterprise Zones; and intensive, residential training programmes for at-risk youth. Strategies that *do not* appear to work include community mobilisation against crime, in high-crime, inner-city poverty areas; gun buy-back programmes operated without geographic limitations on gun sources; summer job or subsidised work programmes for at-risk youth; short-term, non-residential training programmes for at-risk youth; and emphasised specific deterrence such as shock probation and Scared Straight. In fact, a recent review for the Campbell Collaboration found that Scared Straight programmes not only fail to deter young people from committing crime but are actually correlated with increases in offending behaviour (Petrosino *et al.* 2003).

For more specific help, the most useful source of what works in strategic problem-solving comes from the accumulated research conducted on problem-oriented policing strategies, housed at the Center for Problem Oriented Policing (www.popcenter.org). Their free and downloadable response guides, problem-specific guides, and problem-solving tool guides are among the most readable and problem-specific available. The publication 'Crime Analysis for Problem Solvers' is not only one of the most practical guides to analysis, but has also been translated into numerous languages. There are also useful reviews housed with the Campbell Collaboration (www.campbellcollaboration.org). Once police start using their knowledge and intelligence resources in conjunction with these research summaries to influence outside agencies and impact crime vicariously by broadening the range of crime reduction possibilities, it might be possible to move from intelligence-led policing to a more inclusive crime control model of intelligence-led crime reduction (Ratcliffe 2003).

Summary

Understanding the client's business is hugely important in the modern policing arena, given that a police chief makes decisions framed within a broader multiagency governance model with agencies that seek to push police in often conflicting directions. Solutions that will impact on the criminal environment need to be framed within the context of what will be most palatable. Analysts should appreciate that:

Police agencies are steered by a complex array of citizen's groups, police quasi-unions, civilian review boards, various departments of municipal, state-provincial, national and transnational governance, as well as private corporate interests and the mass media. All compete to set the direction and tone of social controlling, using the tools available to them. The result is that policing policy is in disarray. (Sheptycki 2005: 5)

In this environment, crime prevention can appear weak or at least unsexy, even though the benefit of attacking the crime funnel at the top rather than closer to the bottom appears clear when explained to decision-makers. In the end, a combination of enforcement action and prevention are likely to appeal most to decision-makers, be they local commanders in a rural community or key players in the counter-terrorism arena:

> Whether the motivation is religious fundamentalism, anti-government sentiment, or the disaffected loner, radicalized groups or individuals are increasingly perpetrating terrorism. A substantial attack upon U.S. soil is increasingly likely. The answer rests with prevention. ...The only way to prevent radicalization is to end the conditions that foster it. When efforts at prevention are unsuccessful or impractical, a fully trained and seamlessly integrated public safety force is required to recognize preincident indicators and develop interdiction, disruption, or arrest strategies. (Bratton 2007: 6-7)

In the process of demonstrating which tactics analysts could suggest to decision-makers, I have had to be selective in finding key research studies and have inevitably omitted a wealth of research. Such are the constraints of the book; however, useful summaries of research findings can be found in the appendices of reports written for the Center for Problem-Oriented Policing. For example, when I wrote the Center's CCTV guide, I reviewed 20 studies in depth, cited a further 10 in a second appendix, and read dozens of others while preparing the study (Ratcliffe 2006). For analysts, understanding the range of studies that have taken place on an issue is valuable when they make recommendations to decision-makers.

Concerning the lack of training for decision-makers, it is interesting that there are similarities between intelligence-led policing and other policing innovations. As has been noted in the case of Compstat in the Lowell Police Department (but is easily conceptualised to the intelligence-led policing arena), the introduction of a new approach provided 'a classic case of creating a program for which department personnel received relatively little preparation. The prior career experiences of the sector captains did not prepare them well for developing organizational flexibility, data-driven decision making, and innovative problem solving. They received virtually no formal training in these areas before implementation, so they had to adapt and learn on the fly' (Willis *et al.* 2003: 59). If intelligence-led policing is to succeed and develop as the central paradigm of policing in the twenty-first century, then addressing training in crime prevention practice for not only analysts but also police commanders and key decision-makers in the criminal justice system is going to be crucial and may very well be the key determinant in deciding the future of intelligence-led policing.

9

Evaluating intelligence-led policing

> The innovation, if there is one, in Intelligence Led Policing is to realise that the random patrolling of the uniformed officer and the post hoc investigations of the detective are very inefficient methods of dealing with crime and disorder. The police are becoming more proactive in targeting the offender and the potential offender rather than waiting for an offence to be committed and then responding. The difficulty with this approach is that the gathering and analysis of intelligence is a complex and time-consuming activity which demands considerable resources to produce tangible results. It is yet to be demonstrated to be an efficient and cost-effective method of dealing with the type of problems which regularly mar the lives of ordinary citizens as they go about their business. (Sharp 2005: 455)

Efficiency and cost-effectiveness, as mentioned by Sharp above, have been among the driving forces for intelligence-led policing from the outset. If the move towards a more judicious and rational use of police resources and energies is expected to produce tangible results, how does one show that to be the case? Evaluation is essential to the development of any crime reduction strategy, and Don Weatherburn (2004: 36–38) identified five features of a rational approach to crime control:

- adequate investment in measuring and monitoring;
- open access to crime and justice information;
- reliance on evidence in the development of policy;
- commitment to rigorous evaluation;
- a flexible and eclectic approach to control.

Measuring and monitoring crime patterns (Weatherburn's first feature) is essential as a first stage in determining whether policies are successful in combating crime. It also provides government with evidence to address the claims of the more reactionary media and public. Within this framework, the second feature (allowing open access to information) can prevent claims that the police are 'cooking the books' and lay a framework for the sort of honest debate about crime that is required in a democracy. Weatherburn's third feature (evidence-based policymaking) should be an essential function of good government. In other words, before embarking on a new crusade, politicians and other decision-makers should be aware of the research that can inform them of what works and what does not work to reduce particular crime problems. Rigorous evaluation (Weatherburn's fourth feature) is essential if decision-makers are to know whether they have been successful in preventing crime – and that is the subject of this chapter. Finally, without a broader approach to crime control, one that is devoid of ideology or a desire to fixate on one particular part of the criminal justice system, truly imaginative crime reduction is unlikely to occur. As can be seen from Weatherburn's list, evaluation is essential not only to inform existing operations, but also to influence the path of future evidence-based policies.

It might seem strange to dedicate a complete chapter to the idea of evaluating intelligence-led policing, but Gloria Laycock (2001a) is right that a change is under way within policing, a change that is featuring a greater focus on crime reduction as an outcome, greater professionalisation of police, a developing body of knowledge, and a move towards more data- and information-based problem-solving.

The aim of this chapter is to examine the concepts involved in evaluation research and the skills necessary to conduct evaluations. It also looks at the practice of evaluations by drawing on a number of case studies, starting with Operation Vendas and Operation Safe Streets. The chapter also scrutinises the evaluation of Operation Anchorage, a major intelligence-led, burglary-reduction operation conducted in the Australian capital, Canberra, because it contains many key points regarding intelligence-led policing. The remainder of the chapter explores different ways of measuring success, with particular attention paid to the difficulty of measuring disruption and the problems of performance indicators for the future development of intelligence-led policing.

Evaluation concepts and practice

While it may seem complicated, at a very basic level evaluation boils down to two questions: 'Did you get what you expected?' and 'Compared to what?' (Maxfield 2001). The first question asks whether a programme had the impact that it was designed to have, such as reducing drug crime or reducing the recidivism of a group of offenders. The second question addresses an appropriate comparison framework to establish some confidence in the benefit of the programme. One could easily extend this concept to include the cost-effectiveness of the programme.

For example, while research in Australia suggests that increased incarceration can reduce burglary (Weatherburn *et al*. 2006), is it the most cost-effective approach? To Maxfield's two questions, we could add a coda to the first and reframe it slightly. When asking, 'Did you get what you expected?' it is reasonable to ask this not just of the outcome, but also of the programme itself. For example, would one's view of a programme change if it were discovered that the people in charge of the evaluated programme did not know where the crime problem was concentrated?

From a conceptual standpoint, with every operation there is a distinction between the tactics employed and the conceptual framework in which those tactics are selected, and therefore the next section addresses the need to clarify exactly what is to be evaluated.

What are we evaluating?

While particular tactics are often associated with intelligence-led policing, the success of tactics that result from decisions made by senior management is not necessarily indicative of the success of intelligence-led policing. As explained earlier, intelligence-led policing is not a tactic in the way saturation patrolling is, nor is it a crime reduction strategy in the way that situational crime prevention is. It is primarily a business model and information-management process that allows police commanders to understand crime problems in a more strategic manner, and thus make more informed decisions to combat criminality. Within the National Intelligence Model (NIM) these informed decisions are usually gleaned from a strategic assessment report. Traditional evaluation of strategic products is particularly challenging, given that a strategic assessment is not an outcome in itself; as Rogers (1998: 24) points out, its 'meaning and value derives from the contribution it makes to the success of other activities'.

In an intelligence-led policing environment, it is therefore possible that the information processes work well, but the police commander receiving good intelligence makes a poor decision on tactics to resolve the crime problem. In this scenario, the conceptual model epitomised by the 3-i model works – at least until the point of the decision-maker having an impact on the criminal environment. In the end, for the success of intelligence-led policing to be truly assessed, it is necessary to evaluate both the organisational and informational structures that form the 3-i model, as well as the crime reduction strategies and tactics that flow from an intelligence-led decision-making process. Collectively, the interpretation of the criminal environment, the influence on decision-makers, and the impact on the criminal environment all constitute the business model of intelligence-led policing, and all should be assessed for their effectiveness.

Types of evaluations

There are two main types of evaluation of interest; *outcome* and *process* evaluations. An *outcome evaluation* is an assessment that explores whether a programme had the desired effect, such as 'was crime reduced?' or 'was an organised crime group disrupted?' These appraisals of crime reduction programmes are increasingly common as a result of greater access to police data. For example, Compstat is heavily oriented to reducing recorded crime as a measure of success, and evaluation is made possible because police departments record and monitor local crime levels. Although the evaluation sophistication – if it can be termed as such – is fairly basic and short-term, Compstat does pressure police management to be more objective in their assessment of success and to develop a more evidence-based approach to crime control. However, in terms of the broader problems of crime and the policing response, most rigorous outcome evaluations have been conducted by academics rather than internally by police departments. As Herman Goldstein laments, many police departments lack the skill to conduct rigorous evaluation, there is little connection with the academic world who could help in this venture, and there is little pressure either from outside the police or from police leadership to effect a more informed policing field (Goldstein 2003).

Another reason for a lack of internally driven evaluation is that police operations are often initiated with little thought for the broader operational aims and objectives. A number of times I have been asked to conduct an evaluation of a police operation, only to find that opinions within the police department differed as to what the operation was supposed to do. Sometimes the stated operational aims are not directly measurable with the data available, making an effective evaluation essentially impossible.

Even when it is possible to conduct an outcome evaluation, it is often vital to conduct a *process evaluation* to determine why a programme worked or failed. A process evaluation allows a researcher to understand why programmes apparently succeed or fail by examining the underlying processes of what took place during a crime reduction initiative. Process evaluations are especially important for emerging concepts such as intelligence-led policing. For example, a critic might determine that recorded crime has not reduced in an area where the police service claims to be operating an intelligence-led policing model. However, is the fault with the model, or with the way that intelligence-led policing is being implemented? Cope's (2004) qualitative research in two UK police forces found that officers had difficulty in accepting recommendations from civilian police analysts, officers lacked sufficient understanding of analysis to ask the right questions, and crime intelligence products were often ignored when planning operations but were requested afterwards to justify the operations. This is hardly the model of operation that the British architects of intelligence-led policing laid out, and is more indicative of a problem of implementation rather than conceptual design. Process evaluations are therefore important in understanding how programmes work.

Operation Vendas and Operation Safe Streets

As an example of both process and outcome evaluations, a good case comes from Operation Vendas. In three command districts of the Australian state of New South Wales, Operation Vendas sought to increase the risk and speed of capture for offenders by boosting the volume of forensic evidence collection and reducing the time to get samples analysed (Jones and Weatherburn 2004). The idea for Operation Vendas stemmed from a smaller-scale operation in the Bankstown neighbourhood in Sydney, an operation that was lauded as a success internally but was not verified by robust evaluation. Operation Vendas attempted to have crime scene officers visit every single burglary scene and attend to every recovered stolen car in the three command areas for six months. Unfortunately, the outcome evaluation found that the operation was not successful in reducing either burglaries or vehicle thefts, and that the rate of people charged with these crimes did not increase either. So why was the programme unsuccessful?

The answer is found in the process evaluation. While interviewing investigators, analysts and other personnel, the researchers discovered that at one police command the Operation Vendas cases were allocated to investigators with quite limited experience, and that part way through the operation the focus at that area changed from rapid arrest and charging to a more sedate approach of preparing better court evidence. In another area, police had already prioritised the collection of forensic evidence, so it would have been difficult to record an increase in evidence gathering at that location. Furthermore, the stated aim of attending 100 per cent of the crime scenes was never achieved; 60–80 per cent of burglary scenes were attended, and 50–70 per cent of recovered stolen vehicles were examined. Furthermore, for part of the operation, patrol officers were not requesting forensic examination because they had not been informed of the aims of the operation. Finally, a lack of forensic resources was also a factor. One area lacked digital cameras to record evidence, and the analytical laboratory was not sufficiently resourced to provide the turnaround required to provide a rapid capture of an identified offender.

From just the outcome evaluation, one might be tempted to conclude that increasing the speed and scope of forensic examinations was not a suitable tactic to reduce property crime. However, as the process evaluation shows, the actual stated policy of the operation was never fully implemented. It may yet be that a policy of greater forensic engagement may reduce crime in the right context, but it was never fully implemented in Vendas.

A second example comes from Philadelphia. In April 2002, to the surprise of many drug dealers, the Philadelphia Police Department placed officers on static permanent assignment right in the middle of the worst street drug markets in the city; out in force and out on foot. The police had begun Operation Safe Streets, and drug dealers on at least 200 street corners found they had attracted a permanent police presence. The operation had quite a localised affect in the immediate vicinity of the drug corners (Lawton *et al.* 2005). Lawton and colleagues report that areas within a tenth of a mile of the officers' positions experienced less crime. While there was also some displacement of about 23 per cent of drug activity to neighbouring areas, this still resulted in a substantial net gain in terms of reduced drug activity. And the displaced drug activity often moved indoors, thus reducing the visible evidence of drug crime from the streets; analysis of anonymous narcotics tips indicated a significant shift to indoor activity as a result of Operation Safe Streets (Rengert *et al.* 2005), as shown in Figure 9.1. The operation, however, did not significantly reduce city-wide homicide, violent crime or drug crime.

While no formal process evaluation took place and the work of Lawton and colleagues was not sanctioned by the police department, a greater understanding of what really took place on the ground is helpful in figuring out why crime in the city did not fall significantly. Giannetti (2007) reports

Figure 9.1 Change in the structure of drug markets in Philadelphia as a result of Operation Safe Streets, sourced from the number of anonymous narcotics tips and whether the tip related to an indoor or outdoor drug problem (adapted from Rengert *et al.* 2005: 21)

that a considerable degree of what Sherman (1990) refers to as *crackdown decay* took place over the course of Operation Safe Streets. After a while, the officers assigned to corners began to accept emergency calls away from their corners, and assigned Safe Streets foot patrols reverted to roving vehicle patrols. These changes resulted in a decrease in the volume of information being conveyed to narcotics unit intelligence officers. Furthermore, the incentive to arrest was removed. This was because officers who were used to receiving overtime pay for arrests and subsequent court appearances were guaranteed to receive the overtime that came with Operation Safe Streets. Thus, the value of the programme began to wane within a couple of months of the start of the operation.

Evaluation skills

All of these example studies suggest that a high level of analytical dexterity is necessary to conduct robust and rigorous quantitative evaluations, using skills such as proficiency in non-parametric and regression interpretation (Jones and Weatherburn 2004) and spatial analysis (Bowers and Johnson 2003). One advanced technique is a form of time series analysis. ARIMA interrupted time series analysis has been used to evaluate not only the impact of a crackdown on street-corner drug markets (Lawton *et al.* 2005) but also the impact of arrest rates on crime (Chamlin 1991), police attempts to reduce vehicle theft by conducting surveillance of vehicle dumping sites (Krimmel and Mele 1998), an intelligence-led burglary reduction operation (Ratcliffe 2002b; Makkai *et al.*); Compstat (Mazerolle *et al.* 2007a), and the impact of a police sting operation to catch property offenders (Langworthy 1989). Interrupted time series analysis, like many advanced techniques, usually remains in the domain of academic departments rather than police analytical units. These methods are usually taught in advanced postgraduate classes in criminal justice and criminology (if taught at all), and they require specialised software. So, while everyone agrees that the ability to do advanced types of evaluation analysis should be vested within police agencies, the practicality of getting that skill level into departments remains a challenge.

Spatial analysis and crime mapping have also become central to the analytical needs of many police departments, and if we are not there already, 'quite soon, crime mapping will become as much an essential tool of criminological research as statistical analysis is at present' (Clarke 2004: 60). While an increasing number of analysts are learning spatial analysis skills, techniques that are deemed central to intelligence-led policing and to any data-driven crime control model (Chainey and Ratcliffe 2005), it is important that crime be placed in context. Cope points out that while the analysts she interviewed were able to create hot spot maps of crime patterns, the maps lacked inclusion of the crime generators and attractors known by theorists to be influential in causing crime problems. This lack of context meant that the maps were used more for their descriptive value than their analytical power (Cope 2004). Evaluating data-driven models may be a worthy aim, but Cope's work suggests that we may still be some way from data- and intelligence-driven models, and a thorough evaluation will have to wait until the analytical demands can be met.

Even spatial analysis techniques that are fairly simple, at least from a purely statistical sense, require a wealth of experience, software and data. For example, consider the weighted displacement quotient (Bowers and Johnson 2003). This is a simple method by which analysts can determine whether a crime reduction tactic targeted to a specific geographic area reduced crime compared with a buffer area around the target site. The technique can also be used to estimate the level of displacement or diffusion of benefits radiating to the surrounding area. While a powerful tool in the arsenal of any police analyst, it does require access to spatially referenced crime data, an appreciation of likely displacement activity, a geographic information system to conduct the analysis, and knowledge that the technique exists in the first place – all features missing in many police departments.

Pure evaluations and realistic evaluations

Some academic researchers may look down their noses at reasonably simple statistics, such as the weighted displacement quotient analysis, for not being part of the gold standard of evaluation techniques. Yet it is an approach that is accessible to many practitioners and does not require a PhD in statistics.

More advanced methods are certainly possible, and are often encouraged by academia. An influential and widely referenced scale of methodological quality of criminological research is the Maryland Scientific Methods Scale (Sherman *et al.* 1998), which was developed to provide an indication of what works to prevent crime, and was used to assess the quality of the research influencing the findings. Research reports were evaluated across numerous criteria according to a scale of zero (no confidence in the findings) to five (high confidence in the results). The approach is not dissimilar to the method chosen by the UK National Health Service to help reviewers in the health field where a hierarchy of evidence is applied (reported by Farrington 2003). In the health service hierarchy, randomised, controlled, double-blind trials are deemed more scientific than quasi-experimental studies (experiments without randomisation), which in turn are more worthy than controlled observational studies. Collectively, these are all deemed better than observational studies without a control group or the lowest level of scientific rigour, expert opinion! But along with colleagues in Australia, I have argued that, while recognising the value of a well-conducted, randomised, controlled experiment, it is unrealistic to expect police to subscribe to this rigid notion of pure evaluation, and that 'the precise experimental conditions that are a feature of the traditional scientific method are less applicable in a policing research arena where law enforcement does not occur in a vacuum, but is constantly responding to and anticipating activity in the criminal environment' (Makkai *et al.* 2004: 7).

This point is made in greater depth (and with greater eloquence) by John Eck (2006), who argues for the merits of smaller-scale evaluations in circumstances where randomised, controlled experiments are impractical. Calls for greater scientific experimentation will no doubt help to advance the field of criminology (Sherman 2005) but are not necessarily easy to conduct in a policing field where the perceived failures of police chiefs are often rewarded with redundancy. The plain truth is that while evaluations may be logical and considered, the repercussions for police officers and crime prevention practitioners on the receiving end of an evaluation that finds they were unsuccessful in preventing crime are anything but.

An alternative *realistic evaluation* or *scientific realist* approach has been proposed by Pawson and Tilley (1994; 1997). Their central argument is that the pure evaluation approach does not engage enough with the context of the operational environment. Instead, researchers should investigate the relationships between context, mechanism and outcome. These 'configurations' should be examined by more qualitative, narrative, and ethnographic research techniques. The key is to clarify how the choices that people make affect the outcome of the programmes under examination, and to think through the theoretical way that the programmes were expected to work. Pawson and Tilley argue that too many evaluations determine that a programme did not work, but fail to address why it failed. Their approach, which has merit for understanding the flows of information in an intelligence-led policing environment, is concerned with understanding the mechanisms at work and how they function within the context of the operational environment.

In reality, both the scientific and realistic approaches have merit. For a public concerned with crime, the ability to perform a pure technical evaluation that can establish whether public money was well spent and reduced crime is of considerable value. Similarly, a realistic evaluation that understands that programme success is a feature of the personal choices of key players is vital to understanding the result of the technical evaluation.

Police executives will have to address the skill sets of analysts if rigorous evaluations are to be conducted. Managers will also have to allow analysts the time to conduct evaluation work if we want to understand better the impact of police operations on the criminal environment. The rush to address the next urgent problem often prevents opportunity for any evaluation or results analysis. An example of this can be found in the lack (as yet) of a thorough results analysis stemming from the NJSP Operation Nine Connect (Ratcliffe and Guidetti 2008).

To pull some of the threads of this chapter and book together, the Operation Anchorage case study, and the following Viewpoint from Corey Heldon provide a number of useful lessons for the concept and development of intelligence-led policing. From a positive perspective, they show that police can identify prolific offenders, and the targeting of these criminals can be a successful crime reduction strategy. Furthermore, the benefits of incapacitating active offenders can last beyond the time frame of the police operation. On the other hand, it also shows the potential value of situational crime prevention and a more problem-oriented approach to crime control if these short-term gains are to be translated into long-term benefits.

Case study

Operation Anchorage

The Australian capital of Canberra nestles in the hills of the Australian Capital Territory (ACT) not far from Australia's east coast and a few hours' drive south of Sydney. The leafy and affluent suburbs rarely know violent crime; however, there is a property crime problem with which ACT Police (a department of the Australian Federal Police also known as ACT Policing) have to contend. In response to an increase in burglaries in the city and spurred on by the unfortunate break-in at the home of a prominent member of the local judiciary, ACT Policing conducted Operation Anchorage from the end of February 2001 to the end of June 2001. Anchorage placed significant emphasis on senior leadership, the targeting of recidivist offenders through crime and intelligence analysis, and the development of joint operations across different branches of ACT Policing to include all officers in the operation – not just those assigned to the Operation Anchorage team (Makkai *et al.* 2004).

With a local force of about 600 officers, Anchorage consisted of four teams of between 10 and 12 investigators, with six intelligence analysts committed to analysing crime patterns and other information sources (such as covert surveillance and field interviews) (Ratcliffe 2001). Police leadership selected new targets as a result of crime intelligence and changed target lists on a regular basis. Every two weeks, intelligence officers circulated a list of the most prominent suspects and enrolled all of ACT Policing to identify and arrest these targets. This was a considerable change from normal practice in the city, where crime reduction operations were usually short-term and rarely involved significant numbers of officers. It was also unusual to include the whole force in the strategy, isolated squads being the more traditional approach.

Previous attempts to reduce burglary (two operations called Chronicle and Dilute) had achieved short-terms gains that were never sustained. Figure 9.2 shows the frequency of burglaries in the ACT, with the timeline of Operation Anchorage shown as a horizontal bar following the two previous shorter-term operations, Chronicle and Dilute. Chronicle clearly had an impact, but one that was rather short-lived, only lasting for a few weeks. Operation Dilute had a delayed impact that lasted a little longer (about ten weeks), but was unable to sustain the crime reduction benefits. Figure 9.2 shows that Operation Anchorage had a sustained crime reduction benefit that lasted many months after the operation.

Using interrupted time series techniques, we were able to isolate the impact of Anchorage from the previous operations as well as ensure that any crime reductions observed were not simply related to broader regional trends at the macrosocial or macroeconomic level. Our study found that Operation Anchorage was successful in its aim to reduce burglary crime in the ACT. Recorded crime

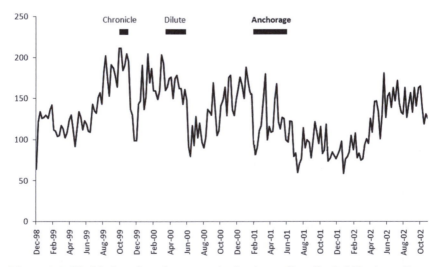

Figure 9.2 Weekly burglary frequency in the Australian Capital Territory, January 1999 to November 2002 (All figures in this case study are sourced or adapted from Makkai *et al.* 2004, and are reproduced with permission)

declined during the operation, and the decline lasted some 45 weeks afterwards. Furthermore, we were also able to calculate that there was no displacement of burglary to the surrounding areas of the state of New South Wales; in fact, we found a diffusion of benefits to the surrounding areas (Ratcliffe and Makkai 2004). We estimated that the operation prevented 524 burglaries while it was operational, with a residual deterrence effect preventing a further 2,445 offences in the 45 weeks after the operation and before burglaries eventually returned to the mean level they had been at prior to Anchorage. These time periods are shown in Figure 9.3.

Using approximations for the cost of burglary calculated by Mayhew and Adkins (2003), we can extrapolate these crime reduction totals to estimate that the financial benefit to society for the crime prevented by Operation Anchorage was approximately AU$1,257,600 during Anchorage, and AU$5,868,000 in the post-operation period, for a total benefit in burglary costs to the ACT of AU$7,125,600.

From the perspective of the operational aims, not only was the operation successful in reducing crime, but Operation Anchorage was also successful in targeting prolific property crime offenders. Of the people arrested during Operation Anchorage, 77 per cent had at least one prior offence, and these recidivists averaged about eight crimes per offender. In fact, 18 per cent of the Anchorage offenders had 15 or more prior offending episodes, this group accounting for the majority (62 per cent) of all prior offending episodes.

To estimate the impact of incarceration, we concentrated on a subset

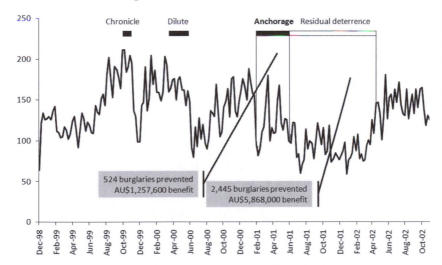

Figure 9.3 Operational benefits for Anchorage and residual deterrence period

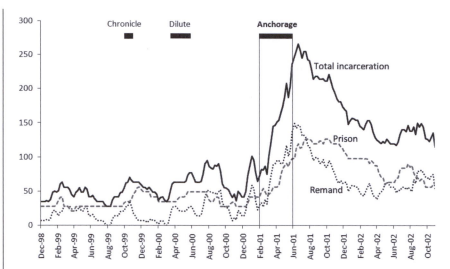

Figure 9.4 Detention rates through remand and prison. Total incarceration also shown

of 119 recidivist offenders who had committed at least one recorded offence prior to the end of 1998, and who were charged with offences during Operation Anchorage. The criminal justice histories of these long-term recidivist offenders were telling. The subjects were drawn from people arrested during the operation, so it was not surprising that they were incarcerated to a greater extent after the operation (Figure 9.4). However, what was of more interest was the realisation of the relationship between the burglary rate and the incarceration rate of the recidivist offenders. In other words, a potentially significant cause of the reduction in burglary after Anchorage was these recidivists being incarcerated. After aggregating the number of days they collectively spent in custody (either in prison or on remand awaiting trial) and plotting this against the weekly burglary counts for the ACT, a pattern emerges. After Anchorage, as the incarceration rate of the offenders begins to decline as they serve their time and are released, the burglary rate begins to creep back up again (Figure 9.5). The overall study left us to conclude that it was reasonable to conclude that a 'non-trivial amount' of burglary offences was prevented through the increased incarceration of prolific offenders during Operation Anchorage (Makkai *et al.* 2004).

Eventually, the weekly burglary frequency returned to pre-Anchorage levels. The problem was that after the incarcerated offenders were eventually released, they returned to the community and found that all their old burglary opportunities still existed: homes

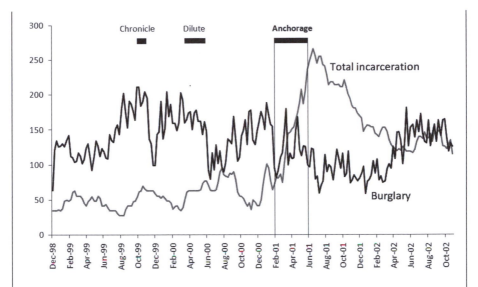

Figure 9.5 Total incarceration rate and weekly burglary frequency

were still left unattended or unlocked, the doors and windows of many properties were still in a dilapidated and unsafe condition, and the housing projects were havens for crime just as before. In response, ACT Police have since been working on long-term crime prevention strategies to supplement the intelligence-led successes (AFP 2005), as explained in the Viewpoint that follows.

Operation Anchorage shows that police are able to target recidivist offenders and proactively work collectively to reduce crime through crime intelligence analysis and focused targeting of the worst offenders. While imprisonment does reduce burglary (Weatherburn *et al.* 2006), it may only be truly cost-effective when targeted on prolific and persistent offenders, as was done in Canberra. However, the operation also shows that without closing down the opportunities for crime, removing offenders may not be sufficient, as Corey Heldon explains in the following Viewpoint.

Viewpoint

Refining strategy after Operation Anchorage

Corey Heldon

That Operation Anchorage was successful there is little doubt. The four-month Operation resulted in an overall decrease in Canberra's burglary rate by around 21 per cent. During the same period the property crime rates in all other Australian jurisdictions increased. Perhaps one of the major reasons behind the success of the operation was the focused effort by ACT Policing. A large number of staff were deployed directly to Anchorage with ancillary effort from other staff in areas such as Traffic Operations.

Ultimately, however, the effort was unsustainable over the long term. The Australian Capital Territory (ACT) is a small jurisdiction. Operation Anchorage drew resources from many different areas including Intelligence, Investigations, General Duties, Traffic Operations and Forensic Services. While the attention was diverted to Anchorage and property crime, there was a reduced ability to concentrate resources on other criminal activity in the region.

As shown in this book, the residual effects of Operation Anchorage lasted approximately 45 weeks. After this time the burglary rates rose to around pre-Anchorage levels. The recidivist offenders who had been targeted and incarcerated as a result of the Operation returned to the community. Fresh out of prison with few legitimate opportunities, the incentive to return to a life of property crime remained. The lack of changes to the opportunity environment (for example unsecured homes that had not been secured) only encouraged offenders to resume burglary in the areas where they lived. It should also be stated that there may have been little that would have altered in the lives of these offenders to divert them away from such activity. Indeed, incarceration may have afforded them few opportunities for rehabilitation. Thus, policing operations can go some way towards alleviating criminal activity; however, sustaining the effort must also elicit a response from other agencies such as corrections, rehabilitation and drug services.

Following Operation Anchorage, ACT Policing commenced Operation Halite in 2002. By 2004 Operation Halite developed its strategy to incorporate three aspects of policing – investigations, intelligence and crime prevention. The strategy was centred on two key facts. First, a minority of offenders commit the majority of crime. Secondly, volume crime makes up around 80 per cent of crime in the ACT.

Operation Anchorage showed that focusing on recidivist offenders would assist in clearing up a reasonable volume of property crime. Operation Halite drew on this lesson and developed strategy based on these findings. The practicalities appear simple. Intelligence identifies hot spots for certain types of crime and possible offenders based on modus operandi and other factors. Investigators and traffic operations target the areas of interest which results in the seizure of property, drugs and the arrest of offenders. Crime prevention officers remain in the area for any follow up with the community for a period after the operation. The result of this strategy was that by 2004 the ACT burglary rate was at its lowest level for six years.

This style of intelligence-led policing operation has had sustained positive results for the Canberra community. Targeting recidivist offenders has enabled ACT Policing to not only clear reported offences but also prevent thousands more.

Corey Heldon is a Superintendent in the Australian Federal Police. She was previously Team Leader of AFP Intelligence training and is currently the Coordinator of the intelligence team supporting the AFP International Deployment Group.

Measuring success in different ways

There is often considerable pressure on police to simply increase the number of arrests, but what is noticeable is that Operation Anchorage did not place emphasis on increasing the volume of arrests, but on arresting the right people. As the Australian Federal Police Commissioner noted in regard to major criminal and terrorist operations, 'not only are we expected to anticipate the next move, but we also have to do something about bringing those involved to justice. This highlights one of the fundamental differences between intelligence that aims to warn and prevent, and investigations for which success is measured by successful prosecution and conviction' (Keelty 2004). The pressure of the legal system tends to push police in the direction of showing value through arrests, and this pressure is not just from outside the police service. Internally, the thinking of police has not yet significantly moved from an investigative mindset to a crime prevention mindset. As Sheptycki (2004b: v) laments, 'Especially notable is the status and prestige that accrues to the detective occupation, the pre-eminence of which has inhibited intelligence-led policing by converting "intelligence" into "detections"'. But if the focus shifts from arrests, are there other ways to evaluate intelligence-led policing?

With some limitations, Operation Anchorage shows that it is possible to calculate a financial value for the social benefits of successful intelligence-led operations. When the costs of the police activity are incorporated in an analysis, it is possible to establish a cost-benefit ratio for policing activity. For example, the Australian Federal Police report that the cost-benefit return on drug operations is AU$5.60 of benefit returned to the community for every dollar spent, and AU$5.10 for fraud investigations (Keelty 2004).

Another example comes from the National Criminal Intelligence Service

(NCIS). Through 2001 and 2002, the UK Home Office funded NCIS to develop an Organised Vehicle Crime Programme, a group of projects designed to address motorcycle theft, the exportation of stolen cars, and cases of 'ringing and cloning' – essentially the rebadging of stolen cars as legitimate sales (Brown *et al.* 2004). With a total cost for the projects of just over a million pounds, establishing the value of the programme was clearly important. The cost-benefits of the intelligence reports created by the NCIS team were greater for the larger of two operations evaluated. A problem profile that addressed the resale of stolen Ford Mondeo cars cost £6,378 to produce, and it fuelled a police operation that cost £221,000. While the operation was estimated to have prevented the theft of 17 vehicles in the following year, the overall operation cost £7.56 for every pound saved. But in a second operation, a target profile produced for an operation to prevent the theft and resale of vehicles to West Africa cost over £12,000, and the subsequent police operation cost about £600,000. This operation is credited with preventing the theft of over 700 vehicles, resulting in a £2.7 million saving at an operational cost of only 23 pence for every pound saved (more than a 400 per cent return on the investment).

Beyond the impact of police operations on social harm, it is also possible to explore the costs involved in particular aspects of work associated with intelligence-led policing and, in particular, the cost-benefit of surveillance and confidential informants, disruption activities, and any benefits accrued through changing business practice.

The cost-benefit of surveillance and confidential informants

Given that intelligence-led policing encourages increased use of surveillance and informant use, it would seem prudent to explore the cost-benefit of these techniques. However, there is a paucity of research or published work on the cost advantages of surveillance activity. While having a surveillance capacity might be an 'indispensable resource' (at least for organised crime investigations, according to Irwin 2001), surveillance is personnel-intensive and involves spending many hours watching offenders who do not commit that much crime on a day-to-day basis. To get some perspective on the effort required for surveillance, consider Operation Nine Connect, described in the opening chapter. Review of time sheets for the operation found that NJSP officers collectively conducted over 8,000 hours of electronic surveillance, spent over 1,200 hours transcribing the wire-taps, and conducted over 2,300 hours of physical surveillance (Ratcliffe and Guidetti 2008). Surveillance is therefore a time-consuming and expensive business.

While coming in and out of favour depending on a variety of reasons

(Ratcliffe 2002d), confidential informants appear once again to be viewed as a cost-effective approach to crime control:

> The effective use of informants is one area that has received much attention, with forces encouraged to concentrate on recruiting and tasking them in greater numbers. Used with discretion and proper supervision, they represent a very cost-effective means of developing operations against crime, compared for example with the costs of deploying a full surveillance team to gather the same information. (HMIC 1997: 17)

The claims from both the Audit Commission (Audit Commission 1993) and Her Majesty's Inspectorate of Constabulary (above) that confidential informants provide extensive value for money have been questioned (for example, Morgan and Newburn 1997; Dunnighan and Norris 1999), but it is difficult to estimate accurately informant costs. While surprisingly little is known about police expenditure on confidential informants, one study did examine the informant finances of a UK police force from 1995 to 1996 (Innes 2000). For an expenditure of £35,910 (about US$56,110 at 1996 exchange rates), the force detected 531 crimes, arrested 528 offenders, and recovered stolen property worth over half a million pounds ($866,521 or £554,574) and drugs worth £842,779 (street value, US equivalent $1,316,842). This translates to less than £70 spent for every arrested offender and crime detected, figures that echo the Audit Commission estimates (Audit Commission 1993). When comparing estimates of the cost of a surveillance operation at the time of £2,500 ($3,900) for a single day, the financial benefits of informants would appear to be substantial.

Yet these figures have to be considered cautiously, as they do not include a variety of associated costs. As Dunnighan and Norris (1999) point out, there are additional costs incurred in the recruitment of the informants, as well as the difficulty in measuring the time and cost involved when recruitment is unsuccessful. Furthermore, in the UK, where informants are registered and assigned primary and co-handlers, the increase in informant use has resulted in concomitant increases in bureaucracy that have pushed up administrative costs. Dunnighan and Norris, based on their interviews with detectives and informants and a survey of officers across more than one force, created revised estimates. These revisions suggest a different and potentially more inclusive view of the costs of informant handling, as shown in Table 9.1.

Given that many officers who handle informants do not record their informants officially, it is impossible to ascertain how much is given to casual or unregistered informants by police officers from their own pocket. Given that the handling of confidential informant handling takes police

Table 9.1 Cost-effectiveness of the use of confidential informants. Adapted from Dunnighan and Norris (1999)[1]

	Reward cost only	Full costs
Cost for each arrest	£54 ($87)	£697 ($1,125)
Cost for each crime cleared up	£27 ($44)	£348 ($561)
Value of property recovered to cost ratio	£34 ($55) to 1	£2.60 ($4.20) to 1

officers closer to ethical boundaries than most other aspects of police work, it may be valuable for police to spend more time evaluating the cost-benefit of greater involvement with confidential sources.

Cost should not be the only measure of the value of an informant. In modern policing, cost-effectiveness is a factor; however, the value of informants to improve our understanding of the criminal environment may have greater strategic benefits that are harder to measure in purely monetary terms. If their use does provide substantial benefit to society, then greater knowledge of both the financial and less tangible costs may help police justify use of informants to a sometimes sceptical public. For all the discussions surrounding the cost of informant handling mentioned above, it is hard to put a value on the intangible benefits of fewer crimes and a reduction in social harm.

Measuring disruption

One of the new words introduced to the lexicon of policing alongside intelligence-led policing has been *disruption*. The existence of disruption as a stated aim of agencies involved in organised crime control is simultaneously an admission of the inability of the criminal justice system to deal with high-level criminality while at the same time finding a pragmatic alternative. Disruption is vaguely defined – where it is defined at all – and it often suits agencies to claim success through disruption when a legal remedy remains expensive or unobtainable. It is also helpful when the real picture of the criminal environment is elusive, negating attempts to establish a benchmark of the target crime against which to evaluate progress.

Very little is known about the true quantitative nature of the organised crime environment (Levi 2002). Recent work from the UK suggests that the social and economic costs of organised crime are approximately £15bn for the drug trade, £3.7bn for excise fraud, and £1bn as a result of the people-smuggling business; however, these estimates are both conservative and vulnerable to large margins of error (Dubourg and Prichard 2007). Therefore, one of the difficulties for SOCA and other agencies in establishing traction against major organised crime groups is establishing the scale of the criminal operations to begin with. For example, in the late 1980s, the DEA set up their own bank in a sting operation to tempt drug traffickers to launder money. Operation Green Ice was so successful that undercover agents laundered US$20 million of Colombian drug cartel money. Operation Green Ice finally led to the arrest of seven of the Cali drug cartel's top financial managers, the seizure of more than US$50 million in assets worldwide, and the arrest of 177 people. A subsequent operation, Green Ice II, netted a further 109 arrests and the seizure of over 13,000 lbs of cocaine and $15.6 million in cash. By most traditional measures, these were successful operations; however, as Levi and Maguire (2004) point out, the seizures were insignificant considering that the United Nations estimated Cali cartel profits to be about *US$30 billion a year*. The impact of these large enforcement operations was fairly minimal in terms of disrupting cartel operations. After reviewing a number of law enforcement operations, Levi and Maguire were left to conclude that few examples of good practice 'appear to have involved sustained efforts to analyze the structure of the organized crime groups that were targeted, or to look in detail at the dynamics of their operations and markets. Similarly, few appeared to be looking beyond immediate operational goals towards a lasting reduction in organized criminal activity' (Levi and Maguire 2004: 457).

In the UK, SOCA are now engaged in developing greater knowledge through their lifetime management of organised crime offenders programme, and the National Policing Improvement Agency are examining gangs at Level 2 of the NIM (force/regional level). However, we still know little about the true magnitude of organised crime and the impact of police operations on this environment. In discussing the draft British government bill that set performance targets for SOCA, Harfield points out that:

> The White Paper proposals are in part premised on the basis that not enough is known about organized criminality to understand yet how best to intervene against it. So the question must be put, how will the impact of SOCA be assessed if the size of the problem itself cannot be quantified? *Detection is simply defined but how will disruption be measured?* (Harfield 2006: 752; emphasis added)

Disruption will continue to be a difficult outcome to measure. One UK agency used to employ a rather optimistic formula: for all drugs couriers caught in the act, an estimate was made of the number of drug-trafficking journeys they might have made in the future if they had not been caught, and then used this to measure disruption (Harfield 2006). More realistic and objective criteria will need to be determined for the future if weight is to put into agency claims that they are disrupting organised crime.

The RCMP has tried to tackle this thorny problem with a Disruption Attributes Tool. The tool uses forms filled out by field personnel to explore perceived disruption of key attributes of organised crime group business (Dawson 2007). Table 9.2 shows the three attributes (core business, financial, and personnel) and four of the six possible indicators (the two remaining indicators are 'not applicable' and 'unable to assess at present or still under investigation'). The Disruption Attributes Tool is still vulnerable to the subjectivity of field personnel, especially when there may be a tendency to overestimate the impact of operations for career benefit; however, the tool is one of the first methodological attempts to articulate the aims and targets of disruption. Usefully, the three attributes implicitly indicate to operational personnel that disruption can occur at different leverage points for different organised crime groups and that different groups can have different organisational and systemic weaknesses.

Measuring success in changing business practice

It may be that a police agency looks first to change their organisational approach to criminality before attempting to reduce crime significantly, and there are ways to measure success in changing business practice. In a 2001 review of police intelligence units in New Zealand, the Office of the Auditor-General found that the intelligence function had staff recruitment and training difficulties, no clear career path for intelligence analysts, did not always feature in district business plans, and generally used rudimentary analytical techniques and systems. They recommended a strategic review to see whether crime and intelligence analysis could be improved to help the New Zealand Police (I helped with that review and the results of the work can be found in various places in this book, as well as in Ratcliffe 2005). As a result of new practices, a further review four years later found that the New Zealand Police had made greater use of intelligence-led policing, raised the profile of intelligence units, implemented and adopted a new crime reduction model (essentially the 3-i model), and increased training opportunities for analysts (Office of the Auditor-General 2006).

Another changing practice is the greater enthusiasm that police have for collaborating with other agency partners. Police are always negotiating a path through different approaches to the governance of crime, and the period since the 1990s has seen the creation of an environment that has become more risk-focused and pluralistic in terms of security provision. For instance, we have witnessed a greater emphasis on regulation and compliance-based approaches to combat money laundering through the global financial system (Levi 2002), as well as the growth of the private and voluntary security industry. Wood and Shearing (2007: 116) describe this as *hybrid governance*, an approach that is 'not simply a story about the incorporation of market logics into the minds of public sector bureaucrats'. They argue that hybrid governance is more than this. There has been an increase in the non-governmental sector playing a greater role in the creation of security. Evaluating intelligence-led policing may therefore be beyond the simple measurement of crime rates before and after an operation. It is possible that an increase in the flow of intelligence products to non-governmental or other criminal justice agencies may justify an investment in the concept and practice of intelligence-led policing. In recognition of this, some agencies are starting to track the number of intelligence products they distribute to other agencies as one of their performance indicators. But performance indicators can have negative repercussions on intelligence-led policing, as the final section of this chapter discusses.

Table 9.2 RCMP Disruption Attributes Tool (version 2)

	Core business	*Financial*	*Personnel*
Attribute description	*The instruments/ process central to the criminal enterprise*	*Financial capacity/ status of the group including profits/ financial assets gained through organised crime*	*Indviduals employed through organised crime (including corporate officials)*
High	Removed the capacity to supply/operate	Removed and/or interrupted the organisation's financial ability to mount large-scale operations	Arrested and/or charged individuals with the majority of the knowledge, contact, expertise, experience, and executive influence
Medium	Interrupted production and/or distribution of supply network	Seizure/restraint of significant proceeds of crime relative to the financial scope of the organisation	Arrested and/or charged support personnel/skilled operators with expertise, knowledge and some contacts
Low	Seized commodities without disrupting production and/or distribution	Seizure/restraint of minor proceeds of crime or interruption of the means to launder and/or legitimise proceeds of crime relative to the financial scope of the organisation	Arrested and/or charged replaceable unskilled operators/ street level operators/ couriers
Nil	No commodities seized	No profits/financial assets seized	No individuals arrested

Measuring success in performance indicators

Performance indicators have become a fixation for a number of police services. Some within the managerial ranks have become fascinated with the (usually false) hope of being able to manage by setting objectives dictated to the lower ranks and evaluated through spreadsheets. When performance indicators were first introduced to UK policing, there were 25 main categories and 60 component indicators (Davidoff 1996). The Police Performance Assessments web page of the Home Office[2] now lists seven key performance areas:

- reducing crime;
- investigating crime;
- promoting safety;
- providing assistance;
- citizen focus;
- resource use;
- local policing.

Not only do these performance areas overlap considerably, but also within these seven areas is a myriad performance indicators, indicators that have grown in complexity and number to the point where some staff are spending their time fully employed in collecting and monitoring internal performance. Performance indicators may have their place in promoting careful management of public funds and achieving centrally set targets; however, for the crime prevention and detection effort, this performance culture can be counter-productive. In research conducted in London's Metropolitan Police, Scott (1998) found that the desire to chase the required figures was returning police to a model of reactive policing and away from proactive policing. Tilley (2004) describes this management through objectives as an 'anathema' by driving police to respond to centrally specified governmental objectives rather than allowing local commanders to focus on local problems, and Smith (1995) lists a number of unintended consequences of the way that many managers interpret the use of performance indicators, including:

- *tunnel vision* – when managers choose the performance indicators that are easiest to measure and ignore the rest;
- *sub-optimisation* – when managers focus on a narrow band of activities that improves some performance indicators but inflicts damage on the performance of the overall system;

- *myopia* – when managers focus on short-term targets only;
- *measure fixation* – when the performance indicator becomes the focus rather than the desired outcome or service;
- *misrepresentation* – when performance data are either misreported or distorted through deliberate corruption;
- *misinterpretation* – when performance data are misinterpreted by higher level managers;
- *gaming* – when managers deliberately underachieve so they can be set lower targets for later assessments;
- *ossification* – when a performance indicator has ceased to be effective but remains on the books.

To this list, Tilley (1995: 5) adds two more:

- *demoralisation* – loss of confidence and commitment among workers delivering services deemed not to count or to be counted inappropriately;
- *discreditability* – public scepticism – brought about through sabotage of enforced performance indicators by disillusioned workers.

Some performance indicators can work in quite subtle ways to draw police away from the core activities of detecting and preventing crime to activities of fighting fear of crime – an altogether different proposition. A couple of years ago, the police in Britain began to notice a 'reassurance gap' (Herrington and Millie 2006) whereby falling crime rates were not reflected in a correspondingly increased sense of public security. The result has been the development of a trend called 'reassurance policing', one where signal crimes that have a disproportionate influence on public fear of crime become a consideration for police response (Innes 2004), and policing becomes responsive to fear of crime rather than crime.

While reassurance policing is a rather amorphous concept that lacks a clear definition, as Innes points out,

> It was precisely the lack of a tightly structured definition that allowed the idea to gain significant levels of support from different interest groups and thus helped to propel it 'up' the political agenda. The malleability inhering in the idea of reassurance meant that different potential supporters were able to interpret it in ways that supported their own agendas. (Innes 2004: 157)

One might argue that this is a situation not that dissimilar to the growth of community policing. How combating fear of crime has become an issue for the police is beyond me, but, in the UK, reassurance has now become a part of the 2002 Police Reform Act and a number of National Policing Plans. Before the National Reassurance Policing Programme's website was renamed the Neighbourhood Policing Programme, Herrington and Millie visited the website and found there a list of core elements to the business plan for reassurance policing, including 'that a targeted, intelligence-led approach is required, focusing the most effective action against the relatively few incidents that cause greatest damage to a community's security' (Herrington and Millie 2006: 155). While the language on the website has now been changed, this is indicative of a desire to return to a more community oriented ethos that is less objectively driven by data and information analysis but more influenced by public perception of crime. As a result, the development of performance indicators for reassurance policing may come into conflict with performance indicators for intelligence-led policing.

Should police use performance indicators to assess crime intelligence-driven activity at all? If so, what performance indicators should be used for intelligence-led policing? These are difficult questions. For many police departments, the first stage is actually realising or agreeing on a definition of 'intelligence-led policing'. As stated earlier in this book, the term is bandied around quite a bit without many people being able to articulate what it means. If the definition and conceptual model from this book are adopted, it may be that the components of the 3-i model will become the grounding for performance indicators that measure not only data and information analysis but also the influence of decision-makers and the impact the whole process has on the criminal environment.

While I open the door to the possibility of performance indicators for intelligence-led policing, caution should be exercised; performance indicators never work in isolation. This point became clear to me during my research in New Zealand. As I wrote a couple of years ago,

> A focus on performance management objectives that are not directly crime related can indicate to lower echelons that monitoring overtime management, monitoring sickness and patrol car mileage are of equivalent importance as the burglary and vehicle theft rate. This was repeatedly mentioned by intelligence personnel and decision-makers, and was reiterated through the pages of the performance management audits. (Ratcliffe 2005: 446)

Summary

From the perspective of many researchers, the death knell for the community policing movement has been the lack of positive crime reduction evaluations (Sherman 1998a; and see Chapter 4). Rigorous evaluation of crime reduction associated with the intelligence-led policing model may be one way to prevent intelligence-led policing from falling into the same sorry state of affairs. If we are to focus here on crime control, and not on the management of public perception through digressions such as reassurance policing, then it is vital to be able to evaluate intelligence-based strategies. That intelligence-led policing and related approaches to crime control are information and data centred is an advantage.

But how should a business model be evaluated? Certainly, it is true that the 'mythical power of subjective and unstructured wisdom holds back every field and keeps it from systematically discovering and implementing what works best in repeated tasks' (Sherman 1998a: 4), and intelligence-led policing should avoid this trap; but not all quantitative research evaluations are of the same quality. Some may argue that it is important to measure such outputs as the number of actioned field intelligence reports, the number of targets under scrutiny, and the number of external agencies supplied with crime intelligence products to support their missions. Use of these measures, while potentially valuable, should not be interpreted as advocating a return to the investigative, reactive approach to policing. Intelligence-led policing retains the strategic aim of informed decision-making about resource allocation and priorities: the evaluation component should equally focus on this overarching aim.

In terms of measuring crime prevention, evaluation may be easier at the local level addressing property and violent crime problems than at the organised crime level (though this depends on the harm caused by the organised crime group under examination). Conceptual approaches to measuring prevention in the form of the tools and techniques that populate strategies such as problem-oriented policing simply do not exist yet for organised crime and transnational crime problems. The result is a tendency to emphasise the language of success in terms of arrests or disruption of individual groups rather than in a more strategic intervention across the broader domain of criminality (Levi and Maguire 2004). This stand is counter-productive in some dimensions of intelligence-led policing. Groups such as joint terrorism task forces rarely make significant numbers of arrests; however, their work may be vital to national security. How are they to be evaluated?

The early developmental stages of intelligence-led policing for many police agencies will involve organisational changes and cultural shifts that are not well captured by quantitative data. In particular, inaccuracies in analysis and interpretation that result in the wrong choice of target not only reduce police effectiveness but can also result in a loss of police legitimacy and the loss of public confidence. Adverse outcome can also include the pressure placed on police officers to make cases when none may exist.

Intelligence-led policing is about informed decision-making, and the impact of intelligence is 'notoriously difficult to measure' (Keelty 2004: 11). Policing takes place in a politically charged environment, and evaluations can spell trouble for some people, especially those involved in unsuccessful programmes where 'the only stakeholders who do not get it in the neck are the research community' (Pawson and Tilley 1994: 292).

While the move towards a more outcome-based accountability in law enforcement has not been uncontested (Wood and Shearing 2007), it is not realistic to expect the management-through-measurement ethos to disappear any time soon. Evaluation is therefore necessary for police to be able to move confidently forward with intelligence-led policing. It can provide objective evidence of progress in crime control, it can provide pointers to bottlenecks in the information flow that is the lifeblood of intelligence-led policing, and it can diagnose problems in analytical processes. But these gains have to be achieved with a thorough understanding of the context of evaluation in the policing domain.

Notes

1 Adapted from Dunnighan, C. and Norris, C. (1999) 'The detective, the snout, and the Audit Commission: the real costs in using informants', *Howard Journal of Criminal Justice* 38(1): 76. UK pound values as reported in original work. US dollar values converted from mean exchange rate for 1999, as sourced from Lawrence H. Officer, 'Exchange rate between the United States dollar and forty other countries, 1913–1999.' Economic History Services, EH.Net, 2002. URL: http://eh.net/hmit/exchangerates/

2 http//police.homeoffice.gov.uk/performance, accessed 12 June 2007.

10

Challenges for the future

Intelligence-led policing is crime fighting that is guided by effective intelligence gathering and analysis—and it has the potential to be the most important law enforcement innovation of the twenty-first century. (Kelling and Bratton 2006: 5)

Even though there has been broad endorsement of intelligence-led policing across the world, I sometimes wonder whether some proponents know what they are supporting. A lack of clarity as to definitions and conceptual direction can be the downfall of some initiatives, while others can founder due to misunderstandings associated with terminology and tactics. It is easily possible for intelligence-led policing to fall by the wayside and become lost in the history of failed attempts of law enforcement to move away from the traditional focus on reactive, investigative policing. One of the significant threats is a misconception among both police and the public that the meaning of *intelligence* retains a suggestion of 'subterfuge, a clandestine and covert activity conducted by officers of a shady disposition and involving a degree of moral ambiguity' (Ratcliffe in press). Although this is not the case, intelligence-led policing does promote increased use of covert information gathering as an adjunct to traditional crime analysis. This chapter therefore explores some of the misconceptions regarding how police employ covert activity and the legislation surrounding these information collection tools.

The chapter also examines the implications of the broadening security agenda. Not only is policing beginning to think more strategically, but intelligence-led policing has also become the lynchpin to merge national security aims with local policing objectives. The chapter, and the book, concludes with a short list of ideas to move intelligence-led policing forward.

The challenges of covert activity

It should be reiterated that there is a fundamental difference between covert information-gathering tactics and intelligence-led policing. As I stated earlier in the book, intelligence-led policing is a business model for prioritising resource allocation while covert information gathering is a tactic that can support the broader mission of intelligence-led policing. With that important caveat in mind, there is a perception within law enforcement that the public are innately wary of proactive policing tactics. Clearly, some people are immediately suspicious when police discuss the use of informants and surveillance. They feel there is something inherently unfair about police using covert tactics to gather information, as if there is some historical notion that police and offenders have to be on a level playing field; however, the assumption of widespread concern may be false. A marketing study conducted on behalf of ACPO identified broad support for proactive policing techniques. Using in-depth interviews with people from a range of socio-economic and racial backgrounds, researchers found that:

- Young people and working adults lower on the socio-economic spectrum favoured proactive, targeted, solution-oriented policing.

- Midlife adults in the middle to higher socio-economic groups, older men, and ethnic groups naturally identified with visible patrolling; however, they could be readily convinced through logical argument that proactive and targeted activities are the most effective and beneficial.

- It was only older women and the retired that retained a connection with visible patrolling as a symbol of reassurance, relating visible patrolling to perceptions of safety.
(Bradley 1998: v)

Regardless of this general support, achieving an objective measure of the criminal environment while simultaneously maintaining police legitimacy in the eyes of the public as a whole does require police to manage the use of covert resources in a way that is both productive and sensitive to the actions of authorities in a democratic system of government. This need for active management is especially important in the UK, where, at least until a few years ago, the legislative response to increased police use of covert sources has been ad hoc, piecemeal and insufficient to address future needs (Maguire and John 1996). Insensitive or unlawful use of covert information gathering has negative repercussions for police services, both financially and in terms of legitimacy. In particular, and as discussed in the following sections, increased use of confidential informants, the proportionality of police activity, human rights, and how information is stored are all relevant to the perceived legitimacy of intelligence-led policing activities.

The risks of greater informant use in covert activities

The use of informers is presented as a cost effective means of solving crime, with few, if any, negative consequences. However, negative consequences abound: crime is facilitated as well as repressed; criminals are licensed to commit crime rather than apprehended for their violations; police rule bending is often organisationally condoned rather than condemned; police morale is sapped as well as boosted; relationships with colleagues are based on distrust and secrecy rather than honesty and openness; the courts are deceived, defendants misled, and in the end justice is as likely to be undermined rather than promoted. The result of these negative consequences is conflict, real and potential, both within and outwith the police organisation. (Norris and Dunnighan 2000: 407-408)

While this is an overly negative portrayal of the influence of informants on the police organisation, it is at least realistic in recognising that there are often negative consequences of informant use. Greater emphasis on using covert human sources to reveal the criminal milieu carries additional responsibilities to check and verify information. Intelligence-led policing emphasises the increased use of covertly gathered information applied in a more strategic manner than the traditional, myopic, investigative role. It is therefore possible that covert information will carry more weight in the decision-making framework of operational policing. This raises issues for police management:

- How do we know that informants are telling the truth?
- How do we place covert information into a wider context of criminality, especially when we may not have confidential sources in other areas?
- How do we manage the wider strategic responsibilities and avoid degenerating into an *informant-led policing* model?

More rigorous monitoring of information-classification systems is necessary if intelligence-led policing is to maintain public confidence. In the UK, the 5×5×5 National Information/Intelligence Reporting System contains components allowing reporting officers to evaluate the validity of the source and the information provided. The analysis unit then considers the appropriate handling code as a measure of the risk associated with sharing the information. Sources are evaluated as one of:

A – always reliable;

B – mostly reliable;

C – sometimes reliable;

D – unreliable;

E – untested source.

The information/intelligence is evaluated as one of:

1 – known to be true without reservation;

2 – known personally to the source but not to the person reporting;

3 – not known personally to the source but corroborated;

4 – cannot be judged;

5 – suspected to be false.

So covert information graded as B1 should carry more weight than information assessed as D4. Handling codes range from 1 (allows dissemination within the UK police service and to other law enforcement agencies) to 4 (originating agency use only) and the most restrictive, 5 (allow some dissemination but with conditions placed on the receiving unit or agency). These grading systems carry a degree of subjectivity, and the overprotective mentality that pervades much of policing tends towards greater information secrecy than information sharing. Education of officers will be essential to promote a more collaborative approach to information management.

Greater use of informants also carries risks if confidential human sources are employed inappropriately, and the early days of intelligence-led policing in the UK certainly suggested that work was required to improve the management, handling and operationalisation of informants (Maguire and John 1995). Cognisant of the risks, Grabosky (1992) argued that informants should be a tool of last resort, one that is only applied for the most serious offences and under supervision, but this was not the view of the Audit Commission (Audit Commission 1993). The reliance on a close relationship between a criminal informant and a police officer is an area fraught with ethical implications (Cooper and Murphy 1997), and sometimes results in outcomes detrimental for police departments by bringing police officers into close contact with the worst offenders.

One salutary example is that of Arthur 'Neddy' Smith. Smith, a heroin dealer and known member of the Sydney criminal underworld, not only asserted that he conducted a number of armed robberies in the Sydney area from 1986 to 1988, but also claimed that he had received a 'green light' from police to commit the robberies and that some even involved police officers (Wood 1997). One officer implicated was Detective Sergeant Roger Rogerson, who was eventually convicted of perverting the course of justice and lying to a Police Integrity Commission inquiry, though not convicted (but strongly suspected) of involvement in the shooting of a fellow police officer, Detective Mick Drury. Drury, who was shot twice while at home feeding his young daughter, alleged that Rogerson had been involved in the attempted hit on him because Drury had refused to accept a bribe from Rogerson in return for failing to provide evidence in a large heroin case.

The activities of Smith, Rogerson and a number of other police officers (for example, Detective Sergeant Robert Irwin, who had a corrupt relationship with a drug dealer and who traded sensitive police information for bribes; see Dixon 1999) were central to the investigation of the Wood Royal Commission. The Wood inquiry concluded that in the New South Wales Police, 'the culture was such, and the management and internal investigative systems were so deficient, that the state of corruption found can only be regarded as systemic and entrenched' (Wood 1997: 130). No doubt hindering attempts to implement intelligence-led policing, the climate that resulted from the Wood Royal Commission had a detrimental effect on informant use and the number of informants recruited (Ratcliffe 2002d).

The New South Wales Police case is not an isolated example. In fact, many large police departments have had damaging public inquiries related to police contact with confidential informants at some point. In London, the perceived mishandling of information from James Grant, pseudonym of an informer with knowledge of the murder of Stephen Lawrence, was brought to light during the Macpherson Report. The public inquiry concluded that the case had been poorly managed and revealed 'a woeful lack of attention to the steps which ought to be taken in respect of an informant' (Macpherson of Cluny 1999: Ch. 19, para. 23).

Informants have been used by police since the inception of modern policing and have been successfully employed in the cause of national security for longer than that. In the UK, the Regulation of Investigatory Powers Act 2000 has helped to codify the use of confidential human intelligence sources and reiterated the concept of proportionality (for example, section 29(2) states that 'the authorised conduct or use is proportionate to what is sought to be achieved by that conduct or use'). However, the intelligence-led policing shift from using them as an investigative resource to employment as a strategic and tactical resource for the whole police service will need careful management, supervision and handling in order for informant use to grow into the collective resource that informants have the potential to become. Furthermore training can limit the subjectivity of systems such as the 5×5×5 scheme, but greater supervision is vital, as are more imaginative ways to verify informant information.

Principle of proportionality

The use of confidential sources to combat criminality is one aspect of policing that has to be measured in proportion to the risks of losing public confidence. A further consideration is the nature of the target. The principle of proportionality (where a response is selected that is commensurate with the situation) has gained greater significance since Ericson and Haggerty (1997) found that police were caught up in a continual process of communicating risk information to public and private agencies. As a result, the day-to-day scope of surveillance has increased and resulted in both the extension of surveillance techniques and covert information collection being targeted at lower-level crimes such as recidivist petty offenders, lower-levels of the drug market, and public disorder (Maguire 2000). Former Commissioner of the Metropolitan Police Sir John Stevens noted that the importance of prominent targets changes with the policing area. He pointed out that the likely target from a crime intelligence assessment of the highest risk for a local police department 'will not be the head of an organised crime syndicate. It is more likely that they will be a prolific 15-year-old thief' (Stevens 2001: 6). Tactics that the public may deem acceptable for organised crime families may therefore not be viewed as appropriate when used to target the boy living in the next street. And proportionality applies not only to target selection but also to the methods of targeting. For example, CCTV footage of a suspect walking through a shopping centre may be personal information, but it is less sensitive than video footage of the suspect in his bedroom gathered through covert surveillance (NCPE 2006).

Proportionality considerations become more of a factor due to the urge, on occasion, to increase the status of a particular group beyond their actual capacity. This is sometimes the case with research into organised crime groups or gangs. Gangs actively try to increase their status and punch above their weight, but this also benefits police officers, who like to feel they are targeting 'worthy' offenders. Realistically, however, most local offenders are unlikely to be involved in a major international crime syndicate, and even possessing a collective gang or family name (either through labelling by the media, public or police, or by themselves to enhance their reputation) does not necessarily suggest an international connection (Stelfox 1998).

Greater analytical work is often required to see through the fog of public concern or gang rhetoric to determine the true nature of a group's criminality. In the UK, the police have adopted ethical standards and codes of practice based on the principle of proportionality and where the level of intrusive work must be justified by the severity of the offence (Neville 2000). This is not universally applied, and police departments need to be cautious of the use of information-gathering tactics that may be frowned on by the public; few people would consider a full surveillance team and wiretaps an appropriate response to a group of disorderly youths at a shopping centre (Ratcliffe 2002d). Without care, there is the possibility of continuing the 'surveillance creep' that Marx (1988) argues has seen an increasing acceptance of intrusion in the name of crime control. The principle of proportionality is therefore a balance of the apposite tactics applied to the appropriate offenders and should be a tenet of intelligence-led policing.

Storing private information

The principle of proportionality is enshrined in legislation in the UK, such that the actions of the police force comply with the human rights principle of proportionality (NCPE 2005b). The principle also applies to the storage of private individual information, an area with considerable legal implications for the development of intelligence-led policing.

In the US, the maintenance and use of criminal intelligence systems is regulated by Title 28 of the Code of Federal Regulations (CFR) Part 23, commonly referred to as 28CFR23. The purpose of 28CFR23 is to ensure that criminal intelligence systems are operated and maintained so that individual privacy and rights are not violated unless in accordance with the law. This places a number of requirements and restrictions on the recording of covert information by police. For example, all information must be reviewed at a minimum of every five years, and any individual, business or group named in a criminal intelligence information system must be suspected of criminal activity. Agencies are, however, permitted to retain information that does not meet 28CFR23 requirements as long as that information is not shared electronically with other agencies. Furthermore, the Bureau of Justice Administration issued a Police Clarification in 1998 that stated:

> Information that is relevant to the identification of a criminal suspect or to the criminal activity in which the suspect is engaged may be placed in a criminal intelligence database, provided that (1) appropriate disclaimers accompany the information noting that it is strictly identifying information, carrying no criminal connotations; (2) identifying information may not be used as an independent basis to meet the requirement of reasonable suspicion of involvement in criminal activity necessary to create a record or file in a criminal intelligence system; and (3) the individual who is the criminal suspect identified by this information otherwise meets all requirements of 28 CFR Part 23. This information may be a searchable field in the intelligence system. (BJA 1998)

It is therefore possible to retain and search non-criminal identifying information on criminal suspects. In the UK, the Data Protection Act 1998 applies eight principles to the retention of personal information. The information must:

- be fairly and lawfully processed;
- be processed for limited purposes and not in any manner incompatible with those purposes;
- be adequate, relevant and not excessive;

- be accurate and where necessary, up to date;
- not be kept for longer than is necessary;
- be processed in accordance with individual rights;
- be stored securely;
- not be transferred to countries outside the EU without adequate protection.
  (NCPE 2006)

These requirements apply not only to computer files but also to structured manual files. There is a general provision in the Act to allow individuals access to information about them that is stored by police, unless restricted for the purpose of safeguarding national security. Section 29 also creates exemptions to certain data protection principles where the data are processed or shared in order to prevent or detect crime, or to assist in the apprehension or prosecution of offenders. From a strategic perspective, section 33 makes provision for the use of personal data for statistical and research purposes. The Act is therefore not as restrictive as many officers believe. The Bichard Inquiry into the handling of intelligence records surrounding the murders of the British schoolgirls Jessica Chapman and Holly Wells by a school caretaker named Ian Huntley, noted that 'police officers were nervous about breaching the legislation, partly at least because too little was done to educate and reassure them about its impact' (Bichard 2004: 4).

For intelligence-led policing to continue to advance, a greater understanding of the legal conditions for covert information gathering and storage is necessary. Police services can then make more effective use of the tools available to them, while staying within legal and ethical boundaries that consider the principle of proportionality in offender targeting and data storage. Without better training and knowledge, police departments will either overstep legal boundaries unknowingly, or fail to employ their skills and resources effectively. If the former, they will lose public trust and confidence; with the latter, they will fail to serve the community as successfully as they could.

Human rights and surveillance

The very process of focusing police tactics is seen by some as a threat to their perceived civil liberties, though public perception of what constitutes civil liberties is often inaccurate and exaggerated. When law enforcement officers concentrate their attention on one group or the residents in one area, it can, not surprisingly, be perceived by that group as harassment. But is a minor and localised infringement of perceived liberties an acceptable trade-off and tolerable if it creates a safer environment and (through a diffusion of benefits) extends the social benefits to surrounding areas? The reality is that people who live in high-crime areas will most likely be a little inconvenienced if the police are to bring down crime. For example, as Weatherburn points out, 'If police are to create a credible threat of apprehension for carrying a prohibited weapon they are bound to conduct searches of a large number of people who, it will turn out, are not in possession of a weapon' (Weatherburn 2004: 98). Related to this, the Kansas City gun experiment did reduce crime (see Chapter 8). However, a gun was found at a rate of one in every 28 traffic stops; on average, the occupants of 27 cars were inconvenienced and searched before a gun was detected. The inconvenience factor is thus fairly high with this tactic. The research on the opposite position is also clear: random and unfocused police activity has no crime reduction benefits and can still be perceived negatively by the public.

This is always an area fraught with potential pitfalls for police. Increased action can reduce crime, but at what cost to public perception of police in a democracy? Even police action conducted in accordance with the law can be perceived as a violation of rights by some members of the public. Considering that when the public have a negative encounter with the police the effects on the perceived legitimacy of the police are anywhere from four to 14 times worse than having a positive experience, the necessity for courtesy and respect and a good bedside manner is paramount (Skogan 2006a). It is therefore vital that police demonstrate respect and courtesy when conducting searches, saturation patrolling or any other activity, not only because it will extend the time that the public are prepared to accept heightened police attention, but also because it makes police work easier by building legitimacy for police within the community.

When police move to more covert forms of information gathering, their contact with the public is often restricted and reduced, often for good reasons of operational security. As surveillance officers monitoring wiretaps discovered in the Brightwood neighbourhood of Indianapolis, Indiana,

> There was evidence suggesting that some of the neighborhood residents who had so vehemently demanded that something be done about the drugs and violence in their neighborhood were the same people heard warning the dealers about possible surveillance. It appears that, in some cases, neighborhood residents wanted rid of the drug problem in their neighborhood—but not their own son, brother, or grandson who might also have been a dealer. (Nunn *et al.* 2006: 81)

Once police begin to operate where much of the police work is not observable by the public, the 'longer-term consequence of the trend to focus policing activity around crime management has been to increase the social distance between police and policed' (Innes 2004: 156). Some legislation is thus designed to provide an oversight role that the public is unable to perform. The Human Rights Act 1998 (HRA) incorporated most of the European Convention on Human Rights (ECHR) and brought to the UK a requirement for police services to act in a manner compatible with the European Convention. Of particular note is Article 8 of the ECHR, which protects an individual's right to privacy except 'in accordance of the law, in pursuit of a legitimate aim; and necessary in a democratic society'. Police must therefore set a clear aim for obtaining personal information and incorporate a test of proportionality to determine how they meet this aim (NCPE 2006). The test works to increase the threshold for allowability as intrusion into the privacy of a suspect increases, and is of relevance to surveillance and the use of informants: the greater the interference with an individual's privacy, the higher the threshold.

All of these controls act to protect the public and in the process build public trust, a vital component necessary to the acceptance of intelligence-led policing, as Russ Porter explains in the following Viewpoint.

Viewpoint

Intelligence-led policing and public trust

Russ Porter

> One of the critical issues that could quickly stop intelligence sharing is the real or perceived violation of individuals' privacy and constitutional rights through the use of intelligence sharing systems. In order to balance law enforcement's ability to share information while ensuring that the rights of citizens are upheld, appropriate privacy policies must be in place. *Fusion Center Guidelines*, Guideline 8 (DOJ 2005: 49)

In a democracy, people generally get the kind of policing that they want. That is to say, they pick up the phone and request it. As such, policing is often a reactive business, in which the police direct their attention to the issues that the public reports, or provide police services that the public requests. In recent years, however, intelligence-led policing – a proactive approach in which intelligence and analysis are at the heart of decision making – has emerged as a promising policing and security strategy. Intelligence activity and analysis, rather than requests for service from the public, become the foundation for many police actions. The need to gather information for intelligence purposes may be especially important for developing strategies related to the control of terrorism, organized crime, drug distribution networks, gangs, and other criminal associations.

But intelligence-led policing also brings with it special challenges. While the police analytical function may be an effective tool for protecting the public from serious crime, information-gathering activities associated with intelligence-led policing may also infringe on the privacy and civil liberties of individuals. This type of information gathering requires the police to use more intrusive procedures, such as informants, undercover operations, electronic surveillance, and sophisticated intelligence analysis. Such intrusive procedures pose threats to civil liberties, privacy, and other rights. In fact, police intelligence practices in the United States repeatedly were the subject of widely-publicized civil liberties complaints, lawsuits, and consent decrees during the 1970s, 1980s, and beyond. The potential threat to civil liberties, privacy, and other rights, therefore, is one of the special challenges facing intelligence-led policing and the development of police information networks. As the Markle Foundation have noted, any attempt to build an information network 'would not be sustainable if the government did not build public trust' (2003: 1).

It is therefore important for police organisations to put the protection of privacy and civil liberties 'up front' when implementing an intelligence-led policing approach. The gathering of information for the police intelligence function is among the critical decision points in policing. Intelligence activity is also an area where law enforcement officers exercise considerable discretion that has seldom been subject to review from outside the police agency. Viewing the intelligence process as a series of discretionary decisions and using policy and training to institute appropriate safeguards, therefore, can help protect privacy and civil liberties.

As with other discretionary decisions in policing, intelligence policies and training that address the protection of privacy and civil liberties should (1) eliminate the unnecessary discretion in the decision-making process, (2) guide the necessary discretion, and (3) continually audit the process to ensure conformance with the policy goals. A number of intelligence policies, laws, and regulations (for example, LEIU File Guidelines; 28 CFR Part 23, known as the Criminal Intelligence Systems Operating Policies; and Article 8 of the European Convention on Human Rights) follow this framework. These policies and others can help police organisations give the protection of privacy and civil liberties the highest priority, build and maintain the public's trust, and therefore sustain their intelligence-led policing approach.

Besides – protecting privacy and civil liberties is the right thing to do.

> *Russ Porter, the Intelligence Bureau Chief for the State of Iowa, has been assigned to the police intelligence function since 1984. He serves on the executive board of the Law Enforcement Intelligence Unit, as an executive adviser to the International Association of Law Enforcement Intelligence Analysts, and on the Criminal Intelligence Coordinating Council.*

The widening security agenda

Much has been achieved in policing in the 20th century, and our concern now is with the future and how we adapt to protect the public in the 21st century....The analysis points to a future policing environment characterised by:

- widespread enterprising organised criminality, proliferating international terrorism and domestic extremism;

- a premium on intelligence, expertise and smart use of capacity;

- an increasingly risk concerned public and intrusive media. (HMIC 2005: 6)

The widening security agenda is a reality in most places. No longer is the provision of crime prevention and security the sole dominion of the police; they share this congested field with a range of state and non-state entities and a public both increasingly informed and alarmed. These can create competing demands on police, but can also provide opportunities for wider information sharing and crime prevention engagement. While the move towards intelligence-led policing took place before 9/11 and while terrorism is still not an issue for the majority of police departments, the development of the intelligence-led policing concept in America has occurred in a political environment where counter-terrorism has been the 800-pound gorilla in the room. The future of intelligence-led policing may well be tied to associated developments.

As technological progress continues to reshape the nature of society, the criminal environment has become more networked and less hierarchically structured. This structural and organisational change has not been matched by law enforcement, still organised as it is along strictly hierarchical lines. As SOCA recognise, 'while helpful in understanding the scale and nature of the various activities and considering the best response, the division of serious organised crime into different sectors (such as drugs trafficking, organised immigration crime, and fraud) is as much a reflection of the law and organisational responsibilities for its enforcement as it is of criminal behaviours' (SOCA 2006: 15). The result is a police organisation that is based upon crime fighting and the status concerns of a rank-structured police bureaucracy (Sheptycki 2007), and not based on a more networked model of operation that is positioned to use information efficiently to combat criminal activity.

Organisational changes are ahead if police are to be successful in reducing and preventing crime, changes that include greater strategic use and application of the resources they command, and the management of the merging of criminal intelligence and national security intelligence.

Greater strategic application

The range of data and information sources available to police analysts might lead one to expect that we are on the brink of a new era of holistic policing, but there is a real possibility that the analytical nucleus of intelligence-led policing can become the victim of paralysis by analysis. As databases become more linked and more encyclopaedic, and contain more non-crime data, this wealth of information requires greater skill on the part of analysts and more patience on the part of decision-makers. Greater volumes of material require longer to bring into focus, especially when much of the material is just noise. Overcoming the frustration of police commanders who do not appreciate that crime intelligence analysis is a time-consuming and technical business can often be a full-time job in itself.

The rewards of a more holistic view of the criminal environment are significant. Greater use of non-crime data will enable police commanders to put different crime threats into perspective. For example, consider a police commander faced with two street drug markets but having the resources to tackle only one. Both drug corners appear similar from the number of drug arrests; however, an analysis of the overdose history of the surrounding neighbourhoods finds that the product from one drug corner causes significantly more harm than the other. A strategic, harm-based decision is now possible. An evaluation of the GMAC PBM (see Chapter 7) – a model that integrates data from numerous agencies – described GMAC PBM as a process that 'supports partners in approaching their shared interests in a strategic manner, basing their decisions on a broad knowledge base – and provides process and structure for actions to be taken in a coordinated manner' (John et al. 2006: 55).

It is with a variation of this approach that we determined that street corners in Camden, New Jersey, had, on average, 100 per cent more violent crime in the immediate vicinity of a drug corner than a non-drug corner, and that corners where more than one gang had been known to deal were 30 per cent more violent again. This strategic insight has helped the local prosecutor's office reconsider their approach to drug corners in the city (Ratcliffe and Taniguchi 2008). Non-crime data such as overdose information or public perception – as measured through public surveys – can also serve to direct police to the appropriate targets. This type of strategic harm approach to prioritisation, one that weighs the impact of crime by its economic and social costs, would appear to be an untapped but potentially productive new development for law enforcement agencies.

However, there is a difference between a strategic harm model and the current modish enthusiasm for prioritising reduction of the fear of crime. In the UK, this manifests itself through the movement for reassurance policing. While being more responsive to the community makes a great sound bite, like community policing, it can move police away from being objective about crime threats to being driven by factors such as media scaremongering. Instead of intelligence-led policing, we end up with *media-led policing* (not far from *stupidly led policing*!). There is insufficient evidence at present that police can significantly influence people's fear of crime, yet this movement has the potential to push police back to reactive policing based on hunches and more abstract notions of crime problems and causes rather than tackling real criminality. While it appears rational, I do worry that reassurance policing is the 'intelligent design' of law enforcement: sounds good but lacks substance.

Public fear of crime is undoubtedly an issue for government; however, the drivers for public concern are often outside the ambit of law enforcement, while tackling actual crime is most certainly the domain of the police. If it is possible to move away from the 'populist' or 'consumerist' focus of reassurance and neighbourhood policing that can pull police to and fro on the whim of 'irrational' public mood swings (Maguire and John 2006: 78), then it may be possible to achieve an objective approach to police priorities and resource issues based on a wider interpretation of police business, as advocated by intelligence-led policing. It is unclear whether this is a marriage that will end happily or in a messy divorce; however, it has been claimed that, 'if successful, both reassurance and neighbourhood policing are potentially of significant benefit to the development of intelligence-led policing, in that improvements in public confidence in the police might serve to improve the quality of criminal and community intelligence' (Maguire and John 2006: 79).

A more holistic, harm-based approach would place national and international threats into context, not just for local crime but also for organised crime activity. In a polemic move, Shepytcki argues that, in the past, 'because policy makers had focused so exclusively on the notion of the "Mr Bigs" of organized crime, the transnational police function had been systematically distorted. Not only have many types of organized enterprise crime been ignored...disorganized transnational crime has also been ignored' (2005: 3). This is a theme that also echoes with the street cop. As Jack Maple, one of the architects of Compstat, said, 'I'm not worried about organized crime; I'm worried about disorganized crime' (quoted in Bratton 2006: 3).

Greater strategic application is also necessary to place the larger environment of the modern world into context. The sense of insecurity and the perception of faceless threats from every corner have increased across society despite crime levels falling and greater levels of access to information than ever before. Greater use of non-crime data and a more inclusive analytical approach can help bring these often abstract areas of criminality and threat into greater focus, enabling police commanders to articulate a clearer vision of the real harms and threats to society, and better manage the associated risks. Not being able to place crime threats into perspective against the broader risk environment leads to tactical, knee-jerk reaction policing. This in turn leads to the creation of ad hoc task forces and units to address immediate tactical concerns, ignores the greater strategic perspective, and undermines attempts to develop a strategic read on the criminal environment that is reliable and valid (Sheptycki 2007). As explained in Chapter 5, strategic can mean different things to different police departments; however, the universal quality of a strategic perspective is one that steps back from the immediate tactical picture and explores actions that can address underlying causes. This is a central component of the problem-oriented policing rationale and one that translates across to intelligence-led policing directly; intelligence-led policing is about identifying, prioritising and intervening with the aim of minimising risk (Cope 2004). The danger of a perspective that is too focused on an investigative, case-specific structure is clear:

> Within the United States, various FBI field offices gathered intelligence on organisations suspected of raising funds for al Qaeda or other terrorist groups. By 9/11, FBI agents understood that there were extremist organisations operating within the United States supporting a global jihadist movement and with substantial connections to al Qaeda. The FBI operated a web of informants, conducted electronic surveillance, and had opened significant investigations in a number of field offices. ... On a national level, however, the FBI never used the information to gain a systematic or strategic understanding of the nature and extent of al Qaeda fundraising. (9/11 Commission 2004: 186)

Merging criminal intelligence and national security

Intelligence-led policing has become a policing paradigm at the same time that national security issues have expanded to become domestic priorities. Prior to 9/11, discussion regarding the future role of the police in the twenty-first century was academic and esoteric. After 9/11, that debate became public, wide-ranging and imbued with a sense of urgency.

Some agencies, possibly with more of an eye to their own organisational benefit than on the evidence, linked terrorism to drugs, organised crime and transnational crime. The linking of organised crime to terrorism has thus enabled law enforcement agencies to expand their information-collation facilities. Indeed, with the greater spread of transnational policing organisations (for example, EUROPOL and Interpol) alongside national law enforcement agencies that have international connections (such as the FBI, New York City Police Department, and the Australian Federal Police), governance and the provision of national security now extends beyond the boundaries of individual nation states, blurring the concept of clear political accountability for police intelligence practices. This is particularly noticeable in the reformatting of serious and organised crime and terrorism as national security concerns (Sheptycki 2007). The police role in this expanding world is unclear:

> It is well established that there is a fundamental and defining tension at the heart of the Anglo-American police institution. The essence of this tension pivots around a debate as to whether the role of the public police should be restricted to the prevention and detection of crime, or whether it should have the rather more amorphous role of engaging in the delivery of security. (Innes 2004: 151)

In this tension, the recent history of the US does suggest caution. The use of detention facilities outside national borders to avoid the civil legal system, rendition flights, and a wealth of new, potentially intrusive legislation places a significant burden of accuracy on crime intelligence analysts working in the 'high policing' domain. In this charged environment, cooperation and information sharing are as essential as political and policy independence. In particular, there is general agreement that counter-terrorism policing relies on cooperation between agencies, a reflection that the context of policing has changed to one of a 'polycentric world of nodal governance' (Wood and Shearing 2007: 114). However, new information-sharing arrangements are never implemented in a virgin environment: there are always existing relationships that were forged prior to the execution of a new directive. These prior relationships dictate the likelihood of success for the future, and success is never guaranteed:

> Unfortunately, federal law enforcement agencies mistrust one another at times. While not directly related to state and local issues, their failure to cooperate in some circumstances influences local police relationships. Many federal law enforcement agencies openly resent the FBI, and this attitude is frequently reciprocated. (White 2004: 44)

The technical environment rarely helps. For example, the current system of information security, with its associated protective markings, classifications and organisational compartmentalisation, was designed in an era where secrecy was necessary to prevent investigations being compromised. The new policing environment is one that places a greater premium on collaborative information sharing and strategic decision-making than on a reactive, investigative ethos. As such, an overhaul of both the governance of information security and the organisational pathologies that support the existing culture may be necessary for the strategic aims of intelligence-led policing to thrive. This overhaul would have to address not only the technical environment, but also the legal, policy, cultural, and organisational conditions that fuel existing organisational pathologies.

In the US, such a refit is under way with the work of the Program Manager for the Information Sharing Environment (in the Office of the Director of National Intelligence) and the Information Sharing Council. The challenges are significant. Intelligence-handling procedures among the various threads of the intelligence, law enforcement, defence, homeland security and foreign affairs communities have all evolved independently, and there is a lack of national strategy or protocols to determine how these federal bodies interact with the fusion centres that provide access to state and local policing resources (McNamara 2006). One of the major challenges is to get the 17 members[1] of the Information Sharing Council to cooperate among themselves in counter-terrorism matters, a situation that has to be resolved before even trying to address their collective interface to the state and local law enforcement levels. For example, even in the area of information that is sensitive but unclassified, among a sample of 20 agencies, it was found that information at this lowest level of the secrecy hierarchy had at least 107 different markings (for example, 'for official use only' or 'law enforcement sensitive') and over 130 different handling procedures for the information (McNamara 2007; Murphy 2007).

More than just procedural encumbrances, there are real conceptual barriers between the various parties. My discussions with different actors at various levels of the US system suggest that some federal agencies still view counter-terrorism as an investigative function, with strategic public safety and crime control considerations as being, to a degree, tangential to their counter-terrorism mission. By comparison, local and state police departments have to incorporate any counter-terrorism activities within the framework of their broader – and equally pressing – mandate to protect the community from violent crime and public disorder. Within these quite different conceptual frameworks, the diverse perspectives make finding common ground for information sharing challenging.

As explained earlier in the book, knowledge and intelligence gain their power through being given meaning and context and, in the latter case, having an actionable component. Whether counter-terrorism intelligence can be acted upon depends on both the nature of the intelligence at hand, and the requirements and priorities of the audience. Each constituent group

– the public, first responders, analysts, police chiefs, politicians, or federal agents – has a different perspective on how intelligence is valuable to their needs. A one-size-fits-all approach to intelligence dissemination only ends up disappointing everyone.

The work of the Program Manager for the Information Sharing Environment is still in progress, and it is too early to say whether his aims will be achieved. If successful, the benefits to counter-terrorism at federal, state and local levels in the US may be significant. If unsuccessful or eternally bogged down in bureaucracy and agency turf protection, there may be some tough questions to answer when the next terrorist incident occurs.

An agenda for the future

It is difficult to conclude this book with a list of the avenues that law enforcement should take to cement intelligence-led policing into the working practices of police departments. The whole book is written to address this need, so identifying a short list of items that should take priority over others is problematic, and different agencies will have different weaknesses to resolve. However, if there are some themes to reiterate, then they are the following: the need for increased training, a better way to promote successes; a realisation that the policing setting is changing to one of greater networks and pluralism, the need for a strategic perspective, and finally the importance of a close relationship between police leadership and analysts.

Conceptual training for analysts and executives

I have previously argued that the police analysis field (through organisations such as IALEIA and IACA) has taken the bull by the horns, recognised the need for education, and started to address the training needs of analysts. It has certainly done so to a far greater extent than police leadership training has embraced educating executives in the latest approaches to crime reduction (Ratcliffe 2004a). Yet, the police analysis industry still provides only limited training opportunities, and the training that does exist is perpetually stuck in introductory mode reflecting the rapid turnover of established analysts constantly being replaced by inexperienced and untrained analysts.

The provision of training is one way that professional organisations can sustain a place alongside the police at the hub of security networks (Dupont 2006), but it is difficult to break out of the rut of rudimentary training when that is the perceived need. A third of large police departments in the US do not offer GIS or crime-mapping training, and about half of the smaller departments (with less than 100 sworn officers) do not offer any crime-analysis training. It is thus not surprising that many analysts are criticised for only counting crimes and not analysing them (O'Shea and Nicholls 2002). With so few development opportunities, it is unsurprising that advanced training in strategic thinking is even rarer. For example, Australia's National Strategic Intelligence Course – an intensive residential course – is one of the few available to advanced analysts; a fact that probably explains the waiting list to get on the course (Walsh and Ratcliffe 2005).

The extant training for analysts tends to focus on technical skills to enable them to do the nuts and bolts of their job. There is a dearth of training that addresses a broader educational approach to the nuances of where they fit into the decision-making framework. In other words, and to use the 3-i model, the existing training is fixated on interpreting the criminal environment, and often with a tactical or investigative mindset. Good crime intelligence analysis is that which identifies the systemic weaknesses that exacerbate crime and provide criminal opportunities to prolific offenders. Showing a decision-maker how to shut down a vulnerable system is of infinitely greater value than assisting one investigation and prosecution while leaving the victimised area vulnerable for the future. Substantial education to show analysts how to understand and operate in a situation where equal importance is placed on influencing decision-makers and making recommendations to help them impact on the criminal environment is in dire need of development.

The analytical education problem is exacerbated by a lack of training for command ranks. Command carries a greater degree of career risk, a point noted by Deukmedjian (2006: 533): 'The burden of processing voluminous and contradictory information falls mainly on mid-management shoulders. ... Since this responsibility creates significant career risks, mid-managers may resist the intelligence-led ideal in ways akin to their resistance to empowerment during the 1990s.' Cope (2004) noted a paucity of training for police officers that affected their ability to use intelligence productively and use products in an operational capacity. It is unreasonable to expect commanders to flounder in the dark without guidance, and therefore without a robust understanding of the overarching philosophy, resistance may become significant.

If intelligence-led policing is to thrive in the future, the training agenda may have to give greater billing to the conceptual aims of intelligence-led policing at both an analytical and a command level. As one of the leading police chiefs in the US has stated, this approach may need to be tackled at the national level:

Recognized as a national way forward, ILP is an all-crimes approach to enforcement that will revolutionize law enforcement. ILP richly integrates existing strategies and technologies into a coherent 'game-plan' approach in allocating resources efficiently. Currently, without a national strategy, or a place where police executives can learn how to implement ILP, it is sitting on the shelf unused. (Bratton 2007: 7–8)

In summary, if there is one critical weakness that exists in the current training environment, it is the development and promulgation of doctrine and best practice managing the link between analysts and decision-makers. The lack of synergy, learning and development addressing this pivotal relationship between the providers and the consumers of crime intelligence is almost certainly one of the main constraints on the growth of intelligence-led policing. If we are to develop a cadre of well-trained analysts that are integrated with decision-making systems, then this has to be an issue for analysts and executives alike.

Disseminating success

As intelligence-led policing moves forward in different police services, it often does so without knowledge of the successes and failures elsewhere. Even though the UK has operated the NIM since 2000 and had been discussing and publishing evaluations of British police service experiments with intelligence-led policing prior to that, I still attended a meeting in 2007 in the US that spent considerable effort deciding that the development of a definition of intelligence-led policing would be a good idea.

For analysts and police commanders wishing to know how to implement intelligence-led policing, there are now multiple information sources on intelligence-led policing, multiple agencies claiming expertise, multiple voices, multiple experts, and yet no coherent message. This problem exists not just for police practice but also for crime reduction generally. One potential solution may be to drag crime reduction knowledge into one place. For example, the Dutch Police Knowledge Net is available to all Dutch police officers through a secure Internet portal. Here police can draw on not just regulations, protocols and background information relating to police operations, but also legislative changes and information on best practice (Bakker 2004). In a similar vein, the value of the Center for Problem Oriented Policing (www.popcenter.org) should not be underestimated. The continued expansion, albeit slow, of problem-oriented policing has been sustained to a considerable degree by the presence of a moderated, central repository of the collected wisdom of the problem-oriented policing movement. Intelligence-led policing would benefit from a similar centralised resource for all things related to intelligence-led policing, or even a collaborative venture alongside the Center for Problem Oriented Policing.

Looking beyond the tactical imperatives

It is understandable why many police departments have no strategic plan. With half the departments in the US having fewer than 10 sworn officers, reactive, tactical policing will probably always dominate the agenda. However, a lack of strategic direction is also a problem for agencies that have greater resources and opportunities. While discussing how to combat organised crime, the researchers Michael Levi and Mike Maguire could easily have been discussing the broader policing field: 'Sophisticated as many of the law enforcement initiatives have undoubtedly been ... they almost inevitably lack the crucial dimension of a focus on longer term outcomes and on the structures and conditions which facilitate organized criminal enterprises' (Levi and Maguire 2004: 410).

When the priorities focus less on investigations and allow a greater role for strategically applied disruption and prevention, new partnerships in the fight against crime become possible. In the UK, agencies with a national security portfolio have been linked to SOCA in a move described as 'consistent with an intelligence-led approach that focused not so much on achieving detections as upon disruption of organized crime businesses through a wide variety of interventions that broaden the "policing" of organized crime beyond the traditional range of criminal law enforcement options' (Harfield 2006: 747). Crime and Disorder Reduction Partnerships (that include not only the police but also local authorities, probation service, health authorities, the voluntary sector, residents and businesses) are another good example at the local level.

Intelligence-led policing was originally sold to and by the police as a way to escape the cyclic nature of response policing, but escaping the gravitational pull of day-to-day reactive needs has still been difficult for some police services. There is evidence that a more strategic approach to crime and community problems is successful, but the need to convince many in law enforcement of this remains.

In developing strategic aims, what are good benchmarks for the selection of priorities? Weatherburn (2004) suggests that the level of public concern should be a criterion in the setting of crime-control priorities, alongside four other criteria: the prevalence of a particular crime, attention to crime types that are becoming more prevalent, the level of harm caused by a problem to individuals or society, and the potential harm of a problem if left unchecked. These criteria are not unrelated to the broader aims of the community policing movement (though Weatherburn articulates them more clearly). Intelligence-led policing is not incompatible with the value set of community-type policing, but only when the right balance is struck. This balance includes considering the community impact of particular strategies, recognising the principle of proportionality, and moving to a harm-based approach. Local police chiefs are answerable to the public, but with good crime intelligence they have access to a more holistic and objective picture of the criminal environment. There is thus a responsibility to convey a version of that picture to the public and explain prioritisation choices. It is probably in this vein, along with a desire to integrate better police knowledge with the wider community perspective, that a number of strategic tasking and coordinating meetings in the UK include representatives from non-criminal justice agencies (John *et al.* 2006; Maguire and John 2006).

Engage the next cohort of police leaders

In 2000, Peter Gill wrote, 'If intelligence-led policing is to become more than a rhetorical justification for traditional policing practices, that is, if it is to become a serious attempt to solve the "knowledge" problem regarding the causes of social damage, then greater efforts are required, especially at the analytical phase of the process' (2000: 261). I do not disagree, but would expand the analytical process to include the management chain. The success of intelligence-led policing lies with the next cohort of police leaders working alongside analysts within the decision-making sphere. Existing leadership has a responsibility to lay the foundations for intelligence-led policing, but the reality is that analytical training, staffing and support are all in a stage best described as 'in progress'. Even if the current levels of top management could appreciate and decipher crime intelligence products, few agencies are functioning at the stage where these products are produced with the consistency and rigour that a strategic, holistic appreciation of the criminal environment from a harm-based perspective demands.

At present, middle management and the ranks of future police chiefs are still swelling with detectives and others with an investigative background. While some investigators have embraced more strategic thinking, spending one's formative years investigating individual cases – and getting promoted on the strength of performance in that area – inevitably drives a tactical frame of mind. It may take some time for this bias to work its way out of the system, and it may require direct action to address the incentive structure of policing to correct this legacy from an investigative era of policing that goes back many decades. It is to be hoped that a background in crime intelligence analysis might be seen as a promotion requirement in the future. The increasing independence of analysis from being an adjunct to investigations helps in developing this future.

One of the significant changes to policing has been the influx of middle management with some degree of tertiary education. From this may flow a greater appreciation for research. This will help enhance the role of the analyst and build the internal capacity for police to evaluate their own strategies and tactics. Without this, the ability to impact on the criminal environment will be hindered, and will end up relying on either external evaluations from other agencies or on the hunches of police commanders

234

unable to articulate whether their tactics will work or not. Some evidence of this greater engagement with research can be seen in the increasing interaction between police agencies and the university research community. While there are always some in academia who regularly criticise police with little constructive purpose other than their own career advancement, there is a growing assemblage of academic researchers who are active in working with police to improve operational responses to crime problems.

Middle management is also increasingly cognisant of the role of data and information in the measurement of their performance. They have moved into the higher ranks during a time of greater oversight and accountability and are more answerable to the public as a result of a new openness in crime statistics. This may have the negative consequence of driving accountability by numbers; however, it does embed a will to tackle emerging crime threats and an acceptance of data as an evaluative tool. This moves the analyst to the hub of both the crime control arena and the response evaluation component.

The 3-i model requires a close relationship between analysts and decision-makers, and as both components grow together, the general public may be the beneficiary. The future may rest on police leadership working in combination with police analysts.

Ten yardsticks for intelligence-led policing

If all of the features described in this book coalesce, what might a police service or police department that embraces intelligence-led policing look like? What sorts of characteristics identify such an environment? While Chapter 4 identified the tenets of intelligence-led policing as a conceptual framework, there appear to be some basic structural and cultural standards that can act as a yardstick for an intelligence-led environment. The following list is likely to be revised as time goes on; however, this initial inventory may serve as a standard against which we can assess the development and growth of intelligence-led policing environments.

Here is my top-10 list of intelligence-led policing yardsticks:

1. There is a supportive and informed command structure.
   - There is 'enthusiastic and energetic leadership' (HMIC 1997: 1) that endorses intelligence-led policing, promotes it actively, and routinely uses crime intelligence analysis as the basis for strategic decision-making.
2. Intelligence-led policing is the heart of an *organisation-wide* approach.
   - Intelligence-led policing has significant differences from some other policing strategies and is therefore incompatible with a piecemeal approach where intelligence-led policing is applied

only in specialised units. While analysis might be a specialised function, it should be directed at, complement and support the whole organisation.

3. Crime and criminal analysis is integrated.
   - An integrated crime intelligence structure has analysts working at the hub of operational policing activities in direct support of decision-makers at all levels of the organisation.

4. The focus is on prolific and serious offenders.
   - The proactive heart of intelligence-led policing is the identification and interdiction of criminal leaders and offenders identified at the strategic level as priority targets.

5. Analytical and executive training is available.
   - Support for the analytical heart of strategic and tactical decision-making is available with appropriate training and resourcing. Support is targeted to a cadre of professional analysts and intelligence staff (source handlers and field intelligence officers), with executive education of the leadership role within intelligence-led policing.

6. Both strategic and tactical tasking meetings take place.
   - With regular meetings, tactical issues can dominate the agenda. Strategic meetings are therefore essential and should be the central focus, allowing decision-makers to draw in a wider range of opinion and explore more considered prevention, enforcement and information-gathering options. Tactical activities should be grounded in these strategic priorities.

7. Much routine investigation is screened out.
   - A move from reactive policing requires less energy spent on the investigation of crimes that are unlikely to result in arrest and prosecution, creating opportunities for more proactive, targeted work.

8. Data are sufficiently complete, reliable and available to support quality products that influence decision-making.
   - Reliable and robust data systems are essential if decision-makers are to place faith in products and if decision-makers are to be persuaded that an intelligence-led approach adds value to their resource-allocation decisions.

9. Management structures exist to action intelligence products.
   - Merely holding meetings is insufficient to warrant the label *intelligence-led*. Intelligence is inherently actionable; therefore, meetings and organisational structures have to see action and resource allocation as the primary function of the impact arm of the 3-i model.

10. There is appropriate use of prevention, disruption and enforcement.

- Not every problem is resolvable by disruption or enforcement, and strategies drawn from problem-oriented policing suggest a number of prevention opportunities.

Summary

If Kelling and Bratton are correct (from the quotation at the start of this chapter) that intelligence-led policing has the potential to be the most important law enforcement development of the century, then sustained effort will be necessary to make this happen. Within the ranks of the police, greater clarity of the aims and mechanisms of intelligence-led policing is essential to staying on target and maintaining pressure on prolific and persistent offenders. Mere adoption of rhetoric, while always easy, is not sufficient as a basis on which to claim operation of an intelligence-led policing model. Making the shift to intelligence-led policing requires organisational and cultural changes that some in policing will resist. Both police executives and analysts will have to demonstrate leadership, ownership and understanding of the tenets of intelligence-led policing for it to succeed.

As important as sustaining focus within policing is the necessity to work in partnership with the community. Intelligence-led policing may help to target the worst offenders, but how do police strike the balance between these proactive activities and the other, more mundane, but equally important, activities and functions that police provide that have little to do with crime? Maintaining essential public support will necessitate a balance between providing the sort of policing that communities in a democratic society expect and find reassuring, and both conducting and explaining the need for the proactive targeting and strategic problem-solving of an effective crime-prevention strategy. One challenge for the immediate future may well be enrolling public support and explaining to communities the value of intelligence-led policing in keeping them safe and secure.

Note

1 Program Manager for the Information Sharing Environment (Chair), Central Intelligence Agency, Department of Commerce, Department of Defense (Joint Chiefs of Staff), Department of Defense (Office of the Secretary of Defense), Department of Energy, Department of Health and Human Services, Department of Homeland Security, Department of the Interior, Department of Justice, Department of State, Department of Transportation, Department of the Treasury, Director of National Intelligence, Federal Bureau of Investigation, National Counterterrorism Center, and Office of Management of Budget.

References

9/11 Commission (2004) *The 9/11 Commission Report*. Washington, DC: National Commission on Terrorist Attacks Upon the United States.

ACC (2004) *Australian Crime Commission Corporate Plan 2004–2007*. Canberra: Australian Crime Commission.

ACC (2006) *Illicit Drug Data Report 2004–05*. Canberra: Australian Crime Commission.

ACPO (1975) *Report of the ACPO Subcommittee on Criminal Intelligence (Baumber report)*. London: Association of Chief Police Officers.

ACPO (1978) *Report of the ACPO Working Party on a Structure of Criminal Intelligence Officers (Pearce Report)*. London: Association of Chief Police Officers.

ACPO (1986) *Report of the ACPO Working Party on Operational Intelligence (Ratcliffe Report)*. London: Association of Chief Police Officers.

Adlam, R. (2002) 'Governmental rationalities in police leadership: an essay exploring some of the "deep structure" in police leadership praxis', *Policing and Society*, 12 (1): 15–36.

AFP (2005) 'Targeting burglary', *Platypus Magazine*, June: 8–11.

Amey, P., Hale, C. and Uglow, S. (1996) 'Development and evaluation of a crime management model', Police Research Group: Police Research Series, Paper 18: 1–37.

Anderson, R. (1997) 'Intelligence-led policing: a British perspective', in A. Smith (ed). *Intelligence Led Policing: International Perspectives on Policing in the 21st Century*. Lawrenceville, NJ: International Association of Law Enforcement Intelligence Analysts, pp. 5–8.

Andrews, P. P. and Peterson, M. B. (1990) *Criminal Intelligence Analysis*. Loomis, CA: Palmer Enterprises.

Audit Commission (1993) *Helping With Enquiries: Tackling Crime Effectively*. London: HMSO.

Bakker, I. (2004) 'Police Knowledge Net: the development of a central knowledge database for the Dutch police', *4th Annual Conference of the European Society of Criminology*. Amsterdam, The Netherlands.

Barnett, A., Blumstein, A. and Farrington, D. P. (1987) 'Probabilistic models of youthful criminal careers', *Criminology*, 25 (1): 83–107.

Barton, A. and Evans, R. (1999) 'Proactive policing on Merseyside: briefing note', Police Research Group: Police Research Series, Paper 105: 1–2.

Bayley, D. H. (1994a) 'International differences in community policing', in D. P. Rosenbaum (ed), *The Challenge of Community Policing: Testing the Promises.* Thousand Oaks, CA: Sage, 278–281.

Bayley, D. H. (1994b) *Police for the Future.* New York: Oxford University Press.

Bayley, D. H. and Shearing, C. D. (1996) 'The future of policing', *Law and Society Review,* 30(3): 585–606.

Bennell, C. and Canter, D. (2002) 'Linking commercial burglaries by modus operandi: tests using regression and ROC analysis', *Science and Justice,* 42 (3): 153–164.

Bennett, T. (1994) 'Community policing on the ground: developments in Britain', in D. P. Rosenbaum (ed), *The Challenge of Community Policing: Testing the Promises,* Thousand Oaks, CA: Sage 224–246.

Bichard, M. (2004) *The Bichard Inquiry Report.* London: House of Commons.

Biderman, A. D. and Reiss, A. J. (1967) 'On exploring the "dark figure" of crime', *Annals of the American Academy of Political and Social Science,* 374: 1–15.

Bigo, D. (2000) 'Liaison officers in Europe: new officers in the European security field', in J. W. E. Sheptycki (ed), *Issues in Transnational Policing.* London: Routledge, 67–99.

BJA (1998) *1998 Policy Clarification.* Washington, DC: Bureau of Justice Administration.

BJA (2005) *National Gang Threat Assessment 2005.* Washington, DC: Bureau of Justice Assistance.

Boba, R. (2005) *Crime Analysis and Crime Mapping.* Thousand Oaks, CA: Sage.

Bond, R. (2004) 'Methods and issues in risk and threat assessment', in J. H. Ratcliffe (ed), *Strategic Thinking in Criminal Intelligence.* Sydney: Federation Press, pp. 119–128.

Borglund, E. and Nuldén, U. (2006) 'Bits and pieces of information in police practice', *IRIS 29 – Paradigms, Politics, Paradoxes: 29th Information Systems Research Seminar in Scandinavia.*

BOTEC (2001) *Assessment of the HIDTA Program: High Intensity Drug Trafficking Areas.* Washington, DC: National Institute of Justice.

Bottomley, A. and Coleman, C. A. (1976) 'Criminal statistics: the police role in the discovery and detection of crime', *International Journal of Criminology and Penology,* 4: 33–58.

Bowers, K. J. and Johnson, S. D. (2003) 'Measuring the geographical displacement and diffusion of benefit effects of crime prevention activity', *Journal of Quantitative Criminology,* 19 (3): 275–301.

Bradley, D., Nixon, C. and Marks, M. (2006) 'What works, what doesn't work and what looks promising in police research networks', in J. Fleming and J. Wood (eds), *Fighting Crime Together: The Challenges of Policing and Security Networks.* Sydney: University of New South Wales Press, pp. 170–194.

Bradley, R. (1998) 'Public expectations and perceptions of policing', Police Research Group: Police Research Series, Paper 96: 1–24.

Braga, A. A. and Weisburd, D. (2006) 'Problem-oriented policing: the disconnect between principles and practice', in D. Weisburd and A. A. Braga (eds), *Police Innovation: Contrasting Perspectives.* New York: Cambridge University Press, pp. 133–152.

Brantingham, P. J. and Faust, F. L. (1976) 'A conceptual model of crime prevention', *Crime and Delinquency,* 22(3): 284–296.

Brantingham, P. L. and Brantingham, P. J. (1990) 'Situational crime prevention in practice', *Canadian Journal of Criminology*, 32 (1): 17–40.

Bratton, W. J. (1998) *Turnaround: How America's Top Cop Reversed the Crime Epidemic.* New York: Random House.

Bratton, W. J. (2006) 'Research: A practitioner's perspective, from the streets', *Western Criminology Review*, 7 (3): 1–6.

Bratton, W. J. (2007) 'Countering the radicalisation threat: an intelligence-led policing challenge'. *Testimony before the Subcommittee on Intelligence, Information Sharing and Terrorism Risk Assessment.* Washington DC: US House of Representatives Committee on Homeland Security.

Brodeur, J.-P. (1983) 'High policing and low policing: remarks about the policing of political activities', *Social Problems*, 30 (5): 507–520.

Brodeur, J.-P. and Dupont, B. (2006) 'Knowledge workers or "knowledge" workers?' *Policing and Society*, 16 (1): 7–26.

Brooks, J. (2001) 'Terrorism, organized crime, money laundering', *International Herald Tribune*, Tuesday, 30 October.

Brown, R., Clarke, R. V., Rix, B. and Sheptycki, J. (2004) *Tackling Organised Vehicle Crime: The Role of NCIS.* London: Home Office.

Brumwell, A. (2007) 'Mapping the cost of crime: area-based analysis of the economic and social cost of crime and implications for police and partnership working', *5th National Crime Mapping Conference.* London: Jill Dando Institute for Crime Science.

Buerger, M. E. (1998) 'The politics of third-party policing', in L. Green-Mazerolle and J. Roehl (eds), *Civil Remedies and Crime Prevention.* Monsey, NY: Criminal Justice Press, pp. 89–116.

Buerger, M. E. and Green-Mazerolle, L. (1998) 'Third party policing: a theoretical analysis of an emerging trend', *Justice Quarterly*, 15 (2): 301–327.

Burgess, E. W. (1916) 'Juvenile delinquency in a small city', *Journal of the American Institute of Criminal Law and Criminology*, 6: 724–728.

Burgess, E. W. (1925) 'The growth of the city: an introduction to a research project', in R. E. Park, E. W. Burgess and R. D. McKenzie (eds), *The City.* Chicago: University of Chicago Press, pp. 47–62.

Carter, D. L. (2004) *Law Enforcement Intelligence: A guide for State, Local, and Tribal Enforcement Agencies.* Washington, DC: Office of Community Oriented Policing Services.

Carter, D. L. (2005) 'The law enforcement intelligence function: State, local, and tribal agencies', *FBI Law Enforcement Bulletin*, 74 (6): 1–9.

Casey, J. (2004) 'Managing joint terrorism', *FBI Law Enforcement Bulletin*, 73 (11): 1–6.

Chainey, S. and Ratcliffe, J. H. (2005) *GIS and Crime Mapping.* London: John Wiley and Sons.

Chainey, S., Reid, S. and Stuart, N. (2003) 'When is a hotspot a hotspot? A procedure for creating statistically robust hotspot maps of crime', in D. B. Kidner, G. Higgs and S. D. White (eds), *Socio-Economic Applications of Geographic Information Science*, London: Taylor and Francis, pp. 21–36.

Chamlin, M. B. (1991) 'Research note: a longitudinal analysis of the arrest-crime relationship: a further examination of the tipping effect', *Justice Quarterly*, 8 (2): 187–200.

Chenery, S., Henshaw, C. and Pease, K. (1999) 'Illegal parking in disabled bays:

a means of offender targeting', Briefing Note 1/99. London: Home Office Policing and Reducing Crime Unit.

Chilvers, M. and Weatherburn, D. (2001a) 'Do targeted arrests reduce crime?' *Contemporary Issues in Crime and Justice.* NSW Bureau of Crime Statistics and Research, Paper 63.

Chilvers, M. and Weatherburn, D. (2001b) 'Operation and Crime Review panels: their impact on break and enter', *Crime and Justice Statistics: Bureau Brief.* NSW Bureau of Crime Statistics and Research.

Christopher, S. (2004) 'A practitioner's perspective of UK strategic intelligence', in J. H. Ratcliffe (ed), *Strategic Thinking in Criminal Intelligence.* Sydney: Federation Press, pp. 176–192.

CISC (2006a) *2006 Annual Report on Organized Crime in Canada.* Ottawa: Criminal Intelligence Service Canada.

CISC (2006b) 'Criminal Intelligence Service Canada's 2006 annual report highlights organized crime threats in Canada', Press release, source http://cisc.gc.ca/media2006/news_release_2006_e.htm (accessed 10 October 2006).

CISC (2007) *Integrated Threat Assessment Methodology.* Ottawa: Criminal Intelligence Service Canada.

Clarke, C. (2006) 'Proactive policing: standing on the shoulders of community-based policing', *Police Practice and Research,* 7 (1): 3–17.

Clarke, R. V. (1992) (ed.), *Situational Crime Prevention: Successful Case Studies.* Albany, NY: Harrow and Heston.

Clarke, R. V. (2004) 'Technology, criminology and crime science', *European Journal on Criminal Policy and Research,* 10 (1): 55–63.

Clarke, R. V. and Eck, J. (2003) *Becoming a Problem Solving Crime Analyst.* London: Jill Dando Institute.

Clarke, R. V. and Eck, J. (2005) *Crime Analysis for Problem Solvers – in 60 Small Steps.* Washington, DC: Center for Problem Oriented Policing.

Clarke, R. V. and Harris, P. M. (1992) 'Auto theft and its prevention', *Crime and Justice,* 16: 1–54.

Clarke, R. V., Kemper, R. and Wyckoff, L. (2001) 'Controlling cell phone fraud in the US: lessons for the UK "Foresight" Prevention Initiative', *Security Journal,* 14 (1): 7–22.

Clarke, R. V. and Newman, G. R. (2006) *Outsmarting the Terrorists.* Westport, CT: Praeger Security International.

Clarke, R. V. and Newman, G. R. (2007) 'Policing and the prevention of terrorism', *Policing: A Journal of Policy and Practice,* 1 (1): 9–20.

Clarke, S. H. (1975) 'Some implications for North Carolina of recent research in juvenile delinquency', *Journal of Research in Crime and Delinquency,* 12 (1): 51–60.

Coleman, C. and Moynihan, J. (1996) *Understanding Crime Data.* Buckingham, UK: Open University Press.

Collier, P. M. (2006) 'Policing and the intelligent application of knowledge', *Public Money and Management,* 26 (2): 109–116.

Collier, P. M., Edwards, J. S. and Shaw, D. (2004) 'Communicating knowledge about police performance', *International Journal of Productivity and Performance Management,* 53 (5): 458–467.

Cooper, P. and Murphy, J. (1997) 'Ethical approaches for police officers when working with informants in the development of criminal intelligence in the United Kingdom', *Journal of Social Policy,* 26 (1): 1–20.

Cope, N. (2003) 'Crime analysis: principles and practice', in T. Newburn (ed.), *Handbook of Policing*. Cullompton: Willan Publishing, pp. 340–362.

Cope, N. (2004) 'Intelligence led policing or policing led intelligence?: integrating volume crime analysis into policing', *British Journal of Criminology*, 44 (2): 188–203.

Cordner, G. W. (1995) 'Community policing: elements and effects', *Police Forum*, 5 (3): 1–8.

Coumarelos, C. (1994) 'Juvenile offending: predicting persistence and determining the cost-effectiveness of interventions.' Sydney: NSW Bureau of Crime Statistics and Research.

CPC (1994) *Understanding Community Policing: A Framework for Action*. Washington DC: Community Policing Consortium.

Crawford, A. (1997) *The Local Governance of Crime: Appeals to Community and Partnerships*. Oxford: Clarendon Press.

Dannels, D. and Smith, H. (2001) 'Implementation challenges of intelligence-led policing in a quasi-rural county', *Journal of Crime and Justice*, 24 (2): 103–112.

Davenport, T. H. (1997) *Information Ecology: Mastering the Information and Knowledge Environment*. New York: Oxford University Press.

Davidoff, L. (1996) 'Police performance indicators', *Statistical Journal of the UN Economic Commission for Europe*, 13 (2): 161–169.

Dawson, D. (2007) 'New tool measures disruption to OC', *RCMP Gazette*, 69(1).

de Lint, W., O'Connor, D. and Cotter, R. (2007) 'Controlling the flow: security, exclusivity, and criminal intelligence in Ontario', *International Journal of the Sociology of Law*, 35 (1): 41–58.

Deukmedjian, J. E. (2006) 'Executive realignment of RCMP mission', *Canadian Journal of Criminology and Criminal Justice*, 48 (4): 523–542.

Deukmedjian, J. E. and de Lint, W. (2007) 'Community into Intelligence: Resolving information uptake in the RCMP', *Policing and Society*, 17 (3): 239–256.

Dixon, D. (1999) 'Reform, regression and the Royal Commission into the NSW Police Service', in D. Dixon (ed.), *A Culture of Corruption*. Sydney: Hawkins Press, pp. 138–179.

Docobo, J. (2005) 'Community policing as the primary prevention strategy for homeland security at the local law enforcement level', *Homeland Security Affairs*, 1(1): Article 4.

DOJ (1977) *Report of the Department of Justice Task Force to Review the FBI Martin Luther King, Jr. Security and Assassination Investigations*. Washington DC: Department of Justice.

DOJ (2005) *Fusion Center Guidelines*. Washington, DC: Department of Justice.

Dubourg, R. and Prichard, S. (2007) 'Organised crime: revenues, economic and social costs, and criminal assets available for seizure', Home Office Online Report 14/07. London: Home Office.

Dunnighan, C. and Norris, C. (1999) 'The detective, the snout, and the audit commission: the real costs in using informants', *Howard Journal of Criminal Justice*, 38(1): 67–86.

Dupont, B. (2003) 'Preserving Institutional Memory in Australian Police Services', *Trends and Issues in Crime and Criminal Justice*, No. 245: 1–6.

Dupont, B. (2004) 'Security in the age of networks', *Policing and Society*, 14 (1): 76–91.

Dupont, B. (2006) 'Mapping security networks: from metaphorical concept to empirical model', in J. Fleming and J. Wood (eds), *Fighting Crime Together: The Challenges of Policing and Security Networks*. Sydney: University of New South Wales Press), pp. 35–59.

Eck, J. E. (1997) 'What do those dots mean? Mapping theories with data', in D. Weisburd and T. McEwen (eds), *Crime Mapping and Crime Prevention*. Monsey, NY: Criminal Justice Press, pp. 379-406.

Eck, J. E. (2006) 'When is a bologna sandwich better than sex? A defense of small-n case study evaluations', *Journal of Experimental Criminology*, 2 (3): 345–362.

Eck, J. E., Chainey, S., Cameron, J. G., Leitner, M. and Wilson, R. E. (2005) *Mapping Crime: Understanding Hot Spots*. Washington, DC: National Institute of Justice.

Eck, J. E. and Maguire, E. R. (2000) 'Have changes in policing reduced violent crime? An assessment of the evidence', in A. Blumstein and J. Wallman (eds), *The Crime Drop in America*. Cambridge: Cambridge University Press, pp. 207–265.

Eck, J. E. and Spelman, W. (1987) 'Problem solving: problem-oriented policing in Newport News'. Washington, DC: Police Executive Research Forum.

Eck, J. E. and Weisburd, D. (1995) 'Crime places in crime theory', in D. Weisburd and J. E. Eck (eds), *Crime and Place*. Monsey, NY: Criminal Justice Press, pp. 1–33.

Edwards, C. (1999) *Changing Police Theories for 21st Century Societies*. Sydney: Federation Press.

Ericson, R. V. and Haggerty, K. D. (1997) *Policing the Risk Society*. Oxford: Clarendon Press.

EUROPOL (2006) *European Organised Crime Threat Assessment 2006*. The Hague: European Law Enforcement Organisation.

Everson, S. (2003) 'Repeat victimisation and prolific offending: chance or choice?'. *International Journal of Police Science and Management*, 5 (3): 180–194.

Ewart, B. W., Oatley, G. C. and Burn, K. (2005) 'Matching crimes using burglars' modus operandi: a test of three models', *International Journal of Police Science and Management*, 7 (3): 160–174.

Farrell, G., Chenery, S. and Pease, K. (1998) *Consolidating Police Crackdowns: Findings from an Anti-burglary Project*. London: Policing and Reducing Crime Unit, Research, Development and Statistics Directorate, Home Office.

Farrington, D. P. (1987) 'Predicting individual crime rates', *Crime and Justice*, 9: 55–101.

Farrington, D. P. (1990) 'Implications of criminal career research for the prevention of offending', *Journal of Adolescence*, 13: 93–113.

Farrington, D. P. (1992) 'Criminal career research in the United Kingdom', *British Journal of Criminology*, 32 (4): 521–536.

Farrington, D. P. (2003) 'Methodological quality standards for evaluation research', *Annals of the American Academy of Political and Social Science*, 587 (1): 49–68.

FBI (2004) *Strategic Plan 2004-2009*. Washington, DC: Federal Bureau of Investigation.

Felson, M. (1998) *Crime and Everyday Life: Impact and Implications for Society*. Thousand Oaks, CA: Pine Forge Press.

Fielding, N. G. (2005) 'Concepts and theory in community policing', *Howard Journal of Criminal Justice*, 44 (5): 460–472.

Firman, J. R. (2003) 'Deconstructing CompStat to clarify its intent', *Criminology and Public Policy*, 2 (3): 457–460.

Fleming, J. and Lafferty, G. (2000) 'New management techniques and restructuring for accountability in Australian police organisations', *Policing: An International Journal of Police Strategies and Management*, 23 (2): 154–168.

Flood, B. (2004) 'Strategic aspects of the UK National Intelligence Model', in J. H. Ratcliffe (ed) *Strategic Thinking in Criminal Intelligence*. Sydney: Federation Press, pp. 37–52.

Flood-Page, C., Campbell, S., Harrington, V. and Miller, J. (2000) *Youth Crime: Findings from the 1998/99 Youth Lifestyles Survey*. London: Home Office Research, Development and Statistics Directorate.

Ford Foundation (1996) *Innovations in American Government 1986–1996 Tenth Anniversary*. New York: Ford Foundation.

Forst, B. and Planty, M. (2000) 'What is the probability that the offender in a new case is in the MO file?', *International Journal of Police Science and Management*, 3 (2): 124–137.

Giannetti, W. J. (2007) 'What is Operation Safe Streets?', *IALEIA Journal*, 17 (1): 22–32.

Gill, P. (1998) 'Making sense of police intelligence? The use of a cybernetic model in analysing information and power in police intelligence processes', *Policing and Society*, 8 (3): 289–314.

Gill, P. (2000) *Rounding up the Usual Suspects? Developments in Contemporary Law Enforcement Intelligence*. Aldershot: Ashgate.

GIWG (2003) *The National Criminal Intelligence Sharing Plan*. Washington, DC: Department of Justice [Global Intelligence Working Group].

GIWG (2005) *The National Criminal Intelligence Sharing Plan* (revised June 2005). Washington, DC: Department of Justice [Global Intelligence Working Group].

Goldstein, H. (1979) 'Improving policing: a problem-oriented approach', *Crime and Delinquency*, 25 (2): 236–258.

Goldstein, H. (1990) *Problem-Oriented Policing*. New York: McGraw-Hill.

Goldstein, H. (2003) 'On further developing problem-oriented policing: The most critical need, the major impediments, and a proposal', in J. Knutsson (ed.) *Problem-Oriented Policing: From Innovation to Mainstream*. Monsey, NY: Criminal Justice Press, pp. 13–47.

Gottlieb, S., Arenberg, S. and Singh, R. (1998) *Crime Analysis: From First Report to Final Arrest*. Montclair, CA: Alpha Publishing.

Goudriaan, H., Wittebrood, K. and Nieuwbeerta, P. (2006) 'Neighbourhood characteristics and reporting crime: effects of social cohesion, confidence in police effectiveness and socio-economic disadvantage', *British Journal of Criminology*, 46 (4): 719–742.

Grabosky, P. (1992) 'Prosecutors, informants, and the integrity of the criminal justice system', *Current Issues in Criminal Justice*, 4 (1): 47–63.

Green, L. (1995) 'Cleaning up drug hot spots in Oakland, California: the displacement and diffusion effects', *Justice Quarterly*, 12 (4): 737–754.

Greene, J. R., Seamon, T. M. and Levy, P. R. (1995) 'Merging public and private security for collective benefit: Philadelphia's Center City District', *American Journal of Police*, 14 (2): 3–20.

Grieve, J. (2004) 'Developments in UK criminal intelligence', in J. H. Ratcliffe (ed.), *Strategic Thinking in Criminal Intelligence*. Sydney: Federation Press, pp. 25–36.

Guerry, A.-M. (1833) *Essai sur la statistique morale de la France: précédé d'un rapport à l'Académie des Sciences*. Paris: Chez Crochard.

Guidetti, R. A. (2006) 'Policing the Homeland: Choosing the Intelligent Option', Masters thesis. Monterey, CA: Naval Postgraduate School.

Gundhus, H. O. (2005) '"Catching" and "Targeting"': Risk-based policing, local culture and gendered practices', *Journal of Scandinavian Studies in Criminology and Crime Prevention*, 6 (2): 128–146.

Hale, C., Heaton, R. and Uglow, S. (2004) 'Uniform styles? Aspects of police centralisation in England and Wales', *Policing and Society*, 14 (4): 291–312.

Harfield, C. (2000) 'Pro-activity, partnership and prevention: the UK contribution to policing organised crime in Europe', *Police Journal*, 73: 107–117.

Harfield, C. (2006) 'SOCA: a paradigm shift in British policing', *British Journal of Criminology*, 46 (4): 743–761.

Heaton, R. (2000) 'The prospects for intelligence-led policing: some historical and quantitative considerations', *Policing and Society*, 9 (4): 337–356.

Heldon, C. E. (2004) 'Exploratory analysis tools', in J. H. Ratcliffe (ed.), *Strategic Thinking in Criminal Intelligence*. Sydney: Federation Press, 99–118.

Herrington, V. and Millie, A. (2006) 'Applying reassurance policing: is it "business as usual"?' *Policing and Society*, 16 (2): 146–163.

Higgins, O. (2004) 'Rising to the collection challenge', in J. H. Ratcliffe (ed.), *Strategic Thinking in Criminal Intelligence*. Sydney: Federation Press, pp. 70–85.

HMIC (1997) *Policing with Intelligence*. London: Her Majesty's Inspectorate of Constabulary.

HMIC (2000) *Calling Time on Crime*. London: Her Majesty's Inspectorate of Constabulary.

HMIC (2005) *Closing the Gap*. London: Her Majesty's Inspectorate of Constabulary.

Hobbs, D. (1997) 'Criminal collaboration: youth gangs, subcultures, professional criminals, and organized crime', in M. Maguire, R. Morgan and R. Reiner (eds), *The Oxford Handbook of Criminology*. Oxford: Clarendon Press, pp. 801–840.

Home Office (2004) *One Step Ahead: A 21st Century Strategy to Defeat Organised Crime*. London: Home Office.

Home Office (2006a) *Criminal Statistics 2005, England and Wales*. London: Office for Criminal Justice Reform.

Home Office (2006b) *Review of the Partnership Provisions of the Crime and Disorder Act 1998 – Report of Findings*. London: Home Office.

Horvath, F., Meesig, R. T. and Lee, Y. H. (2001) *National Survey of Police Policies and Practices Regarding the Criminal Investigations Process: Twenty-Five Years After Rand* (Final report [NCJRS 202902]). Washington DC: National Institute of Justice.

HOSB (1989) *Criminal and Custodial Careers of Those Born in 1953, 1958 and 1963*. London: Home Office.

Hough, M. and Lewis, H. (1989) 'Counting crime and analysing risks: the British

Crime Survey', in D. J. Evans and D. T. Herbert (eds), *The Geography of Crime*. London: Routledge.

IACP (2002) 'Criminal intelligence sharing: a national plan for intelligence-led policing at the local, state and federal levels', *IACP Intelligence Summit*. Alexandria, VA: COPS and International Association of Chiefs of Police.

IALEIA (2004) *Law Enforcement Analytic Standards*. Richmond, VA: Global Justice Information Sharing Initiative.

Indermaur, D. (1996) 'Violent crime in Australia: interpreting the trends', *Trends and Issues in Crime and Criminal Justice*, 61: 1–6.

Innes, M. (2000) '"Professionalizing" the role of the police informant: the British experience', *Policing and Society*, 9 (4): 357–384.

Innes, M. (2004) 'Reinventing tradition? Reassurance, neighbourhood security and policing', *Criminal Justice*, 4 (2): 151–171.

Innes, M., Fielding, N. and Cope, N. (2005) '"The Appliance of Science?": The theory and practice of crime intelligence analysis', *British Journal of Criminology*, 45 (1): 39–57.

Ipsos MORI (2007) 'Research into Recent Crime Trends in Northern Ireland', May 2007. Belfast: Ipsos MORI on behalf of the Northern Ireland Policing Board and the Police Service of Northern Ireland.

Irwin, M. P. (2001) 'Policing organised crime', paper presented to the *4th National Outlook Symposium on Crime in Australia*. Canberra: Australian Institute of Criminology.

Jacobs, B. A. (1993) 'Undercover deception clues – A case of restrictive deterrence', *Criminology*, 31 (2): 281–299.

John, T. and Maguire, M. (2003) 'Rolling out the National Intelligence Model: key challenges', in K. Bullock and N. Tilley (eds), *Crime Reduction and Problem-oriented Policing*. Cullompton: Willan Publishing, pp. 38–68.

John, T. and Maguire, M. (2007) 'Criminal intelligence and the National Intelligence Model', in T. Newburn, T. Williamson and A. Wright (eds), *Handbook of Criminal Investigation*. Cullompton: Willan Publishing, pp. 176–202.

John, T., Morgan, C. and Rogers, C. (2006) 'The Greater Manchester Against Crime Partnership Business Model: an independent evaluation'. Glamorgan: Centre for Criminology, University of Glamorgan.

Johnson, B. D. and Natarajan, M. (1995) 'Strategies to avoid arrest: Crack sellers' response to intensified policing', *American Journal of Police*, 14 (3/4): 49–69.

Johnston, L. D., O'Malley, P. M., Bachman, J. G. and Schulenberg, J. E. (2005) *Monitoring the Future: National Results on Adolescent Drug Use: Overview of Key Findings, 2004*. Bethesda, MD: National Institute on Drug Abuse.

Johnston, R. (2005) *Analytic Culture in the US Intelligence Community: An Ethnographic Study*. Washington, DC: The Center for the Study of Intelligence, CIA.

Johnstone, P. (2004) 'Director General, National Criminal Intelligence Service (NCIS) of the United Kingdom (recently retired), John Abbott', *Police Practice and Research*, 5 (4/5): 407–414.

Jones, C. and Weatherburn, D. (2004) 'Evaluating police operations (1): A process and outcome evaluation of Operation Vendas'. Sydney: New South Wales Bureau of Crime Statistics and Research.

Keelty, M. (2004) 'Can intelligence always be right?' Presentation at the *13th*

Annual Conference of the Australian Institute of Professional Intelligence Officers. Melbourne: AIPIO.

Keelty, M. (2006) 'International networking and regional engagement: An AFP perspective', in J. Fleming and J. Wood (eds), *Fighting Crime Together: The Challenges of Policing and Security Networks*. Sydney: University of New South Wales Press, pp. 116–132.

Kelling, G. L. and Bratton, W. J. (2006) 'Policing terrorism', *Civic Bulletin*, 43: 12.

Kelling, G. L., Pate, T., Dieckman, D. and Brown, C. E. (1974) *The Kansas City Preventative Patrol Experiment: A Summary Report*. Washington, DC: Police Foundation.

Kelling, G. L. and Wycoff, M. A. (2002) *Evolving Strategy of Policing: Case Studies of Strategic Change*. Washington, DC: National Institute of Justice.

Kerlikowske, R. G. (2007) 'Building a partnership strategy: improving information sharing with state and local law enforcement and the private sector'. Testimony before the Subcommittee on Intelligence, Information Sharing and Terrorism Risk Assessment. Washington, DC: US House of Representatives Committee on Homeland Security.

Koper, C. S. (1995) 'Just enough police presence: Reducing crime and disorderly behavior by optimizing patrol time in crime hot spots', *Justice Quarterly*, 12 (4): 649–672.

Krimmel, J. T. and Mele, M. (1998) 'Investigating stolen vehicle dump sites: An interrupted time series quasi experiment', *Policing: An International Journal of Police Strategies and Management*, 21 (3): 479–489.

Kuhn, T. S. (1962) *The Structure of Scientific Revolutions*. Chicago: University of Chicago Press.

Lab, S. P. (1988) *Crime Prevention: Approaches, Practices and Evaluations*. Cincinnati, OH: Anderson.

Lab, S. P. (2004) 'Crime prevention, politics, and the art of going nowhere fast', *Justice Quarterly*, 21 (4): 681–692.

Langworthy, R. H. (1989) 'Do stings control crime? An evaluation of a police fencing operation', *Justice Quarterly*, 6 (1): 27–45.

Lawton, B. A., Taylor, R. B. and Luongo, A. J. (2005) 'Police officers on drug corners in Philadelphia, drug crime, and violent crime: Intended, diffusion, and displacement impacts', *Justice Quarterly*, 22 (4): 427–451.

Laycock, G. (2001a) 'Research for police: who needs it?', *Trends and Issues in Crime and Criminal Justice*, 211: 1–6.

Laycock, G. (2001b) 'Scientists or politicians – who has the answer to crime?' Inaugural lecture of the Jill Dando Institute of Crime Science: University College London.

LEAA (1973) *Criminal Justice System – Report of the National Advisory Commission on Criminal Justice Standards and Goals*. Washington, DC: National Institute of Justice [Law Enforcement Assistance Administration].

Leigh, A., Read, T. and Tilley, N. (1996) 'Problem-oriented policing', Police Research Group: Crime Detection and Prevention Series, Paper 75: 1–62.

Leigh, A., Read, T. and Tilley, N. (1998) 'Brit Pop II: problem-orientated policing in practice', Police Research Group: Police Research Series, Paper 93: 1–60.

Levi, M. (2002) 'Money laundering and its regulation', *Annals of the American Academy of Political and Social Science*, 582: 181–194.

Levi, M. and Maguire, M. (2004) 'Reducing and preventing organised crime: An evidence-based critique', *Crime, Law and Social Change*, 41 (5): 397–469.

Levitt, S. D. (2004) 'Understanding why crime fell in the 1990s: Four factors that explain the decline in crime and six that do not', *Journal of Economic Perspectives*, 18 (1): 163–190.

Loyka, S. A., Faggiani, D. A. and Karchmer, C. (2005) *Protecting Your Community from Terrorism. Vol. 4. The Production and Sharing of Intelligence*. Washington, DC: COPS/PERF.

Mackay, D. and Ratcliffe, J. H. (2004) 'Intelligence products and their dissemination', in J. H. Ratcliffe (ed.), *Strategic Thinking in Criminal Intelligence*. Sydney: Federation Press, pp. 148–162.

Macpherson of Cluny (1999) *The Stephen Lawrence Enquiry, A Report by Sir William Macpherson of Cluny*. London: HMSO.

Magers, J. S. (2004) 'Compstat: A new paradigm for policing or a repudiation of community policing?' *Journal of Contemporary Criminal Justice*, 20 (1): 70–79.

Maguire, M. (2000) 'Policing by risks and targets: some dimensions and implications of intelligence-led crime control', *Policing and Society*, 9 (4): 315–336.

Maguire, M. and John, T. (1995) 'Intelligence, surveillance and informants: integrated approaches', Police Research Group: Crime Detection and Prevention Series, Paper 64: 1–58.

Maguire, M. and John, T. (1996) 'Covert and deceptive policing in England and Wales: issues in regulation and practice', *European Journal of Crime, Criminal Law and Criminal Justice*, 4: 316–334.

Maguire, M. and John, T. (2004) 'The National Intelligence Model: early implementation experience in three police force areas', Working Paper Series, Paper 50. Cardiff: Cardiff University.

Maguire, M. and John, T. (2006) 'Intelligence led policing, managerialism and community engagement: Competing priorities and the role of the National Intelligence Model in the UK', *Policing and Society*, 16 (1): 67–85.

Makkai, T., Ratcliffe, J. H., Veraar, K. and Collins, L. (2004) 'ACT recidivist offenders', *Research and Public Policy Series*, 54: 1–83.

Manning, P. (2000) 'Policing new social spaces', in J. W. E. Sheptycki (ed.), *Issues in Transnational Policing*. London: Routledge, pp. 177–200.

Maple, J. and Mitchell, C. (1999) *The Crime Fighter: Putting the Bad Guys out of Business*. New York: Doubleday.

Markle Foundation (2003) *Creating a Trusted Network for Homeland Security*. New York: Markle Foundation.

Marrin, S. (2007) 'At arm's length or at the elbow?: explaining the distance between analysts and decision makers', *International Journal of Intelligence and CounterIntelligence*, 20 (3): 401–414.

Marvell, T. B. and Moody, C. E. (1996) 'Specification problems, police levels, and crime rates', *Criminology*, 34 (4): 609–646.

Marx, G. T. (1988) *Undercover: Police Surveillance in America*. Berkeley: University of California Press.

Mastrofski, S. (2006) 'Community policing: A skeptical view', in D. Weisburd and A. A. Braga (eds), *Police Innovation: Contrasting Perspectives*. Chicago: Cambridge University Press, pp. 44–73.

Maxfield, M. (2001) 'Guide to frugal evaluation for criminal justice', Final grant report. Newark, NJ: Rutgers University.

Maxim (2006) 'Welcome to Murder City', *Maxim Magazine*, August 2006.

Mayhew, H. (1862) *London Labour and the London Poor*. London: Griffin Bohn.

Mayhew, P. and Adkins, G. (2003) 'Counting the costs of crime in Australia: an update', *Trends and Issues in Crime and Criminal Justice*, 247: 1–8.

Mayne, S. R. (1829) *Instructions to 'The New Police of the Metropolis'*. London: Metropolitan Police.

Mazerolle, L., Rombouts, S. and McBroom, J. (2007a) 'The impact of COMPSTAT on reported crime in Queensland', *Policing: An International Journal of Police Strategies and Management*, 30 (2): 237–256.

Mazerolle, L., Soole, D. and Rombouts, S. (2007b) 'Drug law enforcement: A review of the evaluation literature', *Police Quarterly*, 10 (2): 115–153.

Mazerolle, L., Soole, D. W. and Rombouts, S. (2007c) *Crime Prevention Research Review No. 1: Disrupting Street-Level Drug Markets*. Washington, DC: US Department of Justice (Office of Community Oriented Policing Services).

McCabe, S. and Sutcliffe, F. (1978) *Defining Crime: A Study of Police Decisions*. Oxford: Blackwell.

McDonald, P. P. (2002) *Managing Police Operations: Implementing the New York Crime Control Model – CompStat*. Belmont, CA: Wadsworth.

McDowell, D. (1998) *Strategic Intelligence: A Handbook for Practitioners, Managers and Users*. Cooma, NSW: Istana Enterprises.

McGarrell, E. F., Freilich, J. D. and Chermak, S. (2007) 'Intelligence-led policing as a framework for responding to terrorism', *Journal of Contemporary Criminal Justice*, 23 (2): 142–158.

McGuire, P. G. (2000) 'The New York Police Department COMPSTAT Process', in V. Goldsmith, P. G. McGuire, J. H. Mollenkopf and T. A. Ross (eds), *Analyzing Crime Patterns: Frontiers of Practice*. Thousand Oaks, CA: Sage, pp. 11–22.

McNamara, T. (2007) 'The over-classification and pseudo-classification of government information: the response of the program manager of the information sharing environment'. Testimony before the Subcommittee on Intelligence, Information Sharing and Terrorism Risk Assessment. Washington, DC: US House of Representatives Committee on Homeland Security.

McNamara, T. E. (2006) 'Information sharing environment implementation plan'. Washington, DC: Information Sharing Environment, Office of the Director of National Intelligence.

Mehrabian, A. and Ferris, S. R. (1967) 'Inference of attitudes from nonverbal communication in two channels', *Journal of Consulting Psychology*, 31 (3): 248–252.

Miller, J. (2007) 'In the front line in the war on terrorism', *City Journal*, 17 (3): 28–41.

Moore, M. H. (2003) 'Sizing up CompStat: an important administrative innovation in policing', *Criminology and Public Policy*, 2 (3): 469–494.

Morgan, R. and Newburn, T. (1997) *The Future of Policing*. Oxford: Oxford University Press.

Murphy, W. M. (2007) 'The over-classification and pseudo-classification of government information: the response of the program manager of the information sharing environment'. Testimony before the Subcommittee on Intelligence, Information Sharing and Terrorism Risk Assessment. Washington, DC: US House of Representatives Committee on Homeland Security.

NCIS (1999) *NCIS and the National Intelligence Model*. London: National Criminal Intelligence Service.

NCIS (2000) *The National Intelligence Model*. London: National Criminal Intelligence Service.

NCPE (2005a) *Guidance on the National Intelligence Model*. Wyboston, UK: National Centre for Policing Excellence on behalf of ACPO.

NCPE (2005b) *National Intelligence Model: Code of Practice*. London: National Centre for Policing Excellence.

NCPE (2005c) *National Intelligence Model: Minimum Standards*. London: National Centre for Policing Excellence.

NCPE (2006) *Guidance on the Management of Police Information*. Wyboston, UK: National Centre for Policing Excellence on behalf of ACPO.

Neville, E. (2000) 'The public's right to know – the individual's right to privacy', *Policing and Society*, 9 (4): 413–428.

Nicholas, S., Kershaw, C. and Walker, A. (2007) 'Crime in England and Wales 2006/07', HOSB 11/07. London: Home Office.

Nicholl, J. (2004) 'Task definition', in J. H. Ratcliffe (ed.), *Strategic Thinking in Criminal Intelligence*. Sydney: Federation Press, pp. 53–69.

NJSP (2005) 'New Jersey strategic assessment of organized crime threats'. Trenton, NJ: New Jersey State Police; Intelligence Section.

NJSP (2006a) 'Practical guide to intelligence-led policing'. Trenton, NJ: New Jersey State Police.

NJSP (2006b) 'State Police lead team of 500 officers to decapitate most violent set of Bloods street gang', Press release 25 July 2006. Trenton, NJ: New Jersey State Police.

NJSP (n.d.) 'Gangs in New Jersey: municipal law enforcement response to the 2004 and 2001 NJSP gang surveys'. Trenton, NJ: New Jersey State Police Intelligence Services Section.

Norris, C. and Dunnighan, C. (2000) 'Subterranean blues: conflict as an unintended consequence of the police use of informers', *Policing and Society*, 9 (4): 385–412.

Nunn, S., Quinet, K., Rowe, K. and Christ, D. (2006) 'Interdiction day: covert surveillance operations, drugs, and serious crime in an inner-city neighborhood', *Police Quarterly*, 9 (1): 73–99.

NZP (2002) 'Police strategic plan to 2006'. Wellington: New Zealand Police.

Oakensen, D., Mockford, R. and Pascoe, C. (2002) 'Does there have to be blood on the carpet? Integrating partnership, problem-solving and the National Intelligence Model in strategic and tactical police decision-making processes', *Police Research and Management*, 5 (4): 51–62.

Office of the Auditor-General, NZ (2006) 'New Zealand Police: dealing with dwelling burglary – follow-up audit'. Wellington, New Zealand: Audit New Zealand.

Oliver, W. M. and Bartgis, E. (1998) 'Community policing: a conceptual framework', *Policing: An International Journal of Police Strategies and Management*, 21 (3): 490–509.

Osborne, D. (2006) *Out of Bounds: Innovation and Change in Law Enforcement Intelligence Analysis*. Washington DC: Joint Military Intelligence College.

O'Shea, T. C. and Nicholls, K. (2002) 'Crime analysis in America', Final report. Washington, DC: Office of Community Oriented Policing Services.

O'Shea, T. C. and Nicholls, K. (2003) 'Crime analysis in America: findings and recommendations'. Washington, DC: Office of Community Oriented Policing Services.

Pawson, R. and Tilley, N. (1994) 'What works in evaluation research?', *British Journal of Criminology*, 34 (3): 291–306.

Pawson, R. and Tilley, N. (1997) *Realistic Evaluation*. London: Sage.

Petersilia, J. (1980) 'Criminal career research: a review of recent evidence', *Crime and Justice*, 2: 321–379.

Peterson, M. (2005) 'Intelligence-led policing: the new intelligence architecture'. Washington, DC: Bureau of Justice Assistance.

Petrosino, A., Turpin-Petrosino, C. and Buehler, J. (2003) '"Scared Straight" and other juvenile awareness programs for preventing juvenile delinquency,' (Updated C2 Review). *Campbell Collaboration Reviews of Intervention and Policy Evaluations (C2-RIPE)*. Philadelphia, PA: Campbell Collaboration.

Ponsaers, P. (2001) 'Reading about "community (oriented) policing" and police models', *Policing: An International Journal of Police Strategies and Management*, 24 (4): 470–497.

Prunckun, J. H. W. (1996) 'The intelligence analyst as social scientist: A comparison of research methods', *Police Studies*, 19 (3): 67–80.

Quarmby, N. (2004) 'Futures work in strategic criminal intelligence', in J. H. Ratcliffe (ed.), *Strategic Thinking in Criminal Intelligence*. Sydney: Federation Press, pp. 129–147.

Quetelet, A. (1842) *A Treatise On Man*. Edinburgh: Chambers.

Ransom, H. H. (1980) 'Being intelligent about secret intelligence agencies', *American Political Science Review*, 74 (1): 141–148.

Ratcliffe, J. H. (2001) 'Policing Urban Burglary', *Trends and Issues in Crime and Criminal Justice*, 213: 1–6.

Ratcliffe, J. H. (2002a) 'Aoristic signatures and the temporal analysis of high volume crime patterns', *Journal of Quantitative Criminology*, 18 (1): 23–43.

Ratcliffe, J. H. (2002b) 'Burglary reduction and the myth of displacement', *Trends and Issues in Crime and Criminal Justice*, 232: 1–6.

Ratcliffe, J. H. (2002c) 'Damned if you don't, damned if you do: Crime mapping and its implications in the real world', *Policing and Society*, 12 (3): 211–225.

Ratcliffe, J. H. (2002d) 'Intelligence-led policing and the problems of turning rhetoric into practice', *Policing and Society*, 12 (1): 53–66.

Ratcliffe, J. H. (2003) 'Intelligence-led policing', *Trends and Issues in Crime and Criminal Justice*, 248: 1–6.

Ratcliffe, J. H. (2004a) 'Crime mapping and the training needs of law enforcement', *European Journal on Criminal Policy and Research*, 10 (1): 65–83.

Ratcliffe, J. H. (2004b) 'Intelligence research', in J. H. Ratcliffe (ed.), *Strategic Thinking in Criminal Intelligence*. Sydney: Federation Press, pp. 86–98.

Ratcliffe, J. H. (2004c) *Strategic Thinking in Criminal Intelligence*. Sydney: Federation Press.

Ratcliffe, J. H. (2004d) 'The structure of strategic thinking', in J. H. Ratcliffe (ed.), *Strategic Thinking in Criminal Intelligence*. Sydney: Federation Press, pp. 1–10.

Ratcliffe, J. H. (2005) 'The effectiveness of police intelligence management: a New Zealand case study', *Police Practice and Research*, 6 (5): 435–451.

Ratcliffe, J. H. (2006) 'Video surveillance of public places'. Washington, DC: Center for Problem Oriented Policing.

Ratcliffe, J. H. (2007) 'Integrated intelligence and crime analysis: enhanced information management for law enforcement leaders'. Washington, DC: Police Foundation.

Ratcliffe, J. H. (2008) 'Knowledge management challenges in the development of intelligence-led policing', in T. Williamson (ed.), *The Handbook of Knowledge-Based Policing: Current Conceptions and Future Directions*. Chichester: John Wiley and Sons, pp. 205–220.

Ratcliffe, J. H. (in press) 'Intelligence-led policing', in L. Mazerolle, R. Wortley and S. Rombouts (eds), *Foundations of Environmental Criminology and Crime Analysis*. Cullompton: Willan Publishing.

Ratcliffe, J. H. and Guidetti, R. A. (2008) 'State police investigative structure and the adoption of intelligence-led policing', *Policing: An International Journal of Police Strategies and Management*, 31(1).

Ratcliffe, J. H. and Makkai, T. (2004) 'Diffusion of benefits: evaluating a policing operation', *Trends and Issues in Crime and Criminal Justice*, 278: 1–6.

Ratcliffe, J. H. and McCullagh, M. J. (1998) 'Aoristic crime analysis', *International Journal of Geographical Information Science*, 12 (7): 751–764.

Ratcliffe, J. H. and McCullagh, M. J. (2001) 'Chasing ghosts? Police perception of high crime areas', *British Journal of Criminology*, 41 (2): 330–341.

Ratcliffe, J.H. and Taniguchi, T.A. (2008) 'Is crime higher around drug-gang street corners? Two spatial approaches to the relationship between gang set spaces and local crime levels', *Crime Patterns and Analysis*, 1(1).

Reiner, R. (1997) 'Policing and the police', in M. Maguire, R. Morgan and R. Reiner (eds), *The Oxford Handbook of Criminology*. Oxford: Clarendon Press, pp. 997–1049.

Rengert, G. F., Ratcliffe, J. H. and Chakravorty, S. (2005) *Policing Illegal Drug Markets: Geographic Approaches to Crime Reduction*. Monsey, NY: Criminal Justice Press.

Reuter, P. (1990) 'Can the borders be sealed?', in R. Weisheit (ed.), *Drugs, Crime and the Criminal Justice System*. Cincinnati, OH: Anderson Publishing, pp. 13–26.

Roach, J. (2007) 'Those who do big bad things also usually do little bad things: identifying active serious offenders using offender self-selection', *International Journal of Police Science and Management*, 9 (1): 66–79.

Rogers, K. (1998) 'Evaluating strategic intelligence assessments: some sextant readings for law enforcement', *Journal of the Australian Institute of Professional Intelligence Officers*, 7 (3): 23–36.

Rogerson, P. A. (2006) *Statistical Methods for Geography*. Thousand Oaks, CA: Sage.

Ross, N. (2005) 'Higher up the food chain: putting cops where they belong', paper presented to the *Problem Oriented Policing Conference 2005*. Charlotte, NC: www.popcenter.org.

Scarman, L. L. (1981) *Report of an Inquiry by the Right Honourable The Lord Scarman into the Brixton Disorders of 10–12 April 1981 (The Scarman Report)*. London: Her Majesty's Stationery Office.

Schneider, S. (2006) 'Privatizing economic crime enforcement: exploring the role of private sector investigative agencies in combating money laundering', *Policing and Society*, 16 (3): 285–312.

SCOCCI (1997) 'Guiding principles for law enforcement intelligence'. Sydney: Standing Advisory Committee on Organised Crime and Criminal Intelligence.

Scott, J. (1998) '"Performance culture": the return of reactive policing', *Policing and Society*, 8 (3): 269–288.

Scott, M.S. (2000) *Problem-Oriented Policing: Reflections on the First 20 Years*, October 2000. Washington, DC: COPS Office.

Sharp, D. (2005) 'Who needs theories in policing? An introduction to a special issue on policing', *Howard Journal of Criminal Justice*, 44 (5): 449–459.

Shaw, C. R. and McKay, H. D. (1942) *Juvenile Delinquency and Urban Areas*. Chicago: Chicago University Press.

Sheptycki, J. (2000) 'Introduction', in J. W. E. Sheptycki (ed.), *Issues in Transnational Policing*. London: Routledge, pp. 1–20.

Sheptycki, J. (2002) 'Accountability across the policing field: towards a general cartography of accountability for post-modern policing', *Policing and Society*, 12 (4): 323–338.

Sheptycki, J. (2003) 'The governance of organised crime in Canada', *Canadian Journal of Sociology-Cahiers Canadiens De Sociologie*, 28 (4): 489–516.

Sheptycki, J. (2004a) 'Organisational pathologies in police intelligence systems: some contributions to the lexicon of intelligence-led policing', *European Journal of Criminology*, 1 (3): 307–332.

Sheptycki, J. (2004b) 'Review of the influence of strategic intelligence on organised crime policy and practice'. London: Home Office Research and Statistics Directorate.

Sheptycki, J. (2005) 'Transnational policing', *Canadian Review of Policing Research*, 1: 1–7.

Sheptycki, J. (2007) 'High policing in the security control society', *Policing: A Journal of Policy and Practice*, 1 (1): 70–79.

Sheptycki, J. and Ratcliffe, J. H. (2004) 'Setting the strategic agenda', in J. H. Ratcliffe (ed.), *Strategic Thinking in Criminal Intelligence*. Sydney: Federation Press, pp. 194–216.

Sherman, L. W. (1986) 'Policing communities: what works?', in J. Albert, J. Reiss and M. Tonry (eds), *Communities and Crime*. Chicago: University of Chicago, pp. 343–386.

Sherman, L. W. (1990) 'Police crackdowns: Initial and residual deterrence', in M. Tonry and N. Morris (eds), *Crime and Justice: An Annual Review of Research*. Chicago: University of Chicago Press, pp. 1–48.

Sherman, L.W. (1998) 'Evidence-based policing'. Washington, DC: Police Foundation.

Sherman, L. W. (2002) 'Evidence-based policing: social organisation of information for social control', in E. Waring and D. Weisburd (eds), *Crime and Social Organization*. New Brunswick and London: Transaction Publishers, pp. 217–248.

Sherman, L. W. (2005) 'The use and usefulness of criminology, 1751–2005: enlightened justice and its failures', *Annals of the American Academy of Political and Social Science*, 600: 115–135.

Sherman, L. W., Gartin, P. and Buerger, M. E. (1989) 'Hot spots of predatory crime: Routine activities and the criminology of place', *Criminology*, 27 (1): 27–55.

Sherman, L. W., Gottfredson, D., MacKenzie, D., Eck, J., Reuter, P. and Bushway, S. (1998) 'Preventing crime: what works, what doesn't, what's promising'. Washington, DC: National Institute of Justice.

Sherman, L. W., Shaw, J. W. and Rogan, D. P. (1995) 'The Kansas City gun experiment'. Washington, DC: National Institute of Justice.

Sherman, L. W. and Weisburd, D. (1995) 'General deterrent effects of police patrol in crime "hot spots": A randomized, controlled trial', *Justice Quarterly*, 12 (4): 625–648.

Silverman, E. B. (2006) 'Compstat's innovation', in D. Weisburd and A. A. Braga (eds), *Police Innovation: Contrasting Perspectives*. New York: Cambridge University Press, pp. 267–283.

Silvestri, M. (2006) ' "Doing time": Becoming a police leader', *International Journal of Police Science and Management*, 8 (4): 266–281.

Skogan, W. G. (2006a) 'Asymmetry in the impact of encounters with police', *Policing and Society*, 16 (2): 99–126.

Skogan, W. G. (2006b) 'The promise of community policing', in D. Weisburd and A. A. Braga (eds), *Policing Innovation: Contrasting Perspectives*. New York: Cambridge University Press, pp. 27–43.

Skogan, W. G. and Hartnett, S. M. (1997) *Community Policing, Chicago Style*. New York: Oxford University Press.

Smith, P. (1995) 'On the unintended consequences of publishing performance data in the public sector', *International Journal of Public Administration*, 18 (2/3): 277–310.

SOCA (2006) *The UK Threat Assessment of Serious Organised Crime 2006/07*. London: Serious Organised Crime Agency.

Sousa, W. H. and Kelling, G. L. (2006) 'Of "broken windows," criminology, and criminal justice', in D. Weisburd and A. A. Braga (eds), *Police Innovation: Contrasting Perspectives*. New York: Cambridge University Press, pp. 77–97.

Spelman, W. and Brown, D. K. (1981) *Calling the Police – Citizen Reporting of Serious Crime*. Washington, DC: Police Executive Research Forum.

Spiller, S. (2006) 'The FBI's Field Intelligence Groups and Police', *FBI Law Enforcement Bulletin*, 75 (5): 1–6.

Stelfox, P. (1998) 'Policing lower levels of organised crime in England and Wales', *The Howard Journal*, 37 (4): 393–406.

Stevens, J. (2001) 'Intelligence-led policing'. Paper presented to the *2nd World Investigation of Crime Conference*. Durban, South Africa.

Taylor, B., Kowalyk, A. and Boba, R. (2007) 'The integration of crime analysis into law enforcement agencies', *Police Quarterly*, 10 (2): 154–169.

Taylor, R. B. (2001) *Breaking Away From Broken Windows*. Boulder, CO: Westview.

Taylor, R. B. (2006) 'Incivilities reduction policing, zero tolerance, and the retreat from coproduction: weak foundations and strong pressures', in D. Weisburd and A. A. Braga (eds), *Police Innovation: Contrasting Perspectives*. New York: Cambridge University Press, pp. 98–114.

Tilley, N. (1995) 'Thinking about crime prevention performance indicators'. Police Research Group: Crime Detection and Prevention Series, Paper 57: 1–35.

Tilley, N. (2003a) 'Community policing, problem-oriented policing and intelligence-led policing', in T. Newburn (ed.) *Handbook of Policing*. Cullompton: Willan Publishing, pp. 311–339.

Tilley, N. (2003b) *Problem-Oriented Policing, Intelligence-Led Policing and the National Intelligence Model*. London: Jill Dando Institute for Crime Science.

Tilley, N. (2004) 'Community policing and problem solving', in W. G. Skogan (ed.) *Community Policing (Can It Work?)*. Belmont, CA: Wadsworth, pp. 165–184.

Townsley, M., Johnson, S. and Pease, K. (2003) 'Problem orientation, problem solving and organisational change', in J. Knuttson, (ed.) *Problem-Oriented Policing: From Innovation to Mainstream*. Monsey, NY: Criminal Justice Press, pp. 183–212.

Townsley, M. and Pease, K. (2002) 'How efficiently can we target prolific offenders?', *International Journal of Police Science and Management*, 4(4): 323–331.

Trojanowicz, R. C. (1994) 'The future of community policing', in D. P. Rosenbaum (ed.) *The Challenge of Community Policing: Testing the Promises*. Thousand Oaks, CA: Sage, 258–262.

Vito, G. F., Walsh, W. F. and Kunselman, J. (2005) 'Compstat: the manager's perspective', *International Journal of Police Science and Management*, 7(3): 187–196.

Walsh, P. and Ratcliffe, J. H. (2005) 'Strategic criminal intelligence education: a collaborative approach', *IALEIA Journal*, 16(2): 152–166.

Walsh, W. F. (2001) 'Compstat: an analysis of an emerging police managerial paradigm', *Policing: An International Journal of Police Strategies and Management*, 24(3): 347–362.

Walsh, W. F. and Vito, G. F. (2004) 'The meaning of Compstat: analysis and response', *Journal of Contemporary Criminal Justice*, 20(1): 51–69.

Wardlaw, G. and Boughton, J. (2006) 'Intelligence-led policing: the AFP approach', in J. Fleming and J. Wood (eds), *Fighting Crime Together: The Challenges of Policing and Security Networks*. Sydney: University of New South Wales Press, 133–149.

Wartell, J. and McEwen, J. T. (2001) *Privacy in the Information Age: A Guide for Sharing Crime Maps and Spatial Data*. Washington, DC: Institute for Law and Justice.

Weatherburn, D. (2001) 'What causes crime?' Contemporary Issues in Crime and Justice (NSW Bureau of Crime Statistics and Research) No. 54, 1–12.

Weatherburn, D. (2004) *Law and Order in Australia: Rhetoric and Reality*. Sydney: Federation Press.

Weatherburn, D., Hua, J. and Moffatt, S. (2006) 'How much crime does prison stop? The incapacitation effect of prison on burglary', Contemporary Issues in Crime and Justice (NSW Bureau of Crime Statistics and Research), No. 93, 1–12.

Weatheritt, M. (1986) *Innovations in Policing*. Dover: Croom Helm.

Weisburd, D. and Braga, A. A. (2006a) 'Hot spots policing as a model for police innovation', in D. Weisburd and A. A. Braga (eds), *Police Innovation: Contrasting Perspectives*. New York: Cambridge University Press, pp. 225–244.

Weisburd, D. and Braga, A. A. (eds.) (2006b) *Police Innovation: Contrasting Perspectives*. New York: Cambridge University Press.

Weisburd, D., Bushway, S., Lum, C. and Yang, S.-M. (2004) 'Trajectories of crime at places: a longitudinal study of street segments in the city of Seattle', *Criminology*, 42 (2): 283-321.

Weisburd, D. and Eck, J. (2004) 'What can police do to reduce crime, disorder, and fear?', *Annals of the American Academy of Political and Social Science*, 593 (1): 43–65.

Weisburd, D. and Green, L. (1995) 'Policing drug hot spots: the Jersey City drug market analysis experiment', *Justice Quarterly*, 12 (4): 711–735.

Weisburd, D. and Lum, C. (2005) 'The diffusion of computerized crime mapping in policing: linking research and practice', *Police Practice and Research*, 6 (5): 419–434.

Weisburd, D., Mastrofski, S. D., McNally, A. M., Greenspan, R. and Willis, J. J. (2003) 'Reforming to preserve: CompStat and strategic problem solving in American policing', *Criminology and Public Policy*, 2 (3): 421-456.

Weisburd, D., Mastrofski, S.D., Willis, J. J. and Greenspan, R. (2006) 'Changing everything so that everything can remain the same: Compstat and American policing', in D. Weisburd and A. A. Braga (eds), *Police Innovation: Contrasting Perspectives*. New York: Cambridge University Press, 284-301.

Wellsmith, M. and Guille, H. (2005) 'Fixed penalty notices as a means of offender selection', *International Journal of Police Science and Management*, 7 (1): 36–43.

White, J. R. (2004) *Defending the Homeland: Domestic Intelligence, Law Enforcement, and Security*. Belmont, CA: Wadsworth.

Williams, J. W. (2005) 'Governability matters: the private policing of economic crime and the challenge of democratic governance', *Policing and Society*, (15) 2: 187–211.

Willis, J. J., Mastrofski, S. D., Weisburd, D. and Greenspan, R. (2003) 'Compstat and organisational change in the Lowell Police Department: challenges and opportunities'. Washington DC: Police Foundation.

Wilson, D., Sharp, C. and Patterson, A. (2006) *Young People and Crime: Findings from the 2005 Offending, Crime and Justice Survey*. London: Home Office.

Wilson, J. Q. and Kelling, G. L. (1982) 'Broken windows: the police and neighborhood safety', *Atlantic Monthly*, March: 29–38.

Witzig, E. W. (2003) 'The new ViCAP: more user-friendly and used by more agencies', *FBI Law Enforcement Bulletin*, 72 (6): 1–7.

Wolfgang, M. E., Figlio, R. M. and Sellin, T. (1972) *Delinquency in a Birth Cohort*. Chicago: University of Chicago Press.

Wood, J. (1997) *Final Report of the Royal Commission into the NSW Police Service: Vol. 1. Corruption*. Sydney: RCNSWPS.

Wood, J. and Shearing, C. (2007) *Imagining Security*. Cullompton: Willan Publishing.

Wortley, R., Mazerolle, L. and Rombouts, S. (eds) (in press) *Environmental Criminology and Crime Analysis*. Cullompton: Willan Publishing.

Yokota, K. and Watanabe, S. (2002) 'Computer-based retrieval of suspects using similarity of *modus operandi*', *International Journal of Police Science and Management*, 4(1): 5–15.

Index

3–i model 95, 109–12, 114, 115, 142,
    143, 149, 154, 155, 173, 188, 207, 210,
    231, 235–6
5x5x5 National Information/Intelligence
    Reporting System 215, 217
9/11 12, 22, 25, 26–7, 32, 39, 123,
    124–5, 175, 224, 227
9/11 Commission 5, 96, 125, 133,
    144–5

Abbott, John 9, 145
academics 88, 96, 104, 189, 193, 235
Adkins, G. 197
Air India flight 182, terrorist bombing
    67
al Qaeda 227
analysis models
    3–i 95, 109–12, 114, 115, 142, 143,
        149, 154, 155, 173, 188, 207, 210,
        231, 235–6
    Gill's cybernetic 106–7, 112
    intelligence cycle 81, 95, 104–7,
        108, 112, 113, 114, 116, 127, 152,
        153
    NIM business 107–9, 113, 114, 122,
        135, 141, 150, 156, 177, 188, 205,
        232
    SARA 30, 74, 107, 108, 109, 114
analysis unit, location of 159
analysts 98, 107, 111, 112, 230
    crime 9, 52, 100, 115
    interaction with clients 157
    making recommendations 160–1,
        165

relationship with front line officers
    143–4
secondment of 123, 132
self-directed 116
skill sets of 194–5
structural levels of 99
training for 207, 230–2
understanding the client
    environment 153–4, 173
analytical process, key variables 116–7
analytical techniques 135–7, 139
    'paralysis through analysis' 136
    skills and resources required
        136
Annual Report on Organized Crime in
    Canada 124
arrest logs 52–3
arrest(s)
    alternative to 169–70
    increased rates of 181–2
    targeting 167–8, 195–201
Association of Chief Police Officers
    (ACPO) 33, 92, 214
Audit Commission 36, 37, 42, 64, 83,
    84, 134, 159, 203, 216
Australian Bureau of Criminal
    Intelligence 124
Australian Capital Territory (ACT)
    195–201
Australian Crime Commission (ACC)
    4, 23, 124, 171
Australian Federal Police 23, 40, 59,
    109, 125, 133, 146, 155, 164, 181, 195,
    201, 228

Australian National Strategic
  Intelligence Course 111, 125, 231

Bichard Inquiry Report 97, 220
Boba, Rachel 93, 94, 96, 100, 136, 139
Bratton, William 31, 77, 78, 79, 80, 130,
  184, 213, 226, 232, 237
briefings 23, 141, 161, 162
British Crime Survey (BCS) 43
Brixton Riots 34
burglaries 20, 21, 44, 78, 94, 99, 117,
  190, 195–201

Cali drug cartel 204–5
Cambridge Study in Delinquent
  Development 53–5
Campbell Collaboration 183
CAPRA (Clients Acquiring and
  analysing information, Partnership,
  Response and Assessment) 74
Case Studies
  Calls for service in America's most
    dangerous city 47–9
  Operation Anchorage 195–99
  Operation Nine Connect 11, 120
CCTV 218
Center City District 146–7
Center for Problem Oriented Policing
  30, 75, 161, 183, 184
Center for Problem Oriented Policing's
  CCTV guide 184
Chakravorty, Sanjoy 168
Chapman, Jessica 97, 220
civil liberties 220, 223
civil rights movement 27, 29
Clarke, Ron 94, 107, 161
clearance rates 2, 53
clients
  analysts' relationship with 98–9,
    113–14, 127, 129, 163
  feedback from 105–6
  front-line 143–4
  higher-ranking 141–2
  multiple 111
  understanding environment of
    153–8, 164, 183
  unhappy 102
Cold War 22, 28

collator 23, 94–5
command structure 159, 235
community policing 3, 34–5, 66–70
  core purpose of 66
  counter-terrorism 149
  definition 67, 68
  international phenomenon 68
  lack of positive crime reduction
    evaluations 210
  linked with problem-oriented
    policing 70–1
  origins of 29–30
  programmes associated with 66
  role of public in 148
Community Policing conference 2006
  68
Compstat 3, 4, 76–9, 100, 144, 226
  and crime reduction 77, 78
  definition 76
  Operation and Crime Review 77–8
  rapid emergence of 31–2, 77
  theatrical component 78
  use in evaluation 189, 192
conviction rates 168
Cope, Nina 9, 100, 105, 113, 114, 116–7,
  161, 189, 192–3, 227, 231
cost-effectiveness/ benefit 78, 167, 171,
  186, 188, 199, 201–2, 203–4
Coumarelos, Christine 56, 57
counter-terrorism 79, 124, 134, 149,
  184, 224, 228, 229–30
covert information gathering 134, 138,
  213, 214–20
  understanding legal conditions 220
crime
  desks 34
  fighting 9, 10, 61
  hot spots 51–2, 179, 180
  hot times 180
  management units 34
  mapping 192–3
  unreported 43–4
crime analysis
  definition 93–4
Crime Analysis for Problem Solvers 183
Crime and Disorder Act 1998 150
Crime and Disorder Reduction
  Partnerships 141, 142, 233

crime funnel 42, 43–51, 52, 59, 62, 165,
    166, 177, 182, 184
  lower levels 169
  top-down effect 167
crime intelligence products see
  intelligence products
crime prevention 2, 15–16, 51, 145,
    165, 169–73
  increased directed patrols 178, 180
  lack of enthusiasm for 174
  leaders resistance to 177
  levels of 172–3
  mindset 201
  political will, absence of 170
  situational 30, 51, 75, 195
  threats to 170
crime reduction, non-enforcement
  options
  beneficial 182–3
  non-beneficial 183
criminal careers 52, 53, 57, 63
  length of 55, 171
  studies of 53, 54, 55
criminal intelligence see intelligence
Criminal Intelligence Service Canada
    (CISC) 23, 40, 61, 62, 119–21, 124,
    148
Criminal Intelligence Sharing Summit
    12, 32, 39, 92
Criminal Intelligence System Operating
    Policies (28 Code of Federal
    Regulations) 25, 223
criminal justice system 42–3, 50–1, 52,
    54, 57, 62, 63, 165, 167, 172
Criminal Records Bureau 54
criminal 'triggers' 122
custodial sentence 12, 50, 51, 63, 166,
    167, 168, 169
  cost-effectiveness 171

data 95, 96
  complete and reliable 236
  conviction 54
  criminal justice 17
  evaluative tool 235
  revolution in recording 116
  sharing between agencies 150, 157,
    225–6

storage 219–20
Data Protection Act 1998 219–20
databases 23–4, 96, 126, 133
  more encyclopaedic 225
demand gap 18–20, 33, 35, 178
decision-makers 174, 184
  better informed 146
  defined 141
  educating 154
  identifying 142, 159
  the media as 155
  pressures on 154, 156
  the public as 149
  young people as 162
Department of Homeland Security 23,
    32, 153
detection
  and incapacitation strategy 181
  non-sanctioned 49
  rates 50, 52
  sanctioned 49
DIKI continuum 95, 96–9, 151
disorganized crime 226
disruption 13, 39, 63, 171–3, 182, 204,
    205, 236–7
Disruption Attributes Tool 205–6
'dossier system' 23, 27
Drug Enforcement Administration
    (DEA) 23, 204
drugs
  cost benefits 201, 203, 204
  DARE programme 66
  and organised crime 22
  street corner patrols 71, 180, 191
Drury, Detective Mick 216
Dunnighan, C. 36, 203, 215
Dutch Police Knowledge Net 232
Dutch Police Population Monitor
  surveys 45

Eck, John 30, 31, 94, 107, 194
environmental criminologists 30
environmental criminology 51, 94, 107,
    161
Ericson, R. V. 16, 17, 18, 20, 95, 116,
    147, 151, 217
EU Organised Crime Threat
  Assessment 59

European Convention on Human
   Rights (ECHR) 222, 223
EUROPOL 81, 119, 137, 148, 171, 172,
   228
evaluation
   lack of internally driven 189
   two types 189

Fahlman, Rob 61
Farrington, David 56, 57
Federal Bureau of Investigation (FBI)
   23, 27, 96, 118, 124, 134, 227, 228
   counterintelligence program
      (COINTELPRO) 27–8
Fenian uprising 33
Flood, Brian 10, 18, 38, 101, 134
fusion centers 5, 25, 26–7, 32, 229

gang membership 22, 218
geographical information systems 51
Giannetti, W. J. 191
Gill, Peter 13, 15, 22, 34, 35, 81, 97,
   100, 105–7, 108, 109, 112, 113, 121,
   123, 147, 159, 161, 234
Global Intelligence Working Group
   81
Global Justice Information Sharing
   Initiative (Global) Intelligence
   Working Group (GIWG) 32
globalisation of policing 132
Goldstein, Herman 30, 70, 74, 75, 115,
   189
Grabosky, Peter 216
Grant, James 217
Greater Manchester Against Crime
   Partnership Business Model (GMAC
   PBM) 150, 225
Grieve, John 96
Guidetti, Ray 25, 27
Guiliani, Rudy 31, 80
Gundhus, H. O. 75, 116, 124, 130, 132,
   141, 157, 162

Haggerty, K. D. 16, 17, 18, 20, 95, 116,
   147, 151, 217
Harfield, C, 5, 86, 102, 172, 182, 205,
   233
harm, four types of 120

harassment 220
Heldon, Corey 195, 199–201
Helping with Enquiries: Tackling Crime
   Effectively 36, 38, 42
Her Majesty's Inspectorate of
   Constabulary (HMIC) 37, 203
Herrington, V. 209–10
HIDTAs (high-intensity drug trafficking
   areas) 32, 172
Hobbes, Thomas 151
Home Office 35, 38–9, 54, 57, 83, 84,
   201
   Police Performance Assessments 208
Homeland Security era 5, 26, 32
House Committee on Un-American
   Activities (1937) 27
human rights 214, 219, 220–4
Human Rights Act 1998 222
Huntley, Ian 97, 220
hybrid governance 207

incarceration
   impact on burglaries 171, 188, 198
informants 133–4
   confidential 11, 109, 110–11, 129,
      133–5, 202–4, 214–15, 217
   ethical & legal boundaries 134, 216
   risks 216
information 8, 16, 17, 95, 96
   classification 229
   covert 133–5, 149
   storage of private 219–20
information collation 128–30
   'organisational pathologies' 129
   problems with 129
information sharing 4, 5, 26, 32, 123
   addressing problems 123
   improving 130–2
   informal networks 123–125
   more collaborative approach 216
   Operation Sentry 125
   problems with in the US 122–4
Information Sharing Council 229
Innes, Martin 134, 156, 203, 209, 222,
   228
intelligence 8, 9, 27–8, 114, 158
   cycle 81, 104–5, 112, 113, 114
   definition 76, 86–7, 92, 95

levels of 99
misconception about meaning 213
NIM levels 101–2
operational 100–1
pivotal role 95
requirements 128
strategic 100–1, 102, 128, 138–9
tactical 100–1, 128
terminological conflict 92–3
intelligence-led policing
as business model 188
components of 85–8
definition 89, 182, 210
evolving concept 84–5
information and data centred 211
organisation-wide approach 235–6
original tenets 84
origins of 6, 15–16
intelligence products 26, 78, 81, 98, 99,
111, 114, 124, 141–2, 143, 145, 147,
154, 155, 156, 177, 178, 189, 207, 211,
234, 236
intelligence sharing 4, 26
problems with 97, 123, 133
intelligence units 28
International Association of Chiefs of
Police (IACP 2002) 4, 12, 32, 92
International Association of Crime
Analysts (IACA) 230
International Association of Law
Enforcement Intelligence Analysts
(IALEIA) 92, 93, 136, 230
Interpol 228
investigation, routine screened out 236
Irwin, Detective Sergeant Robert 217

joint terrorism task forces (JTTFs) 124,
133, 139, 157

Kansas City gun experiment 221
Kansas City Police Department, patrol
strategy 21
Kansas City Preventative Patrol
Experiment 21, 178
King, Martin Luther Jr. 27
knowledge 95, 96, 109
converted to intelligence 98, 152,
154, 156

management 98
knowledge workers 95

Lawrence, Stephen 217
Lawton, B. A. 71, 191
lay visitors scheme 34–5
Laycock, Gloria 187
Levi, Michael 205, 233
liaison officers 23, 26, 128, 132

Macpherson Report 217
Maguire, Mike 205, 233
Manhattan Institute 146
Manning, Peter 151
Maple, Jack 80, 226
Markle Foundation 223
Marx, G. T. 218
Massachusetts Association of Crime
Analysts 93
Maryland Scientific Methods Scale 193
Mayhew, P. 197
Mayne, Sir Richard 15, 63
McCarthy, Senator Joseph 27
media 2, 10, 18, 77, 154–5, 170, 183,
187, 218, 224, 226
meetings, strategic and tactical 236
Metropolitan Police 15, 22, 35, 63, 96,
208
mid-management
embrace strategic thinking 234–5
resistance to intelligence-led ideal
231
military intelligence 98, 161
Millie, A. 209–10
mobile phone fraud 147–8
modus operandi 96, 105, 115, 116, 117,
118, 200
money laundering 60, 134, 136, 168,
204, 207
Morgan, Rod 9, 203

National Advisory Commission on
Criminal Justice Standards and
Goals (1973) 25
National Centre for Policing Excellence
(NCPE) 92, 107, 108, 163
National Crime Victimisation Survey
(NCVS) 43, 44, 45, 166

National Criminal Intelligence Service
10, 35, 64, 124, 145, 201
  Organised Vehicle Crime Section
  155
National Criminal Intelligence Sharing
Plan 32, 122
National Health Service 193
National Institute of Justice 28
National Intelligence Model (NIM) 4,
6, 35, 38–9, 52, 63, 64, 85, 96, 98,
107–9, 122, 135, 137, 141, 188, 205,
232
National Policing Improvement Agency
205
National Policing Plans 209
National Reassurance Policing
Programme *see* Neighbourhood
Policing Programme
national security 211, 213, 217, 220
  merging with criminal intelligence
  227–30
'need to know' principle 158
Neighbourhood Policing Programme
209, 226
New South Wales Police 216–7
New York City Police Department 228
New Zealand 207
Newburn, Tim 9
Nicholl, Jonathan 153
nodal governance 146
non-law enforcement 146–8
  examples of 147
Norris, C. 36, 203, 204, 215

offenders
  one-time 53, 54
  potential 56, 57
  predicting 56, 57
  profiling 115
  prolific 53, 54, 58, 165, 170, 236, 237
  self-selection 58–9, 122, 125, 139
  targeting 58–9, 63, 165, 236
Offending Crime and Justice Survey
57
Operation Anchorage 59, 181, 187,
195–201
  operational benefits 197
Operation Green Ice 204–5

Operation Halite 200
Operation Nine Connect 11, 120, 202
Operation Safe Streets 187, 190–2
Operation Vendas 187, 190
Operation and Crime Review (OCR)
77, 180–1
organised crime 22, 59–60 211, 224, 228
  cost of 60
  defining 60
  magnitude of 205
  measuring 204–5
  social and economic costs 204–5
Organised Crime Threat Assessment
81, 137
Osborne, Deborah 8, 82–3, 92, 94, 116,
123, 137, 161

Pacific Transnational Crime Coordination Centre 23
paperwork, burden of 16–17, 20
patrols, increased resources for 178,
180
Pawson, R. 194, 211
performance culture 16, 17, 208
performance indicators 202, 207–10
  conflict of 210
Philadelphia cohort study 54, 58
Phillips, Sir David 6
police, greater professionalisation of
187
Police and Criminal Evidence Act
(PACE) 1984 35
Police and Magistrates Courts Act 33
Police Reform Act 2002 209
Police Service of Northern Ireland
(PSNI) 46
police leadership 144–6
  changing role of 173–5
  grooming for 174
policing
  community 209–10
  'fire brigade' 20
  investigative 2, 17
  knee-jerk 227
  preventative 15, 20, 21, 180
  proactive 42, 63, 208
  public support for 214
  reactive 2, 16, 18, 42, 208, 226

reassurance 209–10, 226
policing models
    confusion between concepts 80–2
    general characteristics 72–3
    networked 224–5, 230
Policing with Intelligence 37, 38
Porter, Russ 222–4
power of information 130
President's Commission on Law
    Enforcement and Administration of
    Justice (1967) 24
President Lyndon Johnson's Crime
    Commission on Law Enforcement
    and the Administration of Justice
    29
private security industry 207, 148
problem-oriented policing 3–4, 31, 35,
    63, 70–6, 107, 142, 182
    broad mandate 75
    central tenets of 71, 74
    concept of 71, 74
    linked with community policing
        70–1
    slow emergence of 30, 74
process evaluations 189–90
Program Axiom 133
Program Manager for the Information
    Sharing Environment 229, 230
promotion 234
proportionality 217–18, 233
public confidence/trust 215, 217, 220,
    222–3, 233–4, 237
public management movement 33–4

Quarmby, Neil 137

recidivism 53–5
    operation Anchorage 197, 200
    predicting 56–8
recorded crime 120–1
recording practices, changes in 166
Regional Information Sharing Systems
    (RISS) 25
Regulation of Investigatory Powers Act
    2000 217
rendition flights 228
Rengert, George 168
reported crime

increase in 18, 46
    paper work associated with 34
    surveys into 43, 46
reporting crime
    delays in 21
    variation in 45
residual deterrence 179, 181
resources,
    allocation and priorities 211
    diverted 200
    increase in 19
risk management 18
Rogers, K. 188
Rogerson, Detective Sergeant Roger
    216
Royal Canadian Mounted Police
    (RCMP) 33, 66–7, 69, 74, 121,
    205–6
Ryan, Peter 180

SARA (Scan, Analyse, Respond, Assess)
    30, 74, 107, 108, 109, 114
    parallel with NIM business model
        108
Scarman Report 34
Scott, J. 208
Scott, Michael 30, 70, 112
security agencies 124, 150
    expanding network 151
security networks 160
sentencing 50
Serious and Organised Crime Agency
    (SOCA) 23, 60, 95, 119, 124, 148,
    182, 204, 205, 224, 233
Sheehy Inquiry 33
Sheptycki, James 10, 13–14, 22, 25,
    85, 86, 113, 119, 121, 128–9, 201,
    226
Sherman, L. W. 3, 21, 52, 66, 112, 149,
    178, 179, 180, 182, 191, 193, 194, 210,
    211
Sleipnir process 61–2, 121
Smith, P. 208
Smith, Arthur 'Neddy' 216
spatial analysis 92, 191, 192, 193
Spelman, William 30
spy networks 33
standard model of policing 16, 65

limitations of 20
Stevens, Sir John 165, 218
sting operations 121
stop and search powers 34–5
strategic analysis 137–8
Strategic Intelligence Requirements
  (SIRs) 128
strategic social harm approach 10
Sullivan, William C. 27
surveillance
  cost benefits 202–3

Tactical Intelligence Requirements
  (TIRs) 128
targeting
  available resources 179
  criminal elite 167–8
  investigative 120
  known offenders 120–2, 181
  recidivists 58–9, 169, 180, 181
technology, changes in 23
terrorism 22–3, 26–7, 39, 86, 184, 222
  see also counter-terrorism; 9/11
  challenge to criminal justice system
    5
  community policing and 149
  global concerns 151
  Homeland Security era 32
  informants 134
  information sharing 122–5
  joint task forces 157, 211
  organised crime and 228
  origins of ILP and 12
Terry stop 179
The Challenge of Crime in a Free Society
  29
Tilley, N. 20, 65, 70, 86, 194, 208, 209,
  211
time series analysis 191–2
training 145–6, 236
  lack of 161, 165–6, 184–5
  need for increased 230–2
  programmes 146
threat assessments 118–20
Tilley Awards 35
transnational crime 22, 59, 211, 228
  see also organised crime
Transnational Crime Units 23

transnational policing 151
Treatise on the Police of the Metropolis
  126
Trends and Issues in Crime and Criminal
  Justice 162

Uniform Crime Reports 117
United Kingdom Threat Assessment of
  Serious Organised Crime 124
unreported crime 43–6
  reasons for 44–5
urban riots 29
US law enforcement 24–32

vehicle crime 201–2
Vietnam War 27
  demonstrations 29
Vidocq, Eugène-François 33
Viewpoints
  A practitioner's perspective on
    the National Intelligence Model
    103–4
  Fragmented policing and the role of
    fusion centres 26–7
  Information sharing at the national
    level 126–127
  Intelligence-led policing and public
    trust 222–4
  Policing conceptual frameworks
    from the analyst's perspective
    82–3
  Refining strategy after Operation
    Anchorage 199–201
  The leadership role in intelligence-
    led policing 175–6
  The responsibilities of intelligence-
    led police leadership 152–3
  Threat measurement techniques for
    organised crime 61–2
Violent Criminal Apprehension
  Program (ViCAP) 118
Vollmer, August 29

Watergate Scandal 28
Weatherburn, Don 171, 186–7, 221,
  233
weighted displacement quotient 193
Wells, Holly 220